IMAGES
of America

FRISCO AND THE TEN MILE CANYON

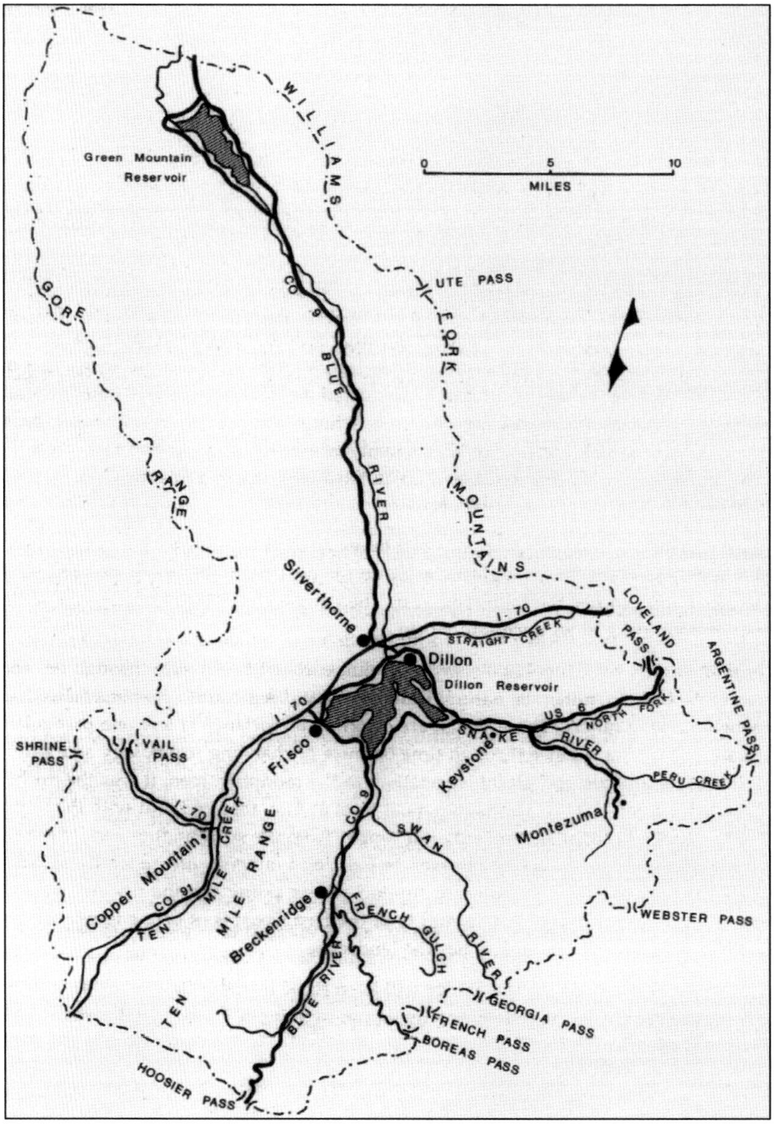

SUMMIT COUNTY, COLORADO. Summit County, located approximately 75 miles west of Denver, is home to 60 mountain peaks over 11,000 feet, four ski resorts, two reservoirs, and numerous high-altitude mountain passes. Frisco is located on the southwestern shore of Lake Dillon, a reservoir built by the City of Denver, with the Ten Mile Canyon extending to the southwest. (Map drawn by author.)

ON THE COVER: Life at home offered a stark contrast to that of the streets. Women worked to counter the corrupting influences of the saloons, dance halls, and red-light districts by extending their Victorian values beyond the front doors of their homes. Still, the intermixing of the values of an earlier generation with the realities of Western life caused conflicts that persisted through adulthood for children such as these. (Courtesy Town of Frisco Historic Park & Museum.)

IMAGES
of America

FRISCO AND THE TEN MILE CANYON

Sandra F. Mather, PhD, and
the Frisco Historic Park & Museum

ARCADIA
PUBLISHING

ISBN 978-0-7385-7549-0

Published by Arcadia Publishing
Charleston, South Carolina

Printed in the United States of America

Library of Congress Control Number: 2011921612

For all general information, please contact Arcadia Publishing:
Telephone 843-853-2070
Fax 843-853-0044
E-mail sales@arcadiapublishing.com
For customer service and orders:
Toll-Free 1-888-313-2665

Visit us on the Internet at www.arcadiapublishing.com

This book is dedicated to all those who have helped preserve Frisco's heritage and continue to share this valuable legacy with others.

CONTENTS

ACKNOWLEDGMENTS

The author wishes to express her heartfelt thanks to Peggy Alexander; Ed and Nancy Bathke; Simone Belz; Jerry Dziedzic; Bill Eloe; Bill Fountain; Tom Klinger; Kris Ann Knish; Caitlin Lewis; Bob Schoppe and the Denver, South Park & Pacific Historical Society; the Colorado Historical Society; the Denver Public Library; and the Frisco Historic Park & Museum. Unless otherwise noted, all images appear courtesy of the Frisco Historic Park & Museum.

Introduction

The story of Frisco and the Ten Mile Canyon began millions of years ago—long before the miners, long before the Utes or their ancestors, long before humans began modifying the landscape. As the Rocky Mountains rose, tremendous forces pushed preexisting rocks deep into the crust, recrystallizing them into the metamorphic rocks seen today in the Ten Mile Canyon. These same forces created cracks and fissures in those rocks that mineralized fluids filled with gold, silver, lead, and zinc.

More recently, glaciers filled the canyon and some tributary valleys such as Mayflower Gulch, carving bowl-shaped cirques and U-shaped valleys while exposing the mineral wealth found centuries later by prospectors.

The human story begins with the Utes, whose ancestors lived in the area for generations. Early explorers told of the herds of American bison that inhabited the meadows along the Ten Mile Creek and the Utes who depended on them for food, shelter, and clothing. With the arrival of prospectors in 1859, the lifestyle of the Utes rapidly disappeared.

Frisco and the Ten Mile Canyon experienced little of the first gold rush of 1859. Prospectors entered the canyon from Leadville but after not finding ample rewards for their efforts, many left for richer strikes. Those who remained quickly exhausted the gold they found in the gulches of the southern Ten Mile Canyon. For this reason, the canyon escaped the devastation from hydraulic gold mining found elsewhere in Summit County.

Hard rock or lode mining dominated in the Ten Mile Canyon. Miners returned in 1879, this time searching for the silver they had seen earlier. The first silver rush followed, but individual miners and prospectors did not fuel the stampede. Removing the minerals required advances in technology and strong financial backing that only large ventures could provide. Men worked for companies; the individual prospector played a small role in the development of silver mining in the Ten Mile Canyon. The usual "boom and bust" cycle repeated itself many times. Mines prospered, only to close when conditions suffered. Hopes rose with new owners or the infusion of money from investors. The Sherman Silver Purchase Act of 1890 and ensuing silver panic of 1893 caused irreparable damage to the economy. Men lost jobs and moved away. As years passed, the mines continued a slow but steady decline.

When profit-hungry mining companies arrived in 1879, so too did land developers who platted Robinson, Kokomo, Recen, Wheeler, and Frisco. The towns provided housing and other necessities for residents. Hastily constructed buildings dotted the landscape. At first, merchants sold just the basics—food, clothing, and mining supplies. Only later, when towns promised longevity, did specialty stores arrive. Saloons were among the first businesses in the towns. Offering liquid refreshment, games of chance, and companionship, they filled a need and bolstered the male ego. Men could find comfort and a refuge from loneliness. Patrons could exchange news and gossip, discuss local and national topics, get a haircut, attend to civic duties, vote in elections, file claims, attend religious services, or receive rudimentary medical attention from visiting doctors or dentists.

Saloons often functioned as the first courtrooms, with the barkeeper perhaps serving as a judge. Some saloons rented mailboxes, posted employment notices, or offered hot and cold baths to dusty, weary travelers. Many saloons advertised fireproof safes to protect valuables.

The whiskey sold in the earliest saloons was called rotgut for good reason. To stretch their supply, saloon keepers added things like tobacco, water, red pepper, or lye to the drinks they served. Some sold colored liquid and called it whiskey. Diluted, doctored, or legitimate, whiskey was the preferred drink of the men in the Ten Mile Canyon.

Fraternal and benevolent organizations flourished in these towns, filling a need during a time of great societal change. Westward migration, the influx of European immigrants, and improved transportation all created a more fluid society that still searched for and socialized with those of similar values, political leanings, and religious and ethnic backgrounds. The Masons, Odd Fellows, and Rebekahs met regularly in Robinson, Kokomo, and Recen. Informal social clubs such as a kitchen, literary, or sewing club provided an entrance to the community for newcomers, a way to feel part of the town or camp. Women could discuss local affairs, promote civic programs, and make friends more quickly. These organizations supported charitable efforts on behalf of their members as well as others. On a lighter note, they sponsored dances, parties, dinners, and cultural events such as lectures and shows.

In 1880, the Denver & Rio Grande Railroad laid rails through the canyon from Leadville, eventually reaching Frisco, Dickey, and Dillon. The Denver, South Park & Pacific, constructing its tracks over Boreas Pass, arrived from Breckenridge. At Dickey, the main line turned toward Frisco and the Ten Mile Canyon. With the arrival of the railroads, mining prospered as it had not done before. Stores sold fresh fruit and vegetables brought by the railroads. Cheaper transportation helped make the low-grade ore more profitable.

While mining dominated the economy of the Ten Mile Canyon and Frisco, ranching occurred east and north of town. Cattle, sheep, and horses grazed on lush meadows that had so recently fed the herds of bison. The residents of Frisco and the Ten Mile Canyon eagerly purchased the milk, butter, and cheese produced by the ranches.

The economy of Frisco and the Ten Mile Canyon did not develop in isolation. Financial support for the mines came from Boston, New York, and as far away as Great Britain. Engines for both the Denver, South Park & Pacific and the Denver & Rio Grande arrived from Pennsylvania and Ohio. Immigrants from eastern states and northern Europe worked in the mines or for logging companies. Summit County produced minerals purchased by industries throughout the United States.

Cultural values influenced those living in Frisco and the Ten Mile Canyon. Mining was important, not scenic beauty or the environment. Hillsides stripped bare of timber, dilapidated buildings, mine dumps, and polluted streams were of no consequence. Economic reality took precedence.

A philosophical difference existed between the Native Americans and later residents. The Utes and their ancestors used the resources provided by nature, while those who came later sought to subdue the land. Miners, ranchers, merchants, developers, and land speculators saw the land as capital. They assigned a value to it and, in turn, helped to advance settlement.

The optimists stayed through good times and bad; the next mineral strike was a shovelful away, the long-sought investor on the next train, the prices for ore and agricultural products bound to rise the following year. The people were bold. They left the familiar for the unknown and took risks in an uncertain world. Some succeeded; some did not. But they all had a hand in writing the history of Frisco and the Ten Mile Canyon.

Changes to and on the landscape since the time period covered in this book have been truly monumental. Sometimes fast, sometimes slow, change is a constant. Many of the features of the late 1800s and early 1900s are gone—replaced by those of a new economic landscape. But the old landscape lives on in fading memories and photographs; remnants remain for those who look.

The Utes are gone, relocated to the Ute Reservation in southwestern Colorado. Yet their legacy remains, in the names of passes, roads, and housing developments.

Robinson, Kokomo, and Recen are gone. Tailings from the Climax molybdenum mine flooded the valley after 1959. Mine tailings bury the town site of Robinson; parts of the Kokomo and

Recen town sites remain but are on private property. What the silver panic of 1893 did not accomplish, the tailings did.

Wheeler is gone, replaced by the Copper Mountain resort that opened in 1971. The developers held a simple philosophy: the ecosystem is a single, closed system. Nature should be duplicated whenever and wherever possible. Trees became a "timber harvest." The Environmental Sawmill cut the timber for firewood, and the Thick and Thin Lumber Company of Copper Mountain sold it on the local market. The Pretty Lumpy Concrete Company of Copper Mountain used the four million tons of sand and gravel recovered from the rechanneling of the West Ten Mile Creek to make concrete for a variety of projects.

The two narrow-gauge railroads are gone, but the canyon, once a conduit for a wagon road and those two railroads, remains an important part of the transportation network. Interstate 70 follows the Denver & Rio Grande right-of-way, while a recreational path has been built on the Denver, South Park & Pacific right-of-way. Before construction could begin on the interstate highway, the meandering, swampy Ten Mile Creek had to be rechanneled. Despite being polluted by mining operations in the early 1900s, the stream supported a small population of brown and brook trout. Beginning in 1976, crews moved and stored vegetation. Bulldozers dug a new channel that meandered around existing rock formations. Log and rock dams and deflectors created pools of varying depths that provided shelter and food for fish. When the new 16,000-foot channel was completed and vegetation replanted, construction could begin on the roadway.

Dickey is gone. The water of Lake Dillon drowned the railroad facilities constructed there. The railroad's right-of-way turning toward Frisco appears when the water level drops at the end of summer.

The mines of the Ten Mile Canyon are gone, but mine dumps, mill tailings, foundations, and crumbling buildings dot the landscape. After numerous periods of dashed hopes, the mines closed permanently when prices for the minerals produced no profits for investors.

The ranches are gone. Businesses cover the pastures where cattle once grazed. Bill's Ranch remains as a subdivision of Frisco. The Giberson Preserve, which now includes only 179 acres, became part of the Continental Divide Land Trust in 1998.

Frisco still guards the entrance to the Ten Mile Canyon. It is not gone. The vibrant town offers summer and winter visitors a variety of recreational activities while striving to preserve its heritage. Buildings moved to the Historic Park tell the story of those living and working in the town during the late 1800s and early 1900s. The Frisco Bay Marina offers visitors opportunities to see the spectacular scenery surrounding Lake Dillon. The reservoir, which impounds over 85 billion gallons of water, provides water for the city of Denver.

What does the future hold for Frisco and the Ten Mile Canyon? Only time will tell. Undoubtedly, change—constant change, sometimes rapid, sometimes slow, for many decades—will be part of the story.

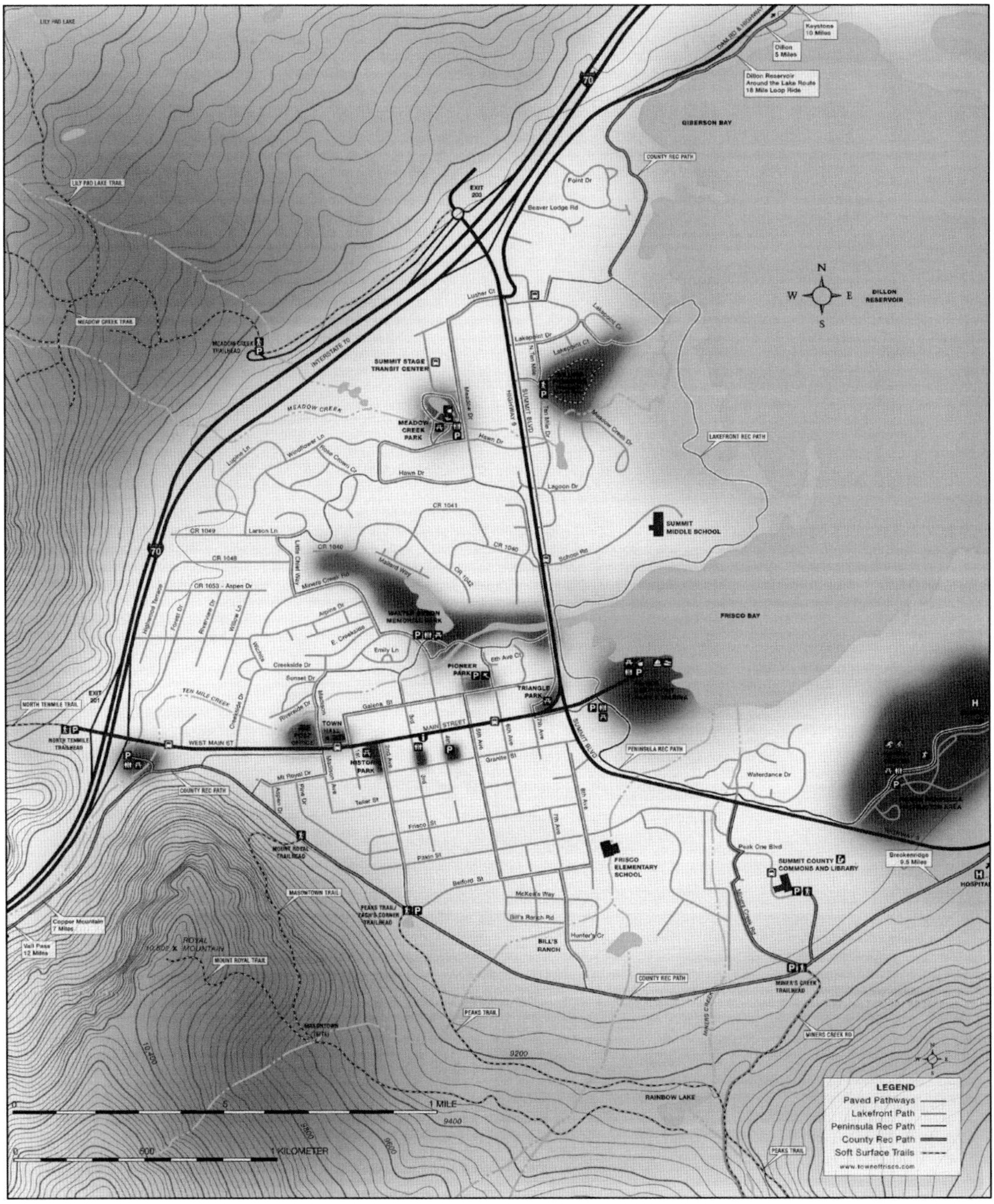

FRISCO, COLORADO. Surrounded by towering Mount Royal, Wichita Mountain, Chief Mountain, and the flanks of Buffalo Mountain, all rising over 10,000 feet, the town of Frisco is nestled between Lake Dillon and I-70 at an elevation of just over 9,000 feet. At the western end of Frisco, I-70 enters the Ten Mile Canyon. (Courtesy Town of Frisco.)

One

The Utes
The First Inhabitants

For centuries, the land that would become Summit County provided the necessities of life for humans. As long as 12,000 years ago, hunters roamed the area in search of food. Projectile points, knives, scrapers, and charcoal from campfires tell of the continuous occupation of specific sites. These people were the ancestors of the Utes encountered by the trappers, travelers, miners, merchants, and others coming to Summit County. Because of the isolation provided by the mountainous terrain and deep valleys, the bands of Utes in Summit County were quite distinct from those living in Utah. Those living here adopted many cultural traits of the Plains Indians, who were at various times their rivals, allies, or enemies.

The Ute way of life left distinct marks on the landscape as the bands followed the bison between summer grazing lands along the Blue River and winter quarters at lower elevations. The passes used by the Utes became the early wagon roads. Present-day highways follow some of these same routes.

The biggest legacy of Ute civilization came from their use of fire. The Utes burned the valley bottoms annually to encourage the growth of the short, tender grasses that the bison and horses preferred. Besides improving pasturage, the fires facilitated travel, removed unwanted trees, and improved visibility. The fires destroyed species that could not tolerate repeated burning and encouraged the growth of lodgepole pines, whose cones open only after being subjected to heat. The bison further changed the vegetative character of the county. Large herds stripped the ground of most of the grasses, trampling anything not eaten. Therefore, much of the vegetative landscape in place when the miners and others arrived resulted directly from the Ute lifestyle.

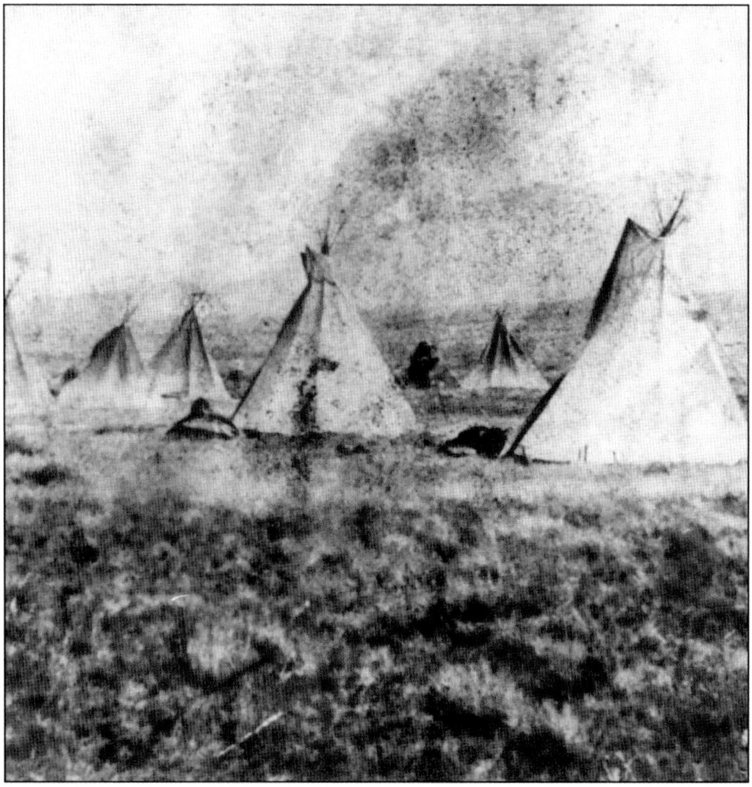

A Ute Village in 1899. The Utes lived in groups of various sizes. Shelters reflected their hunter-gatherer lifestyle. Winter homes were tepees built in the style of the Plains Indians, using the lodgepole pines so abundant in the county. In summer, the Utes built shelters called wickiups made of brush and willow arranged over a wooden frame.

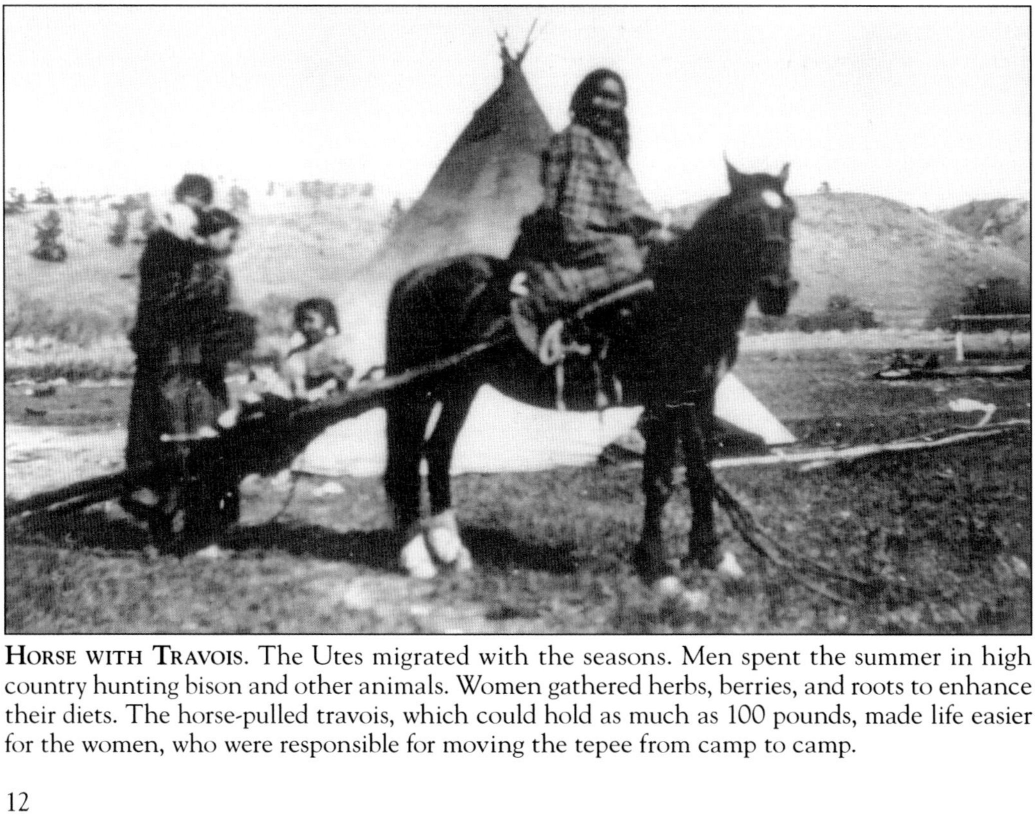

Horse with Travois. The Utes migrated with the seasons. Men spent the summer in high country hunting bison and other animals. Women gathered herbs, berries, and roots to enhance their diets. The horse-pulled travois, which could hold as much as 100 pounds, made life easier for the women, who were responsible for moving the tepee from camp to camp.

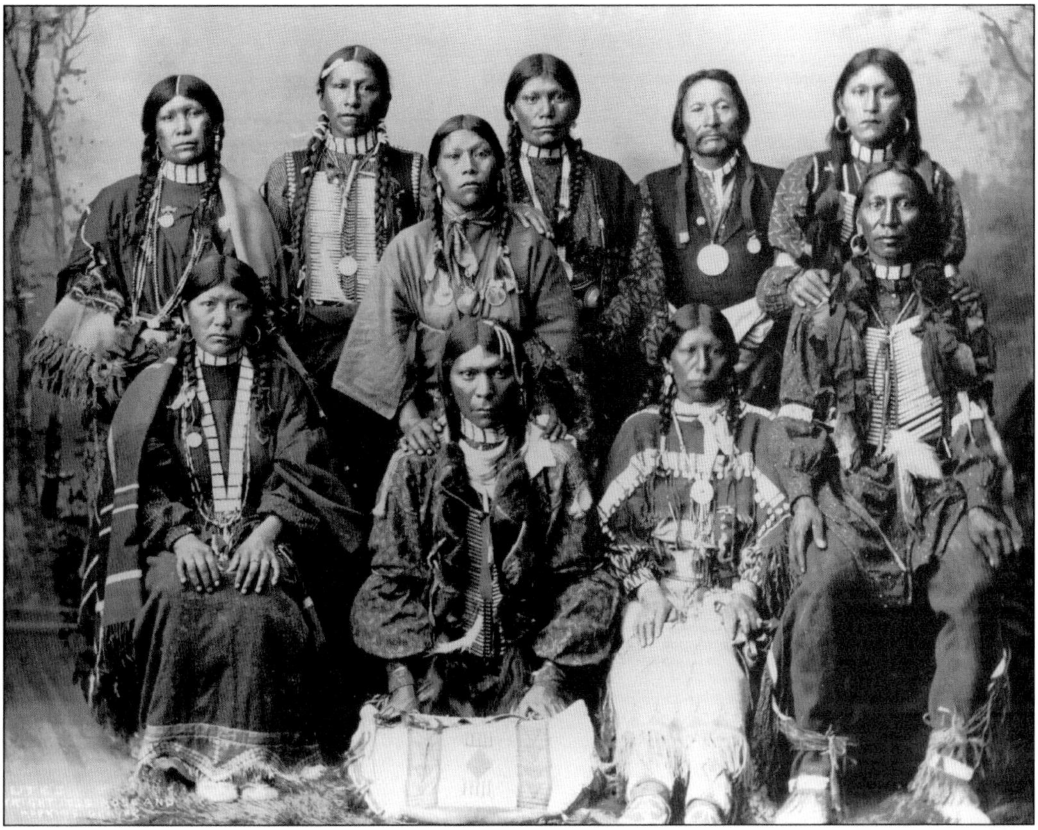

Ute Clothing. Men and women wore highly decorated clothing made of hides tanned by the women, who then added quills, beads, earth-tone paints, and fringes to the softened hides. Decorative bags hung from their waists. Moccasins protected their feet. Making and decorating the clothing was just one of many roles assumed by Ute women on a daily basis. (Courtesy Denver Public Library, Western History Collection, Rose & Hopkins, H-427.)

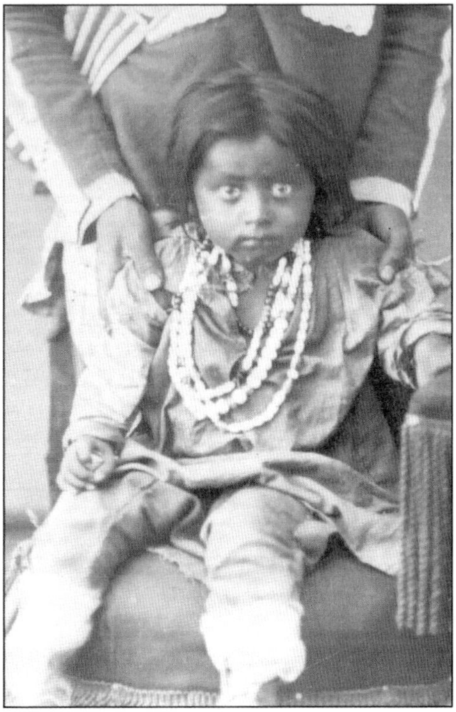

Ute Children. The Utes valued children—often pampering them. All adults shared responsibility for the children, who in turn learned expected behavior by following examples set by adults. Children spent most of their first year in a cradleboard carried by their mother or sister. Older women made the boards from a wooden frame covered with soft hides, embellishing the boards with elaborate beadwork and fringes. (Used with permission from the Ed and Nancy Bathke Collection.)

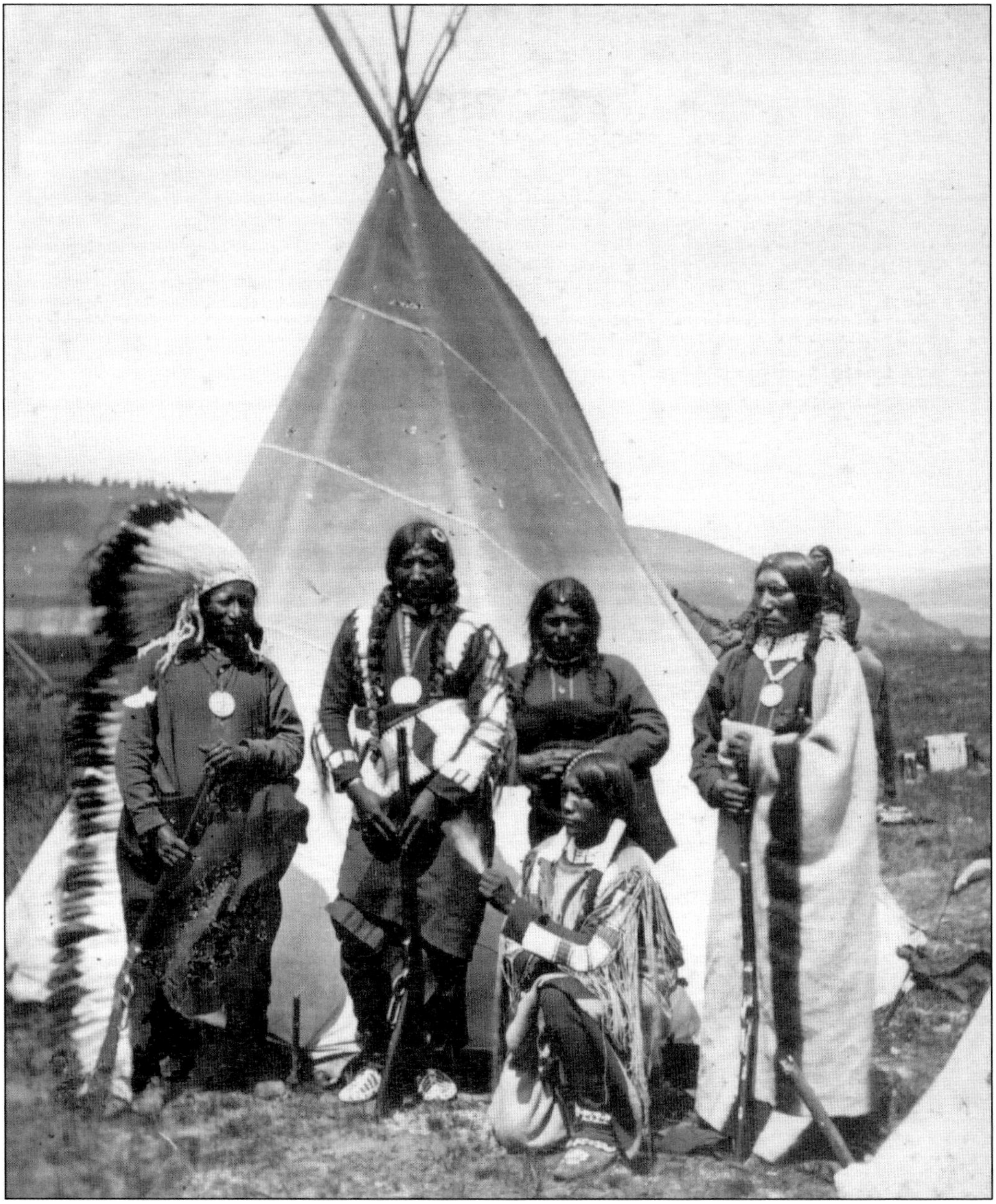

Ute Men, c. 1874. Ute men did not cut their hair, but wore it in long braids. Women fashioned deer, sheep, and bison hides into shirts, moccasins, and leggings and bison fur into blankets. Masters of the bow and arrow, the men also used rifles obtained from traders for hunting. Ute men only wore feather bonnets when waging war on their enemies. (Used with permission from the Ed and Nancy Bathke Collection.)

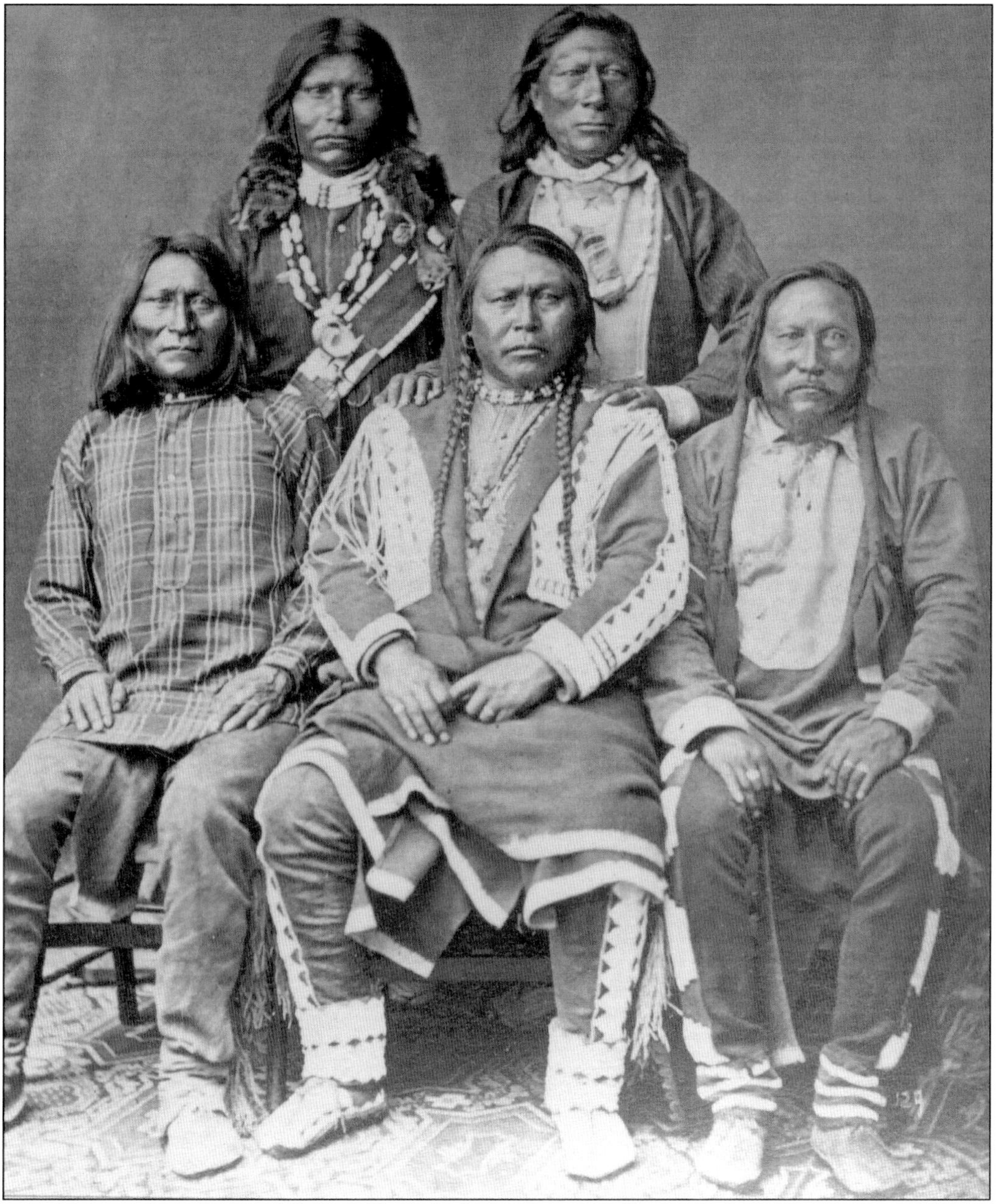

Ute Chiefs. Utes did not use the word "chief." For each task, they chose an appropriate leader. When the role no longer existed, the leader no longer held power. Only white settlers used the word chief. In this photograph taken in Washington, DC, the leaders included Ouray, sitting in the center of the front row. Under his leadership, the Utes preserved their identity but lost the majority of their homeland in Colorado. (Used with permission from the Ed and Nancy Bathke Collection.)

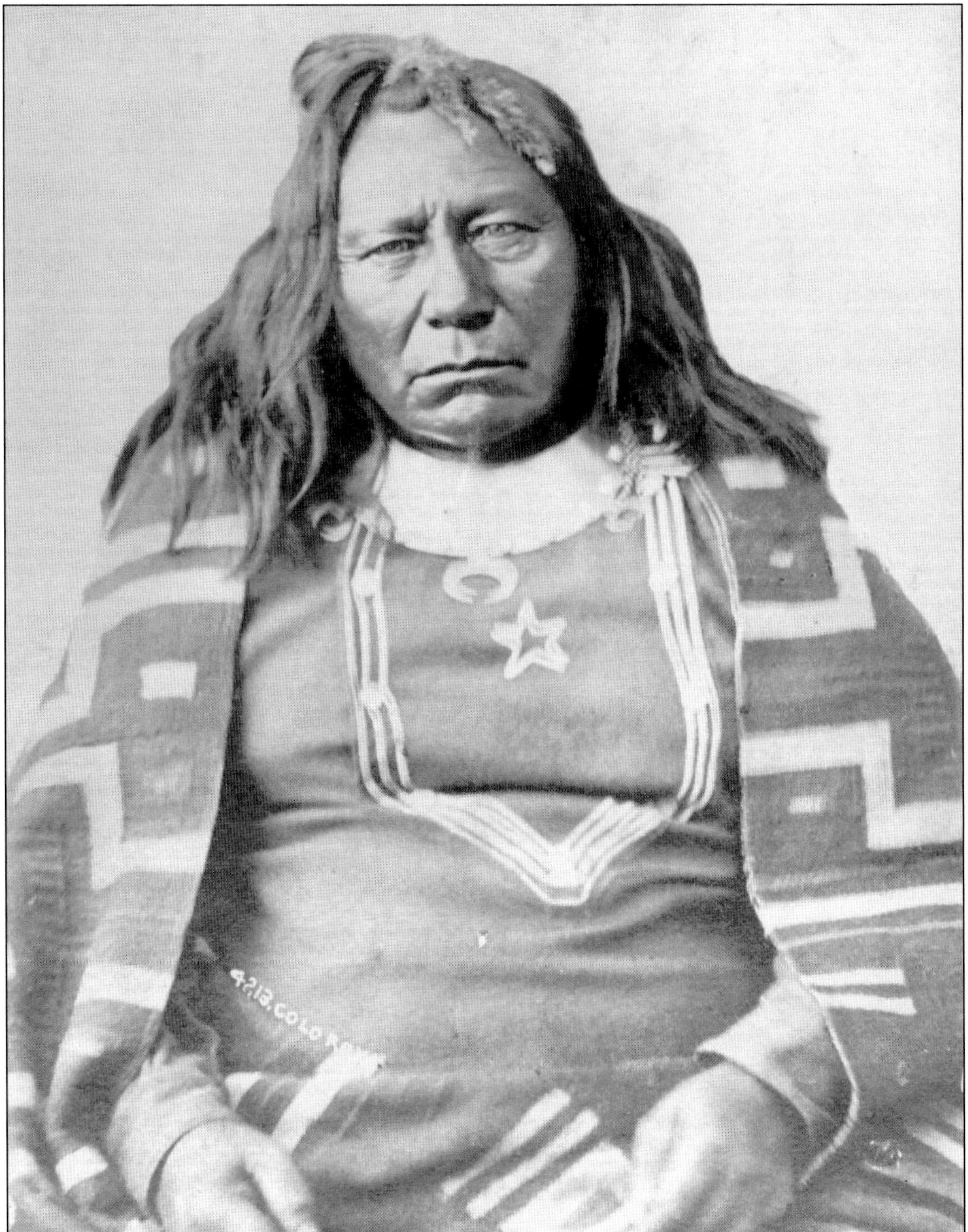

COLOROW IN 1887. Weighing about 300 pounds, Colorow was a common sight in Summit County. Residents had no reason to fear the Utes. Although they were generally friendly to white settlers, the Native Americans considered other tribes, such as the Arapaho and Cheyenne, their mortal enemies because these tribes living on the eastern plains entered Ute territory to hunt game and cut lodgepole pine trees for their tepees. (Used with permission from the Ed and Nancy Bathke Collection.)

Two

FRISCO
THE TOWN AND ITS PEOPLE

Location determined the destiny of the town of Frisco, dictating that it would serve those living and working in the Ten Mile Canyon.

Frisco developed at the same time as the other towns in the Ten Mile Canyon—all of them dependent on mining. One of the earliest residents, Henry Recen, a Swedish-born miner who arrived in 1873, built a cabin on what is now Ten Mile Island. In 1875, Henry Learned posted a sign on Recen's cabin naming the settlement "Frisco City." It is thought that Learned, an agent for the St. Louis-San Francisco Railway Company, hoped to draw the railroad into the town and canyon by naming the town for the railroad. The word "Frisco" is derived from the "fr" in Francisco, the "is" in St. Louis, and "co" in company. When the town incorporated, "City" was dropped from the name.

While some towns grew in a haphazard fashion, Frisco did not. Charles Walker surveyed the town, laying out the streets in a grid pattern, the most common pattern for mining towns. A May 1, 1888, map shows east–west streets named Galena, Main, Granite, Teller, Frisco, Pitkin, and Belford. Each block consisted of 12 lots facing the named streets and an alley dividing the block from numbered street to numbered street. Inside lots sold for $5; corner lots cost $10.

Frisco, first governed by the amended rules of Chihuahua, a town on Peru Creek in eastern Summit County, and later the amended rules of Breckenridge, had a mayor and board of trustees.

Frisco became an important transportation hub. Mail, mining supplies, food, clothing, and people all passed through, riding on wagons and stagecoaches at first and later on the two railroads that built through the town.

At the turn of the 20th century, the town reflected the federal government's devaluation of silver. Mines closed. Smelters accepted no ore. Men lost jobs. The railroads curtailed operations. Unemployment rose. It was not until decades later that Frisco came to life again thanks to an economy based on summer and winter recreation.

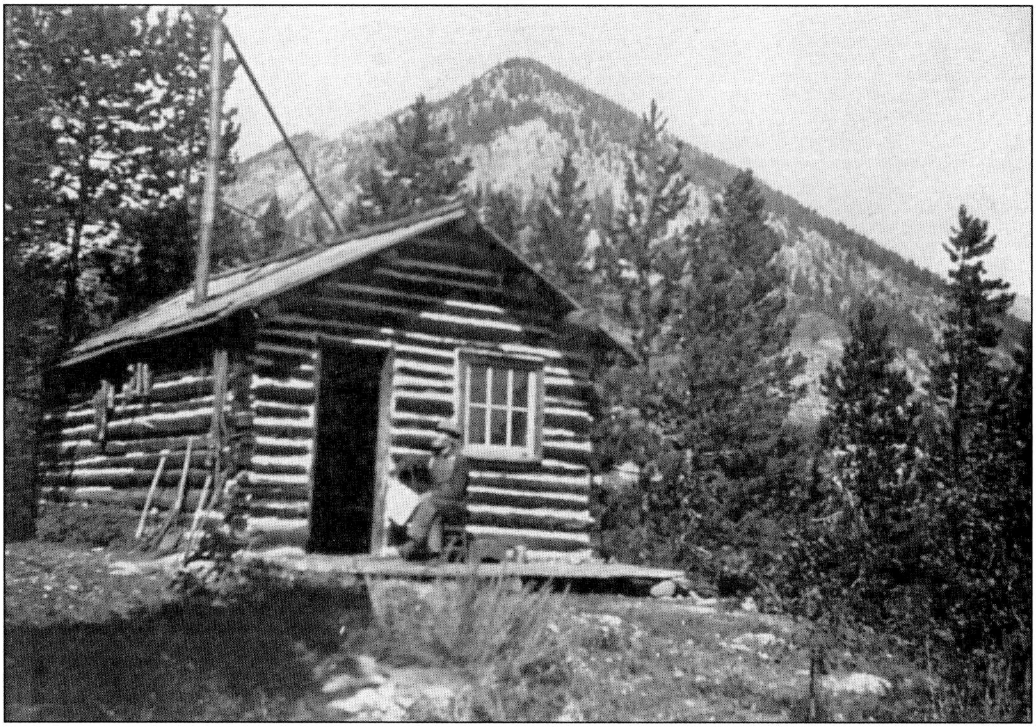

Where It All Began. In 1875, Henry Learned, an agent for the St. Louis-San Francisco Railway Company, posted a sign on Henry Recen's cabin along the Ten Mile Creek that read "Frisco City." No matter the size of the settlement, people in the American West added the word "city" to the name of a town to indicate permanence and future growth.

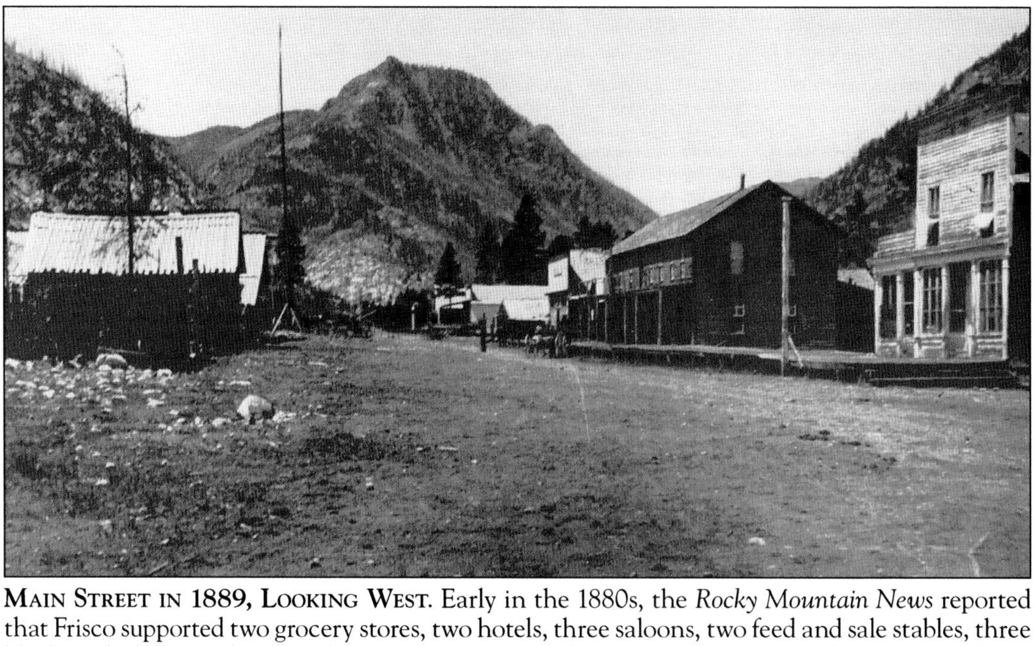

Main Street in 1889, Looking West. Early in the 1880s, the *Rocky Mountain News* reported that Frisco supported two grocery stores, two hotels, three saloons, two feed and sale stables, three blacksmith shops, and every other shop except that of a lawyer—the town had no "undesirables," such as lawyers, gamblers, fallen women, and ministers.

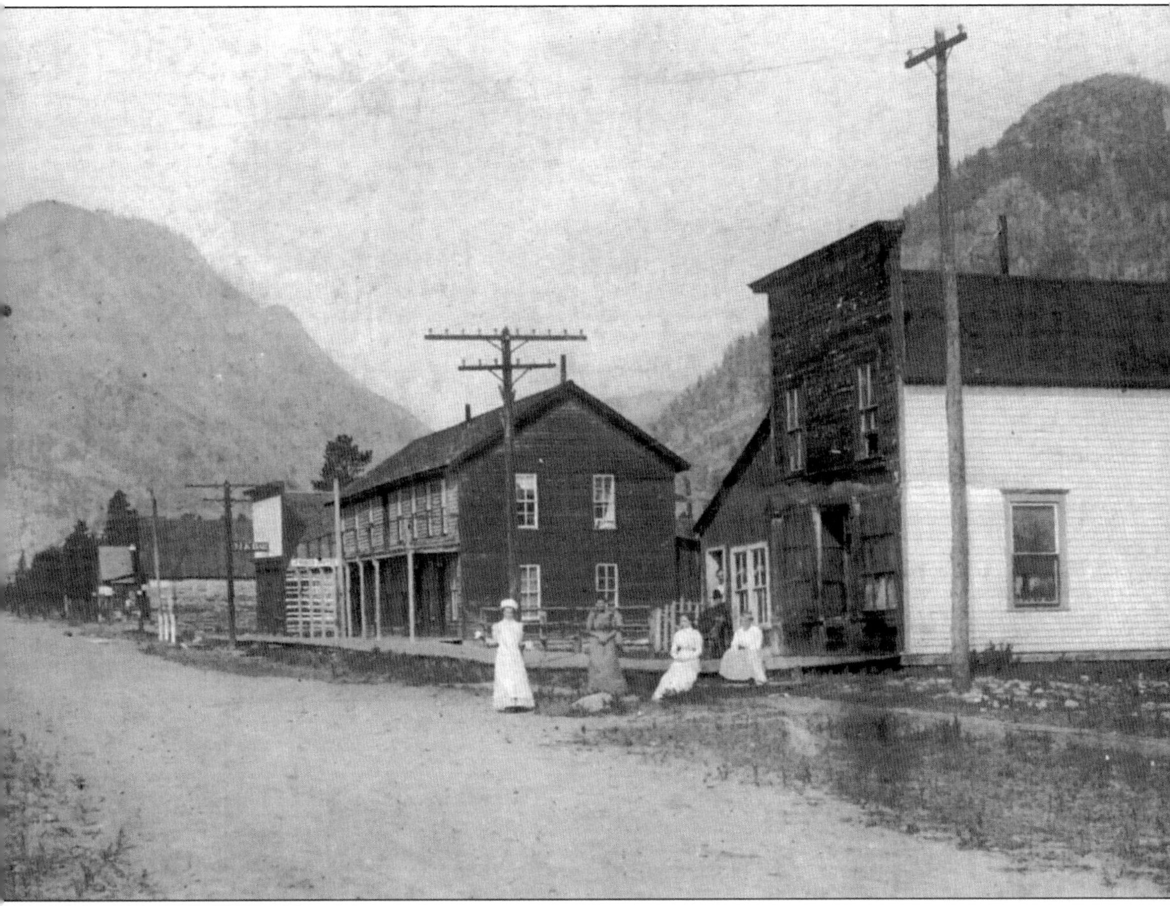

Main Street in the Early 1900s. Kitty Ecklund, in the white hat, and friends pose in front of the Frisco Hotel. Kitty's husband, Con, sits on the boardwalk behind the women. In 1919, before women won the right to vote nationally, Kitty served as mayor of Frisco. She took over after the all-male town board had not fulfilled its responsibilities for months. Note the electric light hanging over the intersection.

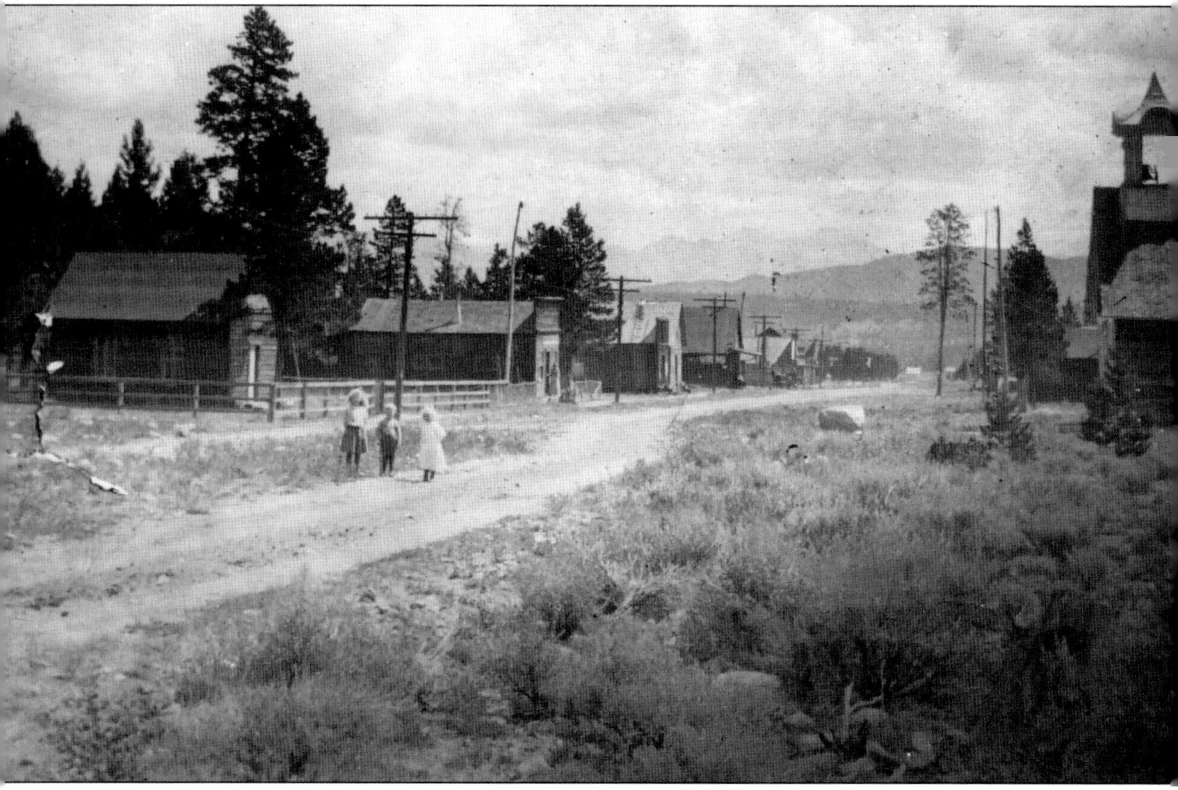

Main Street in 1910, Looking East. At the turn of the 20th century, Frisco consisted of two east–west streets (Main and Galena). Businesses and residences lined Main Street, but there were only residences on three-block-long Galena. Boardinghouses, hotels, general stores, livery stables, blacksmith shops, and the post office could be found on Main Street. (Courtesy History Colorado.)

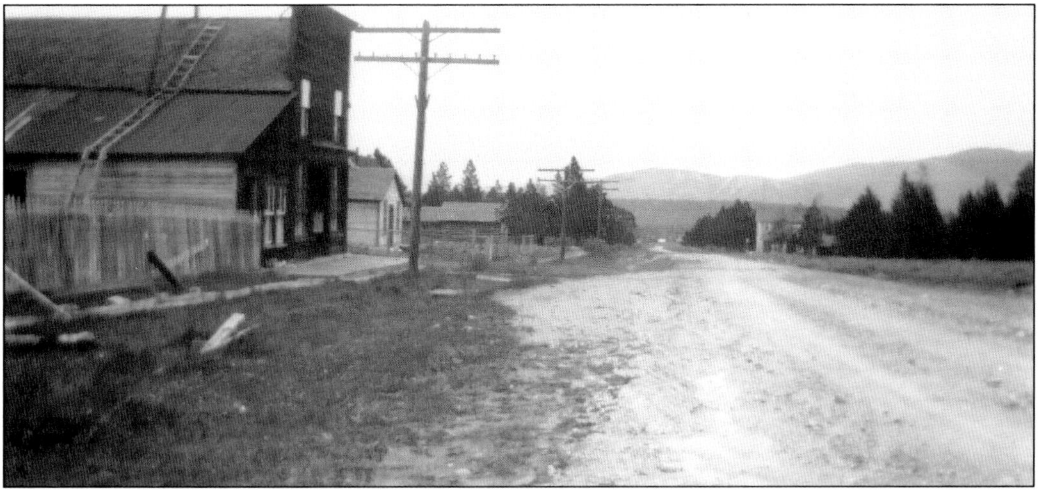

MAIN STREET IN 1934, LOOKING EAST. The buildings along Main Street indicate the effects of the depression on the economy. The mines had not recovered from the devaluation of silver in 1893; businesses closed and families moved away. The Frisco Hotel still stands but other buildings and residences have disappeared. Electric and telephone wires no longer stretch from pole to pole. Note the fire ladder rising to the roof crest.

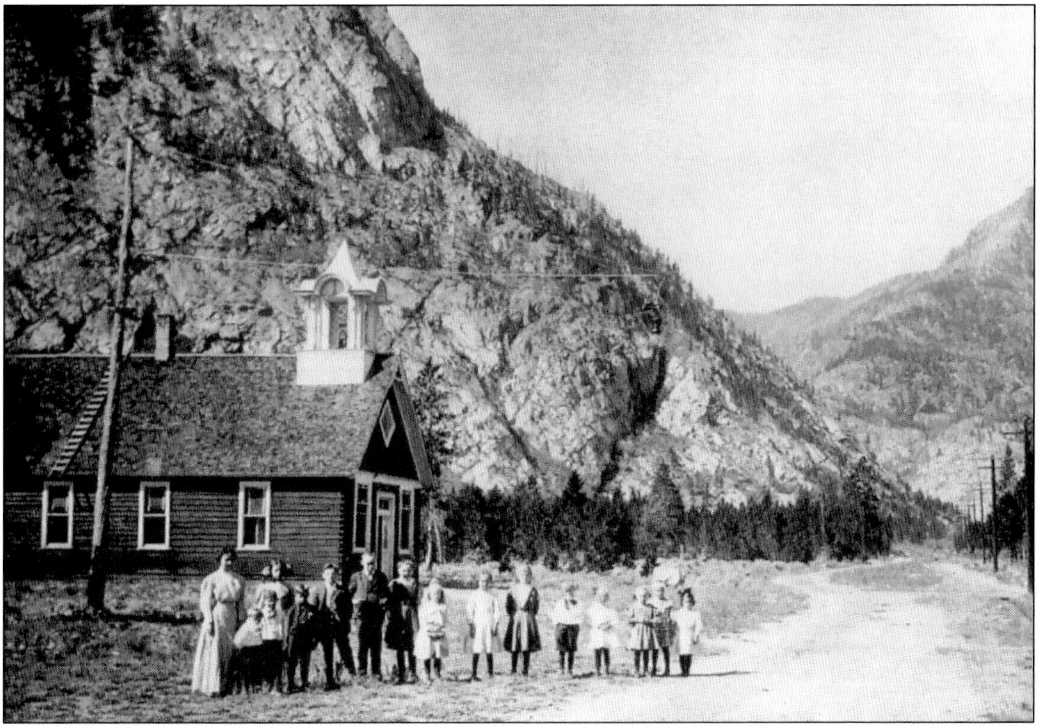

FRISCO SCHOOLHOUSE IN 1911. Teacher Atta Lynch and her class pose in front of the schoolhouse originally built by Oliver Swanson as a saloon. Note the ladder on the roof. In many towns, ordinances required ladders as an aid in dousing roof and chimney fires. The bell tower, installed on the Frisco schoolhouse in 1909, was moved from the 1882 schoolhouse in Breckenridge where it had called scholars to their studies. (Courtesy Denver Public Library, Western History Collection, X-8560.)

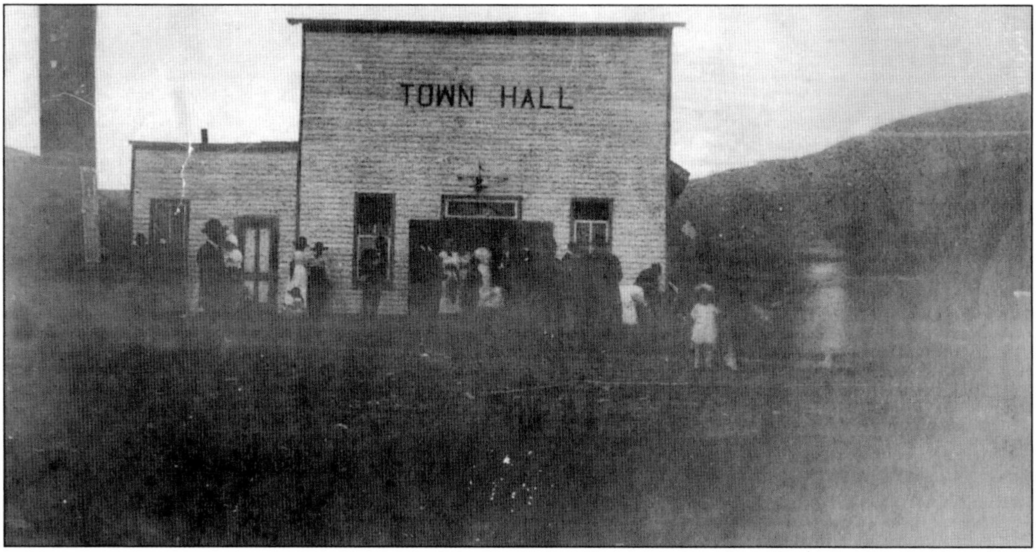

Frisco Town Hall. In this undated, post-1899 photograph, Frisco residents gather for a festive occasion. People came to the town hall to conduct business, vote, and exchange news and gossip. Over the years, people enjoyed square dances and potluck dinners in this building constructed in 1899 by volunteers. Note the electric light above the front entrance.

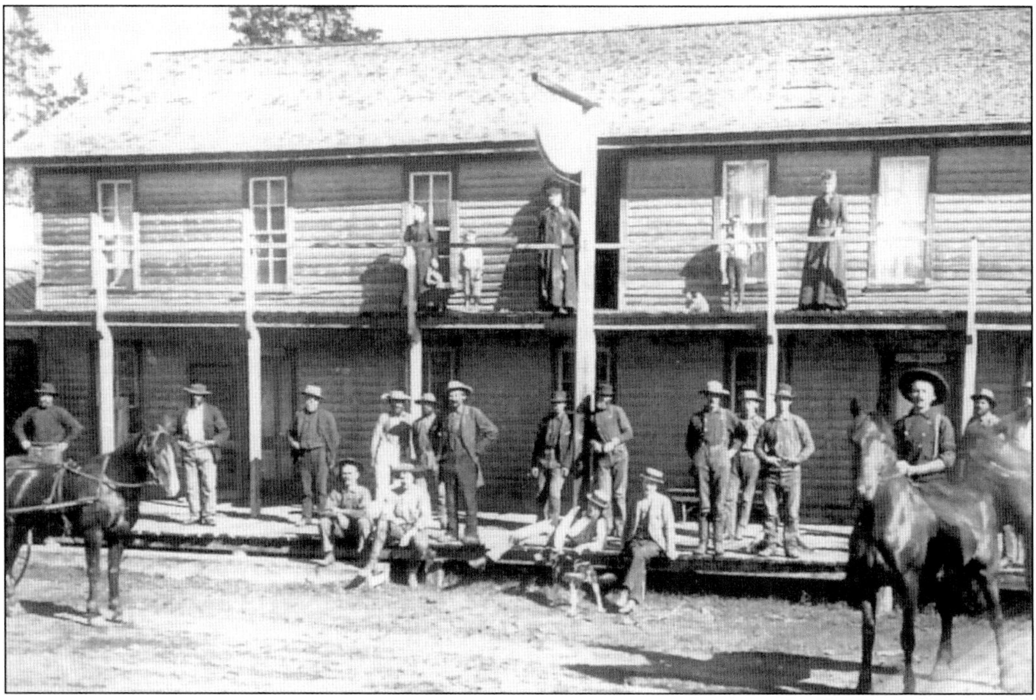

Leyner's Hotel. Visitors and men who came west without their wives in the late 1880s and early 1890s could stay in Leyner's Hotel, one of several hotels and boardinghouses in town that offered lodging and home cooking. The ratio of men to women in the picture reflects the imbalance in most mining towns and camps, where men far outnumbered women.

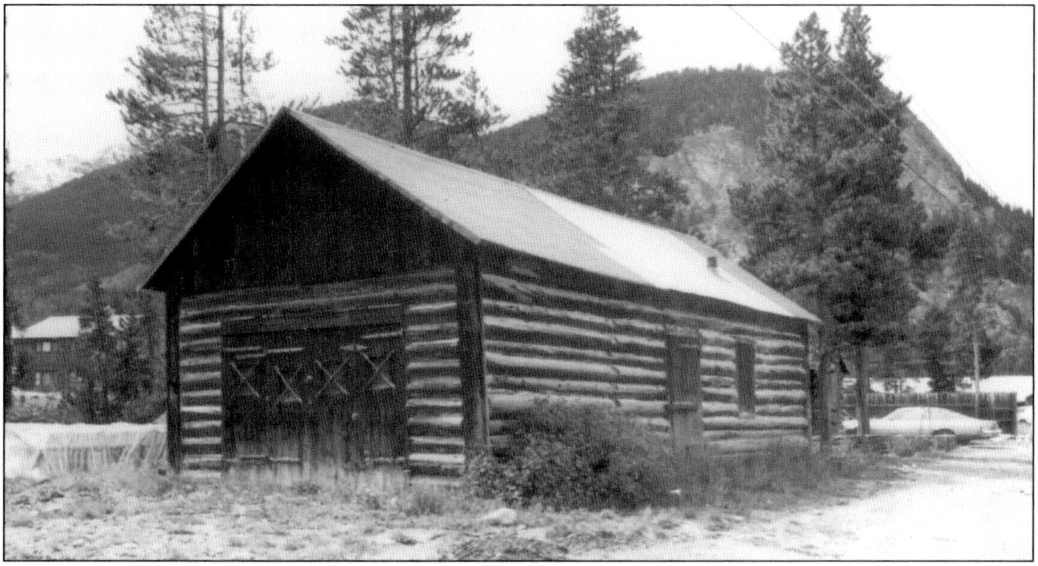

Frisco Calaboose. To deal with those who visited the saloons too frequently, Frisco needed a calaboose, or jail. In 1881, the town board appointed a committee to locate a site, pay for, and build the lockup. Approved supplies included a heating stove, three mattresses, four blankets, two comforters, lamps, and locks. A badge was ordered for the marshal. The jail was located south of Main Street on the east side of Fifth Avenue.

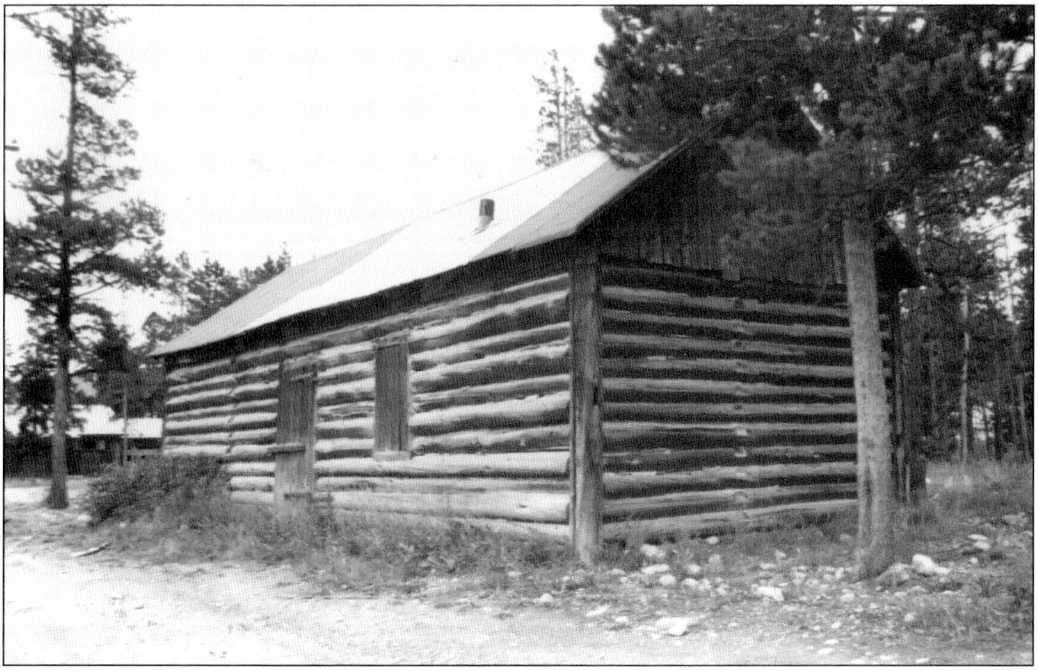

Frisco Jail. The number of individuals residing in the calaboose, with its four 7-by-10-foot cells, warranted further purchases, including two more comforters, two single mattresses, one double mattress, one large lock, one lantern, one oil can, one water pail, three tin cups, two pairs of handcuffs, one set of prison books, and a second marshal's badge.

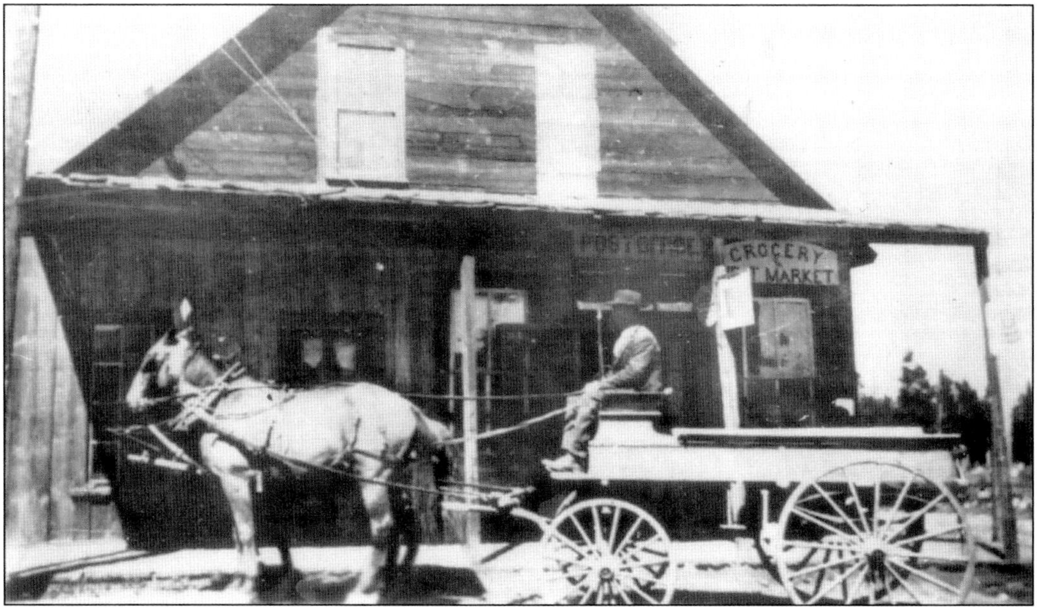

MAIN STREET POST OFFICE IN 1907. As in so many western towns, the post office served as a social center for the residents of Frisco. Wagons and trains brought their precious cargo. Receiving mail from home was so important that men and women planned their day so that they would be nearby when the postmaster or postmistress finished sorting the letters and packages.

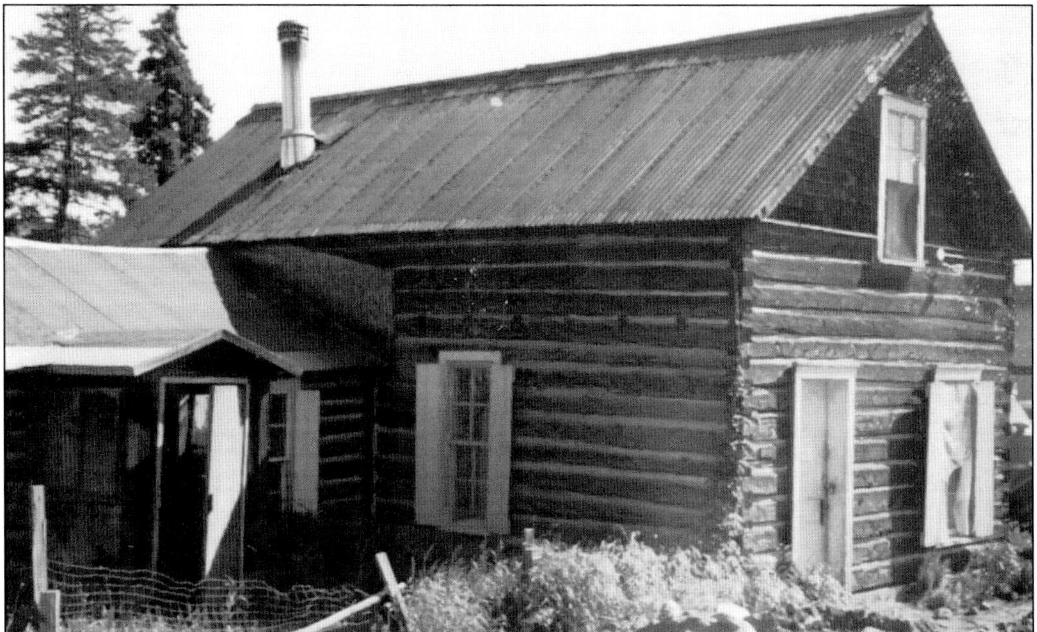

THE BAILEY HOUSE. This hand-hewn two-story log house typifies the homes built in Frisco in the late 1890s. To keep their homes warmer in winter, people inserted chinking of wood, cloth, or clay between the logs. Newspapers covered the interior walls as extra insulation. If they could afford it, residents added wallpaper to walls and ceilings. Originally, this house stood on the northeast corner of Fifth Avenue and Main Street.

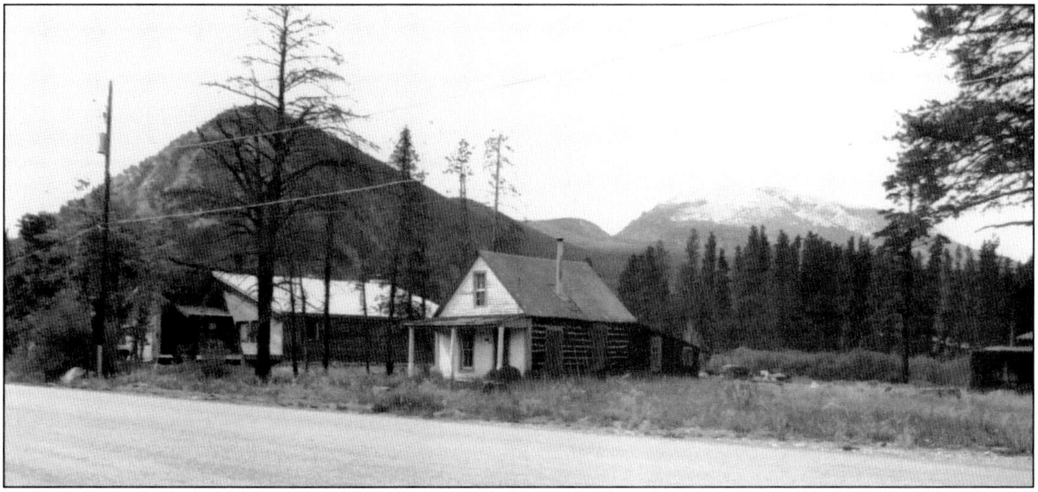

The Prestrud-Staley House. With Chief and Buffalo Mountains behind it, the Prestrud-Staley house sat on the northwest corner of Fourth Avenue and Galena Street. Built in 1899 with logs and clapboard siding, the structure exemplified the type of home in which a middle-class mining family lived. Peter Prestrud and Eyvind Flood built one of Colorado's first flotation mills, used for separating valuable metal ore from waste materials.

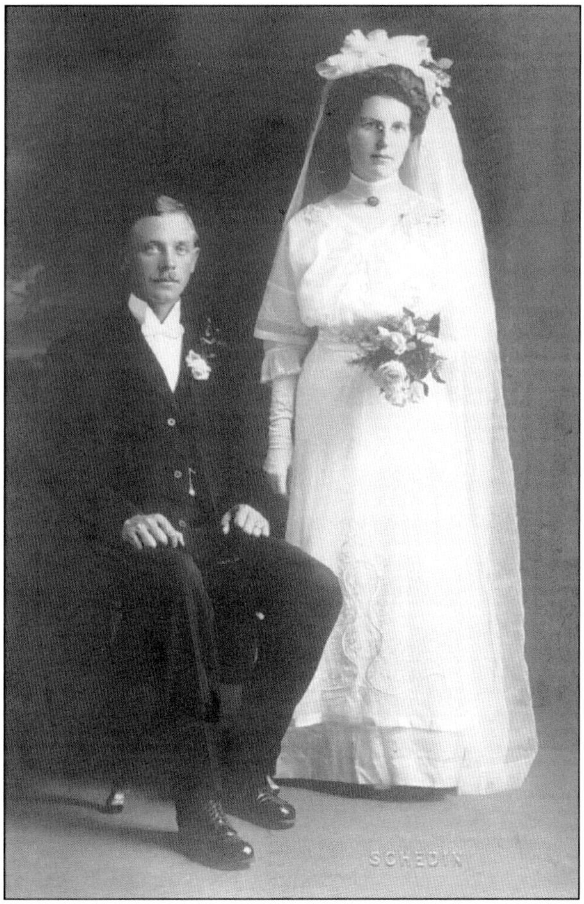

Peter and Alice Prestrud on Their Wedding Day. Peter Prestrud, born November 7, 1883, in Hamar, Norway, immigrated to the United States in 1906. On a return trip to Norway, he met his future wife, Alice Herseth. Alice's father, with mining interests in Frisco, asked Peter to settle in the town and look after his investments. Peter and Alice married on September 10, 1911.

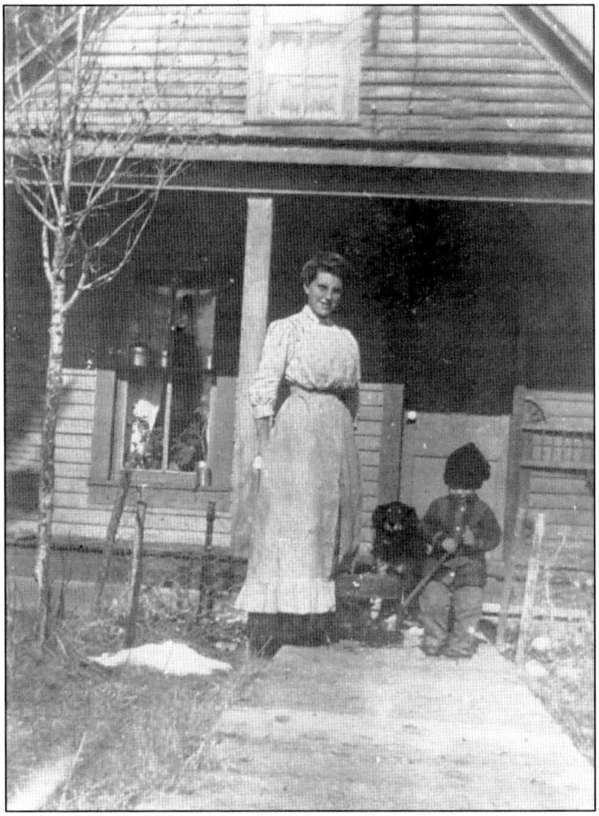

Alice Herseth Prestrud, Buster the Dog, and Son, Lars. Like many women in Frisco, Alice's primary roles were wife and mother. Few opportunities for employment outside the home presented themselves to women. Some found jobs as teachers or clerks while others owned stores or pursued professional careers such as teaching piano. Still others worked in laundries or opened boardinghouses and cooked for men who arrived without their families.

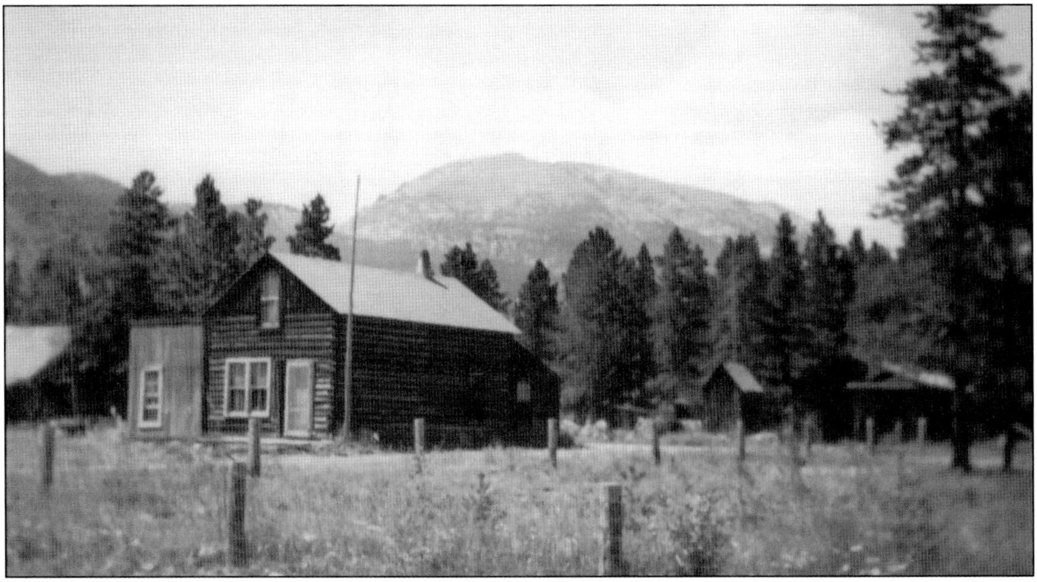

Frank and Annie Ruth House. This residence, first built on Main Street as a barn around 1890, features hand-hewn logs, square nails, a root cellar, and board and batten gables. Square nails indicate construction prior to 1900. Many homes had root cellars. Instead of keeping food cool, as in the eastern United States, root cellars in Summit County kept food from freezing during winter months.

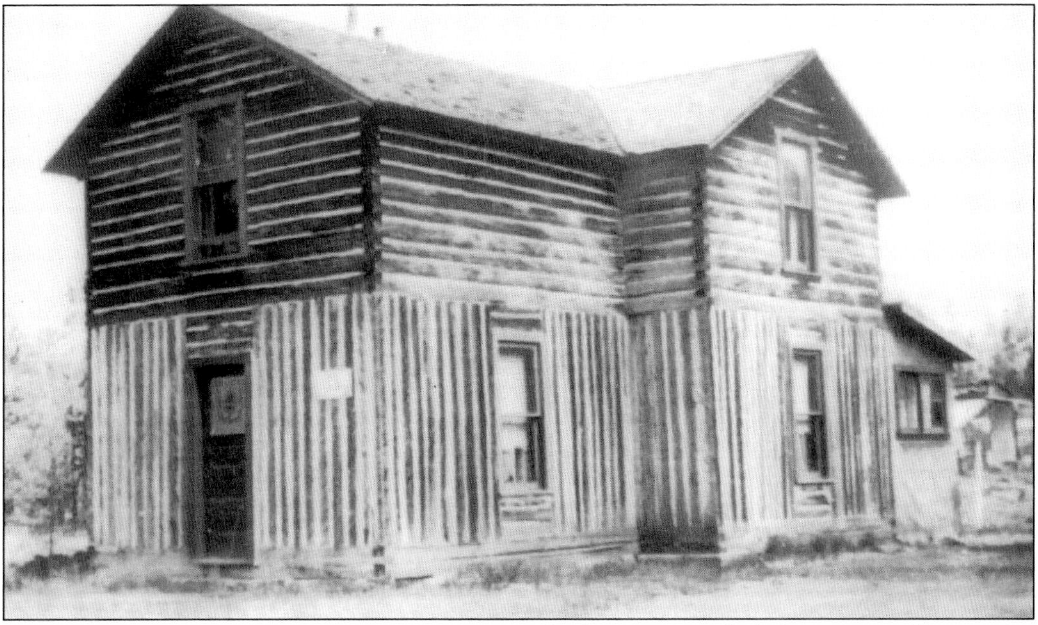

Staley-Rouse House. Located at 518 Main Street, this home originally belonged to William Staley and his wife, Alvarena. The use of both vertical and horizontal logs for the outside walls makes this a very unique structure in the state of Colorado. The key-notching at the joints of the horizontal logs indicates Nordic, possibly Finnish, influences in the house's design and construction.

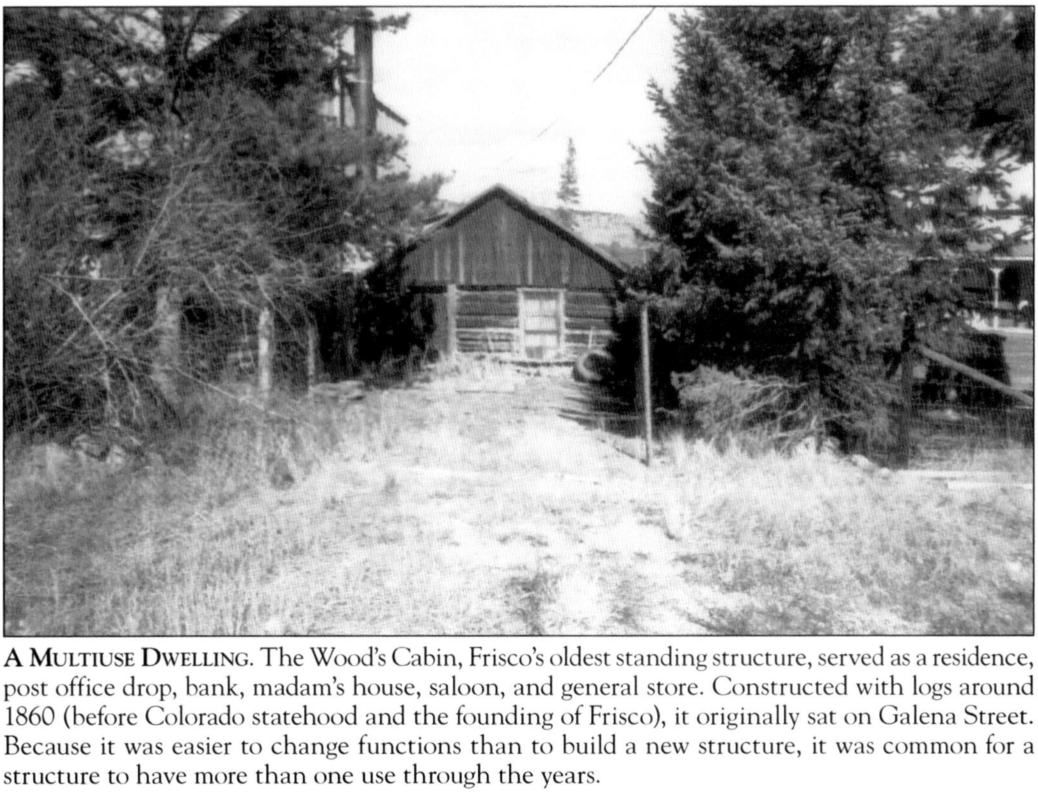

A Multiuse Dwelling. The Wood's Cabin, Frisco's oldest standing structure, served as a residence, post office drop, bank, madam's house, saloon, and general store. Constructed with logs around 1860 (before Colorado statehood and the founding of Frisco), it originally sat on Galena Street. Because it was easier to change functions than to build a new structure, it was common for a structure to have more than one use through the years.

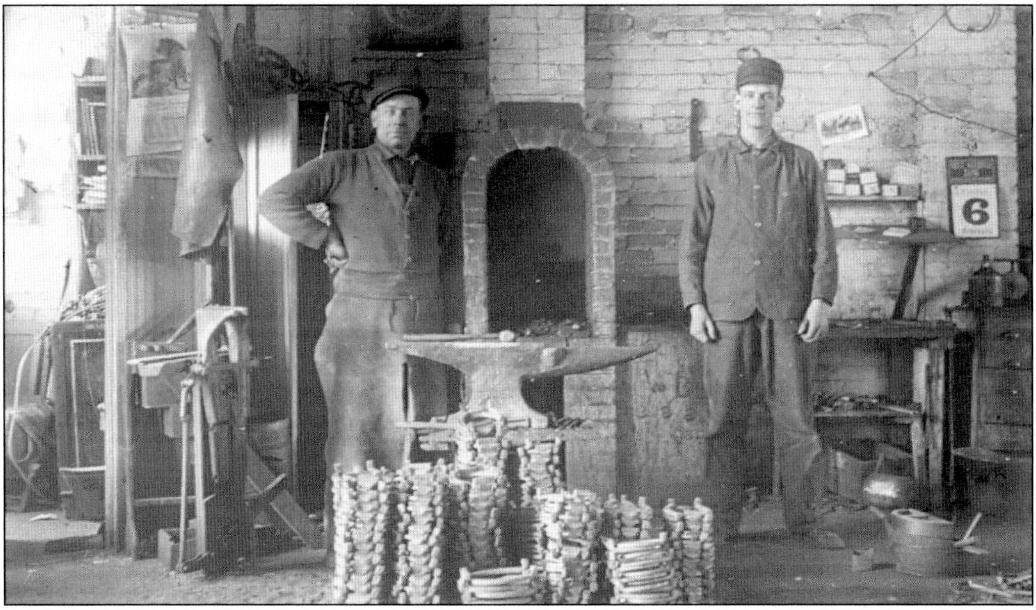

Blacksmiths at Work. The blacksmith was one of the most important men in a town or at a mine. Making horseshoes and shoeing horses occupied much of his time. Note the horseshoes stacked in front of the men. Mining operations depended heavily on blacksmiths for quick repairs to pipes, hand tools, and drill steels. Railroads hired blacksmiths to make equipment used by crews to repair engines and lay track.

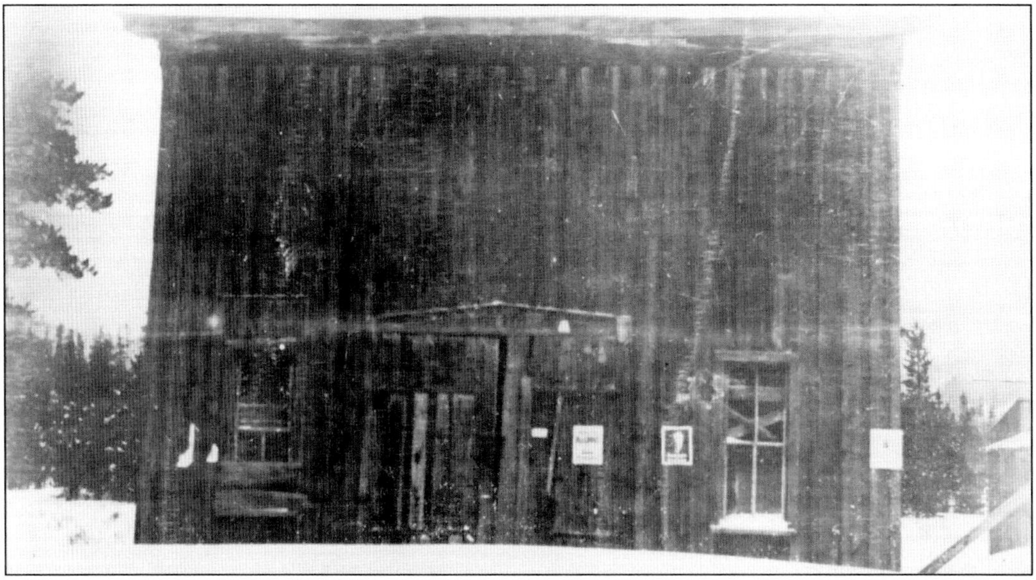

Ballif Blacksmith Shop. A trained veterinarian, Adolphus "Tip" Ballif opened his first blacksmith shop in Frisco. He drove stagecoaches and owned a dairy ranch east of Frisco with his wife, Emma. Later he served the town as marshal. In December 1883, with no money to pay his salary, the town board told him to tax the ladies of the night $5 per month. He collected $9 for that month. (Courtesy History Colorado.)

SUSAN EMERY BADGER. Known to everyone as Miss Badger, she arrived in Frisco in 1934 and served as director of the county department of public welfare, deputy sheriff, marriage counselor, employment officer, and tireless worker for those who needed her help. Never without a hat when on the job, she pumped her own water, chopped her own wood, enjoyed a glass of whiskey, and smoked on occasion.

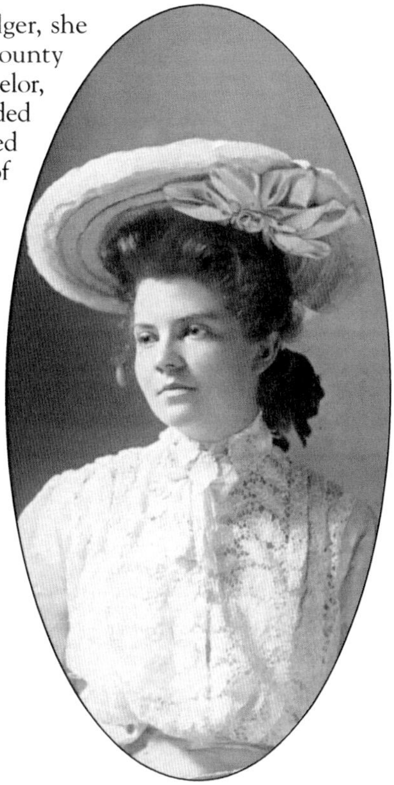

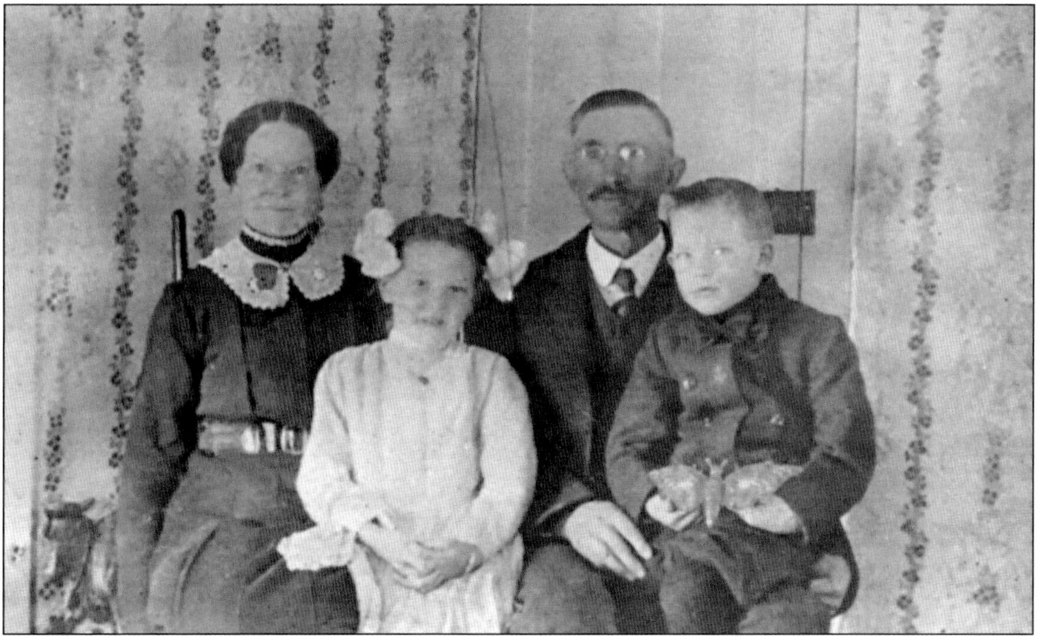

THE WILDHACK FAMILY IN 1914. Louis A. Wildhack, like many men living in Summit County, filled many roles. A miner, mining engineer, and mine surveyor, he also served as Frisco's postmaster from 1914 until 1935. Individuals who served as postmaster while continuing other occupations included Peter Leyner, Henry Learned, and Peter Prestrud.

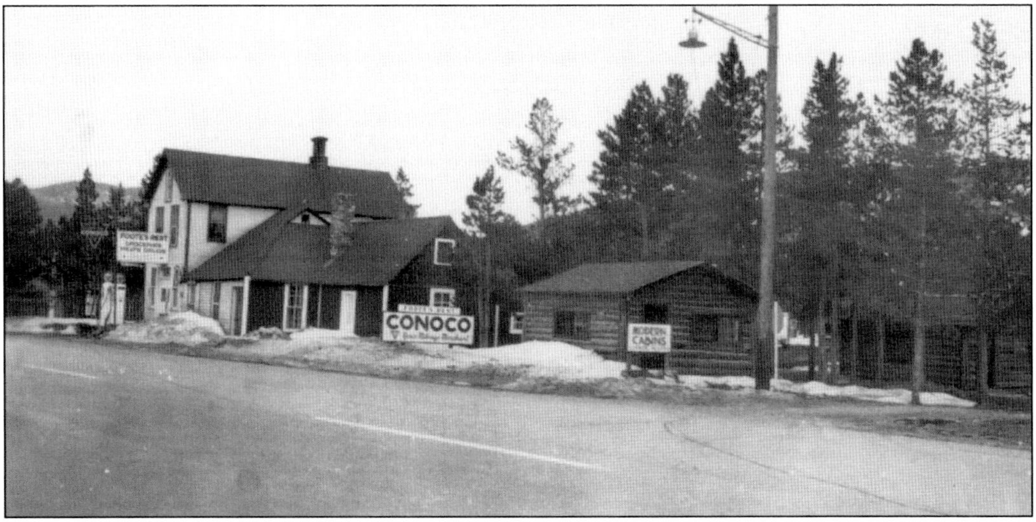

Foote's Rest. Louis Wildhack began constructing the original log-plank part of this structure in 1882. He added rooms as he needed more space for the store and post office. In 1920, he used lumber from the shuttered Admiral Mine to construct the two-story addition. When the Foote family purchased the entire building, they renamed it Foote's Rest.

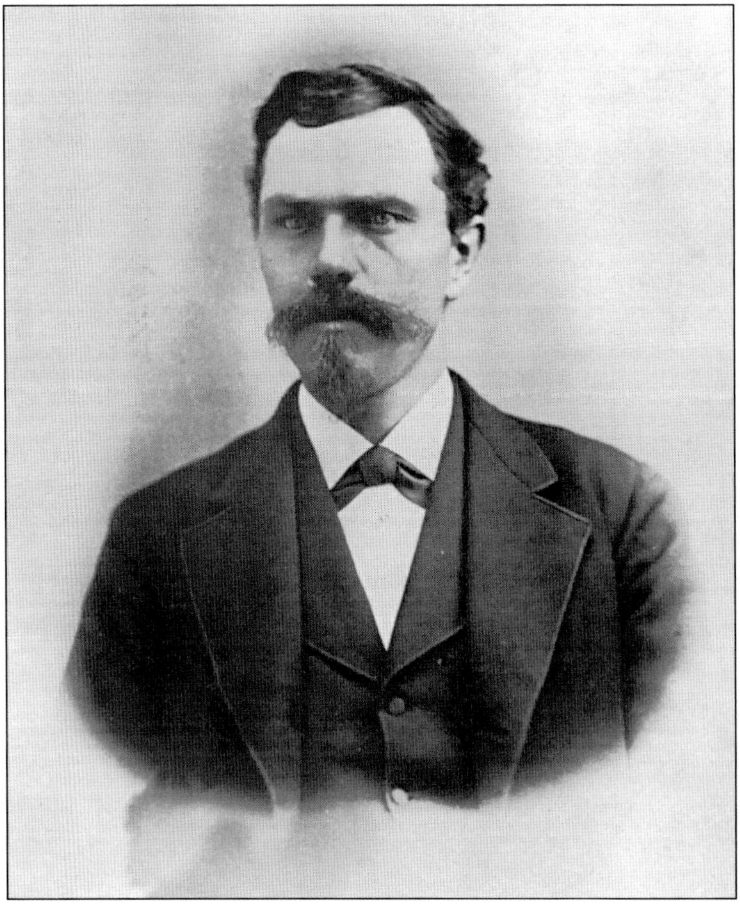

A Man of Many Talents. Chauncey Warren, during his years in Frisco, served on the town's school board and in 1887 as mayor. A miner, he later owned the Monroe Mine in the Ten Mile Canyon. He and his wife, Mary, both born in New York state, moved to Dillon and established the Warren Hotel and livery stable. Chauncey also served as mayor of Dillon.

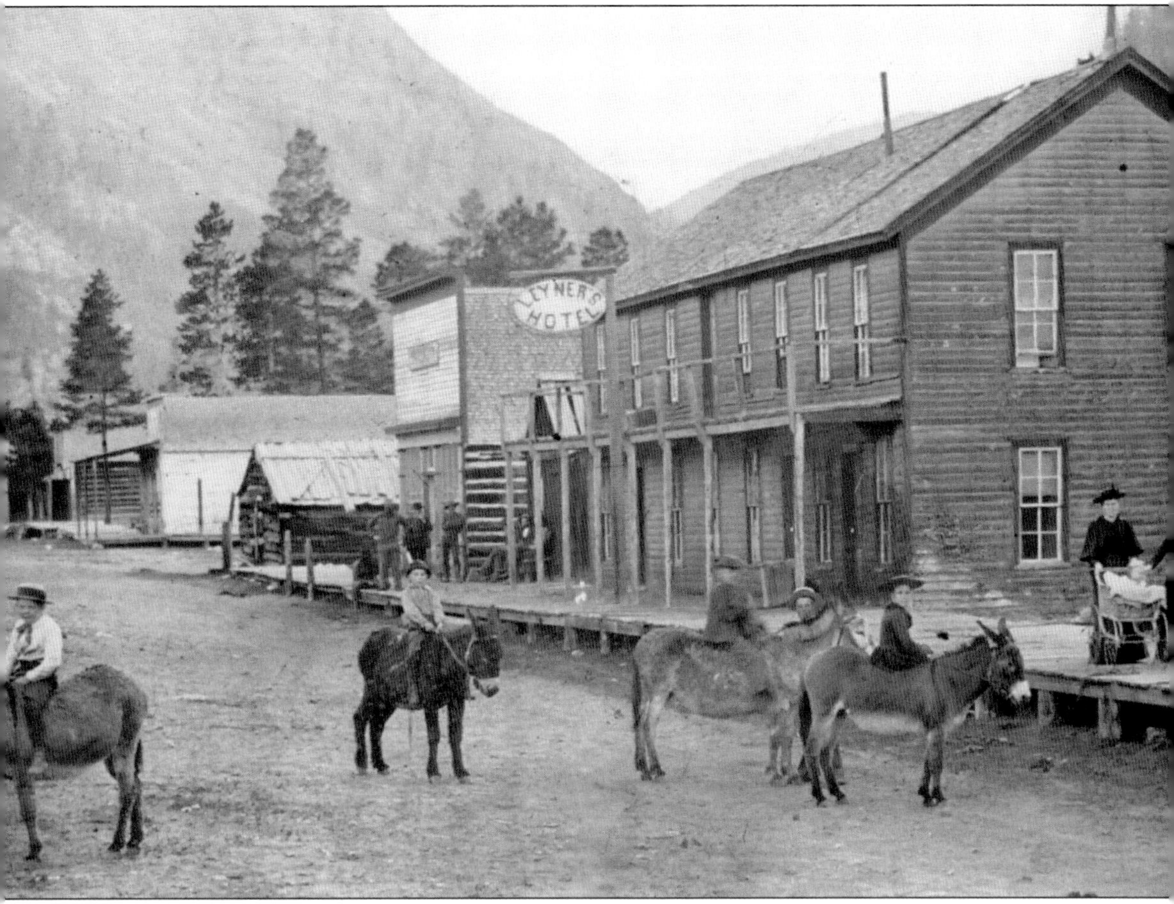

Children Riding Burros. Children faced many difficulties in the mining era. Unsanitary conditions and diseases such as diphtheria, influenza, smallpox, pneumonia, chicken pox, and measles claimed boys and girls of all ages. Early residents told of the absence of doctors, stressing that "none were needed, thank you." Of course, this was untrue.

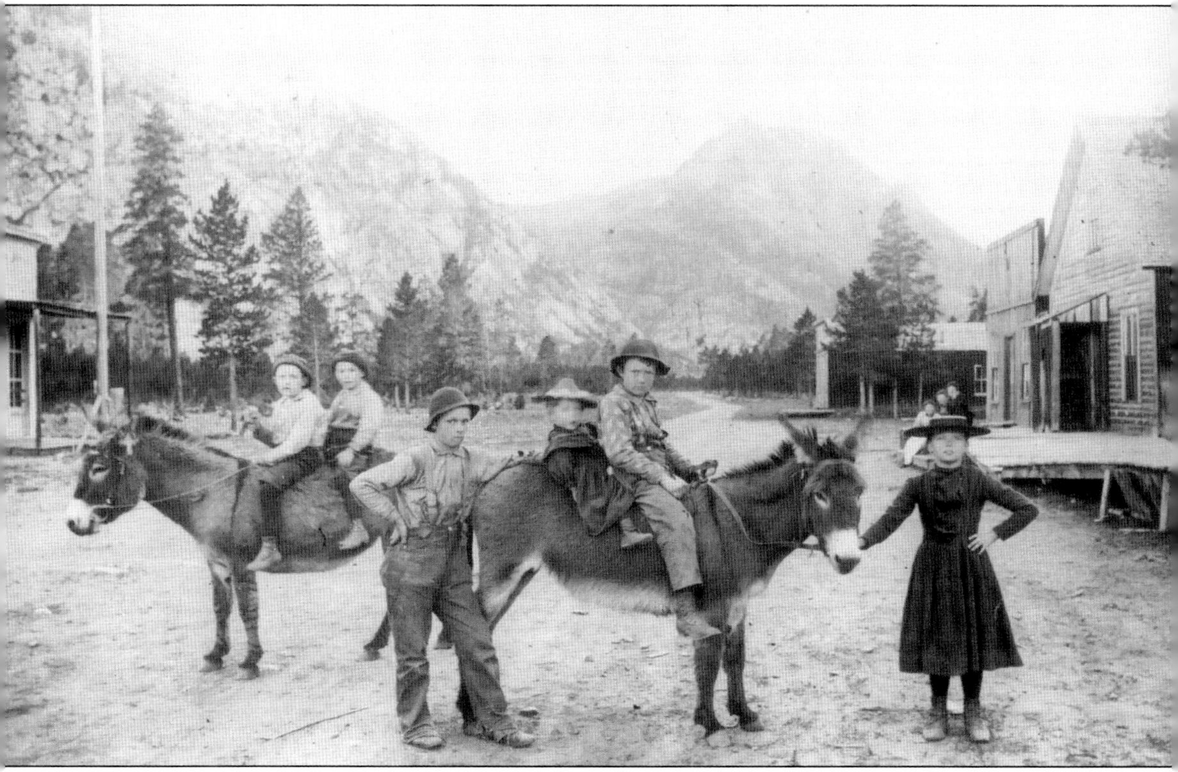

A Free Moment for the Photographer. School work and chores kept youngsters in Frisco and the Ten Mile Canyon fully occupied. At an early age, girls helped their mother maintain the home. At work, men taught the boys responsibility, integrity, and honesty, as well as less-endearing habits.

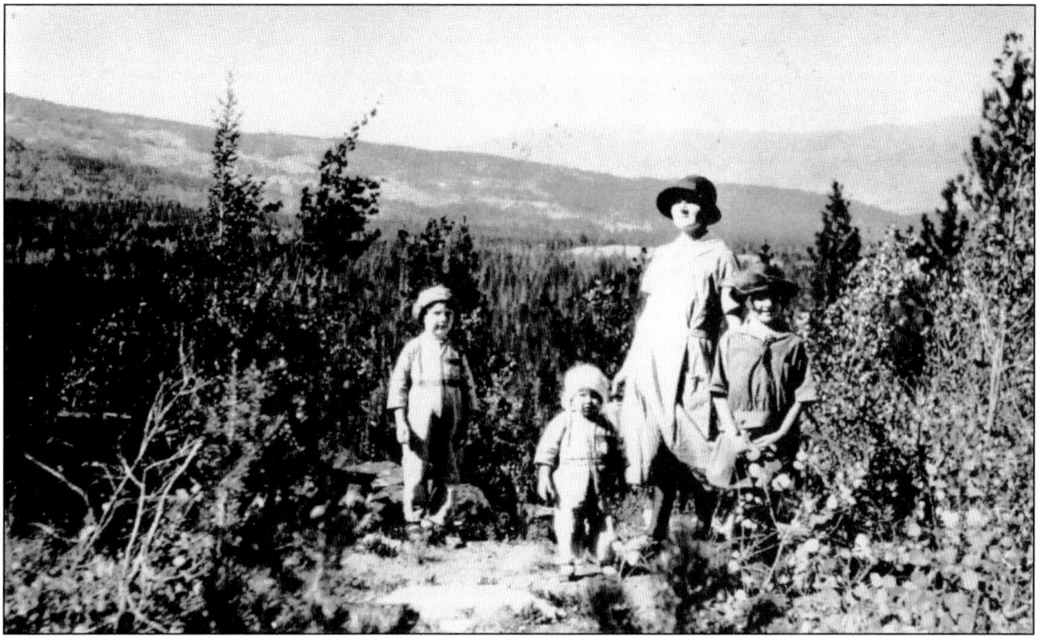

Searching for Berries. Every woman had her secret berry patch. Adults and children harvested a variety of berries every autumn. Those not eaten out of hand became jams, jellies, and syrups that tasted so good during the snowy winters. Bears in the berry patches posed a real danger for those not aware of their surroundings.

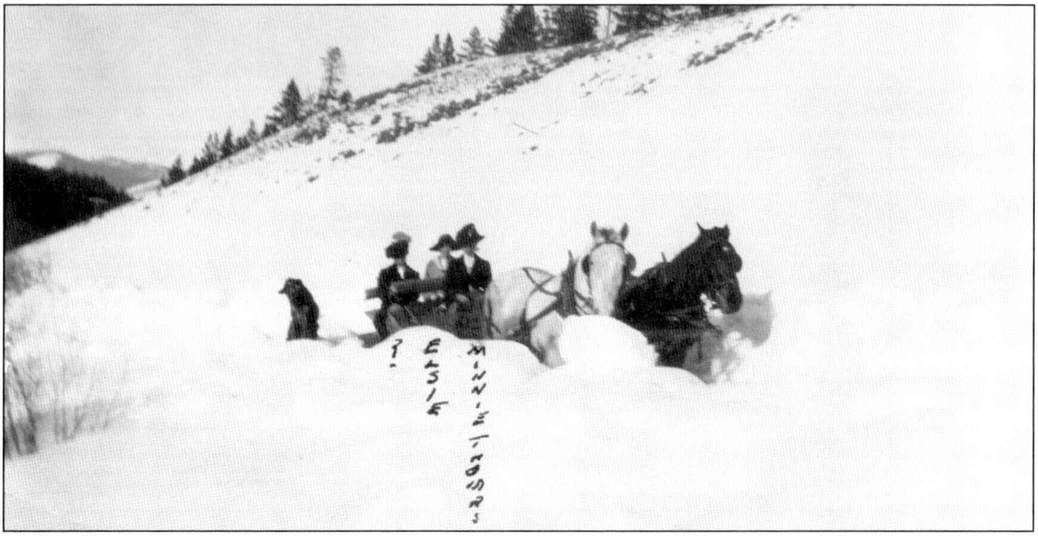

Winter Travel in 1914. Heavy, deep snow created obstacles for horse-drawn carriages. With no plows for roads, horses struggled to push through the drifts. Despite the difficulties, the women of the county considered the snow just one more problem to face during the long, cold winters. While some faced the winter cheerfully, others fell victim to deep depression during the days with little sunlight.

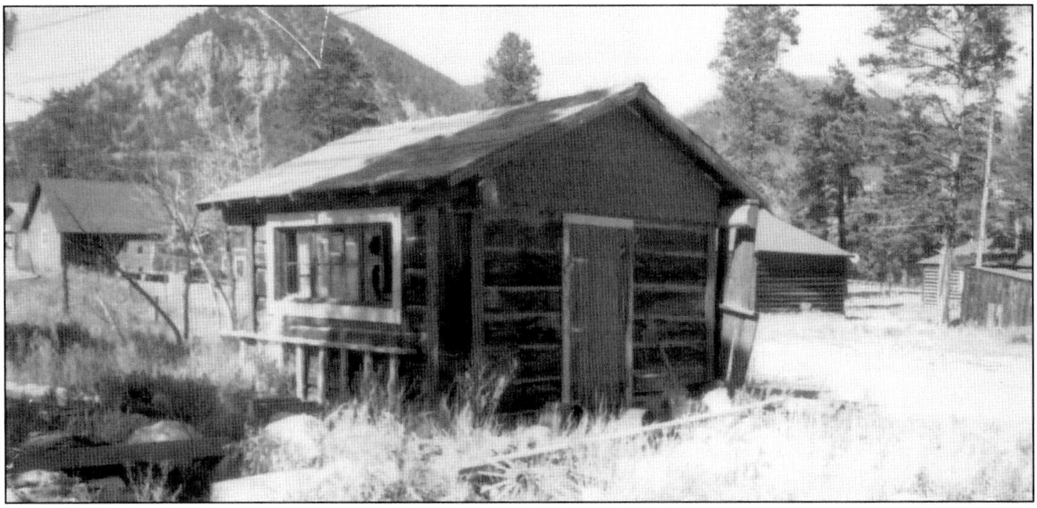

A Frisco Cabin. Between 1820 and 1850, mountain men harvested the fur-bearing animals for the fashion houses of Europe. High altitude and cold winters assured the desired thick pelts. The era of the mountain men ended when the fashion houses switched to silk, but trapping did not. Men built cabins like this one for shelter while tending their traps. The animals provided fur for clothing and meat for the table.

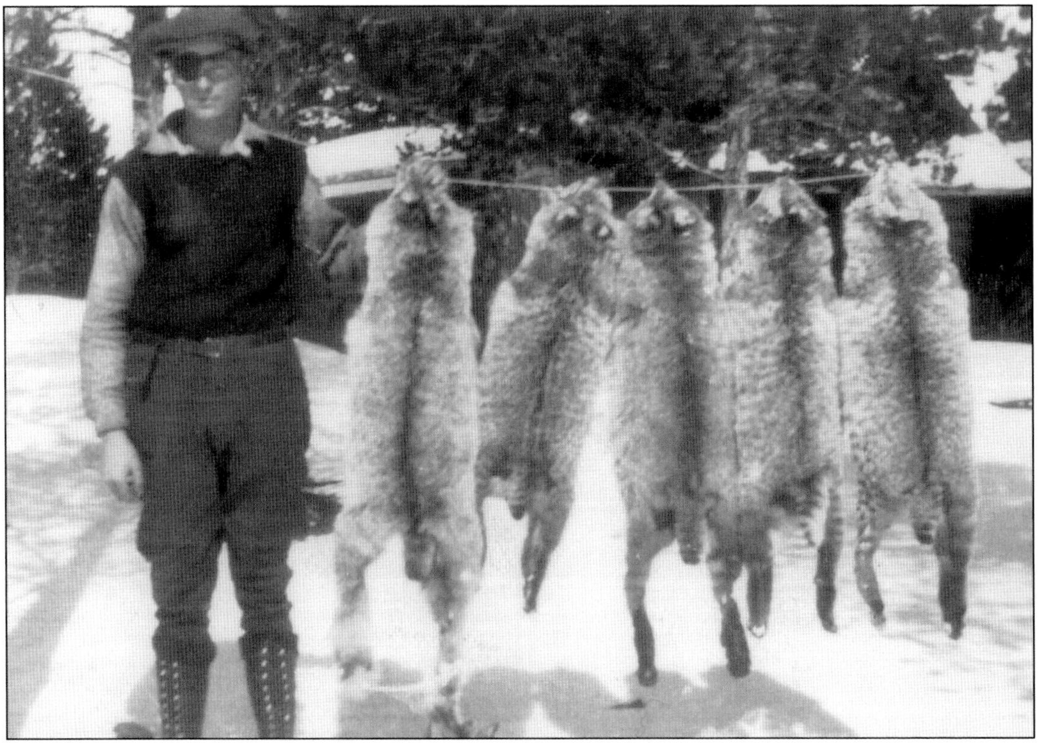

Bob Deming with Furs in 1925. Despite an accident that caused him to lose an eye as a teenager, Bob Deming became known as a crack shot. Knowing well the dangers of trapping in the winter, he tended his trap lines and earned much-needed money for his family. Using snowshoes (sometimes called Indian feet or webs), he often walked through heavy snow from trap to trap to collect the furs.

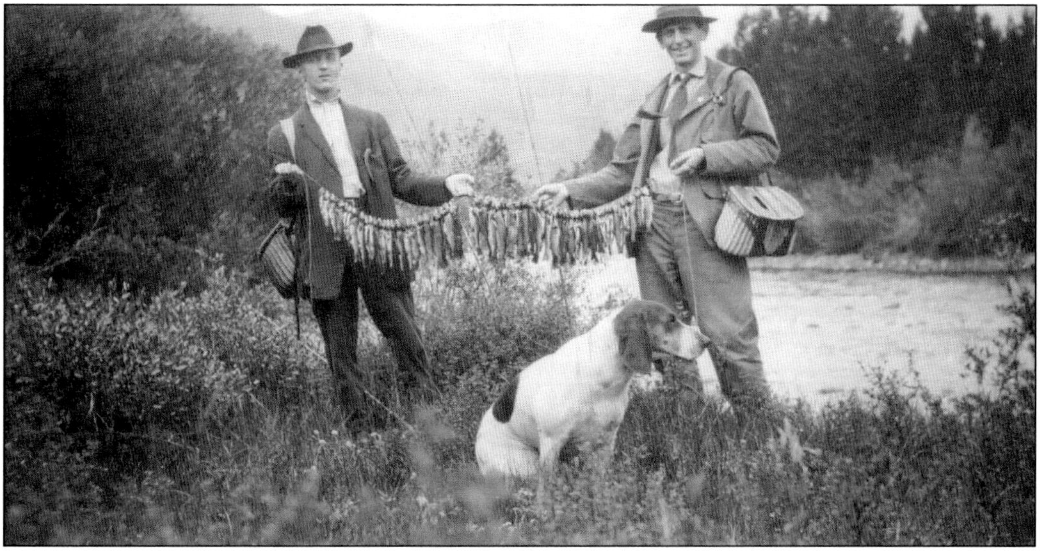

A Bountiful Catch. Erick Rathbun (left) and Leonard Pridy display their catch in 1912. Anglers harvested a variety of fish from the streams around Frisco and in the Ten Mile Canyon. For some, fishing was a pleasurable way to spend the afternoon; for others, it provided necessary food in hard times. The promise of a tasty meal drew many to the area.

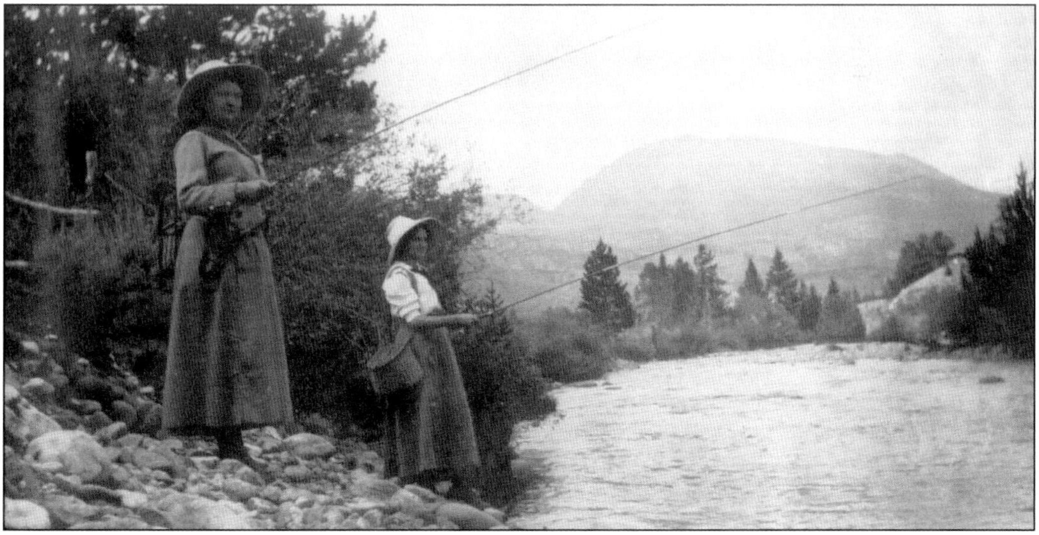

Women Anglers in 1912. Evelina Pridy (left) and a friend tried their luck while Pridy's husband fished nearby. When necessary, women supplemented their family's diets not only with fish but with quickly maturing vegetables and fruits raised in small gardens, chickens that provided meat and eggs, and wild berries gathered in autumn.

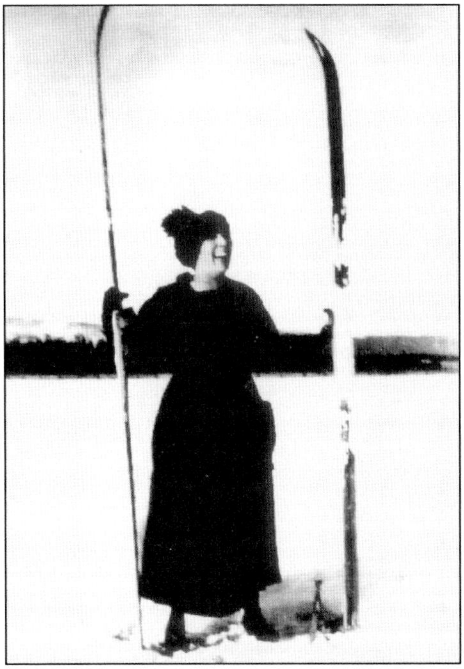

Learning to Ski in 1920. Prior to recreational skiing, people used skis that measured up to 12 feet in length to travel downhill over heavy winter snow. To stop, they placed the pole between their legs and sat down. To turn, they used the pole like a rudder on a ship. Bertha Tate enjoyed her experience.

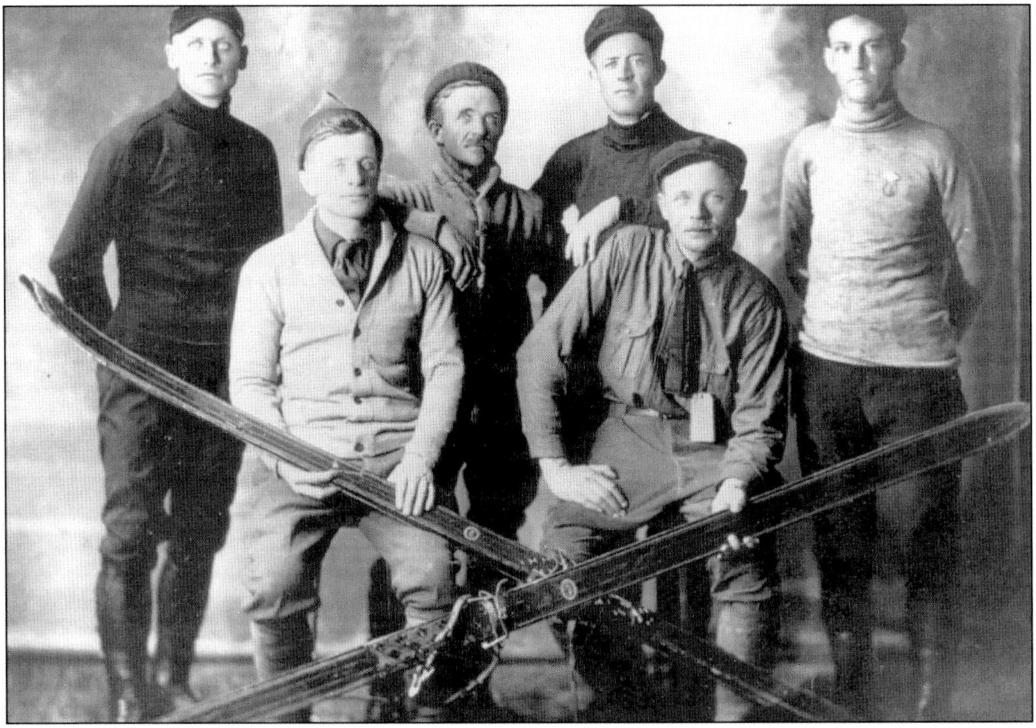

Ski Jumping. In 1910, Peter Prestrud introduced ski jumping to the residents of Summit County. It soon became a favorite sport among the men and young boys. The Dillon ski jumping team in 1919-1920 included, from left to right, Hans Hansen, Eyvind Flood (seated), Carl Howelsen, Anders Haugen, Peter Prestrud (seated), and Lars Haugen. (Courtesy Denver Public Library, Western History Collection, F-22846.)

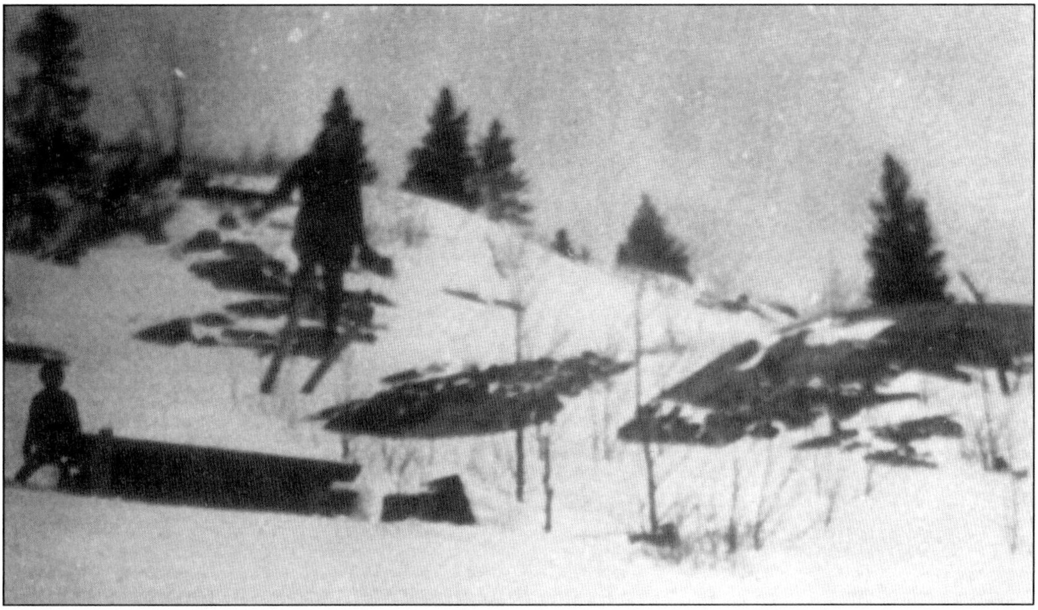

Ski Jumping, c. 1920. Because of the popularity of the sport around Frisco, skiers built small jumps like this one at Excelsior Mine where young men such as Willie Wildhack, seen here, practiced their skills. The thin atmosphere at 9,000 feet helped the "flyers" to travel great distances. On the large ski jump in Dillon, Anders Haugen set a world record in 1920 with a jump of 214 feet.

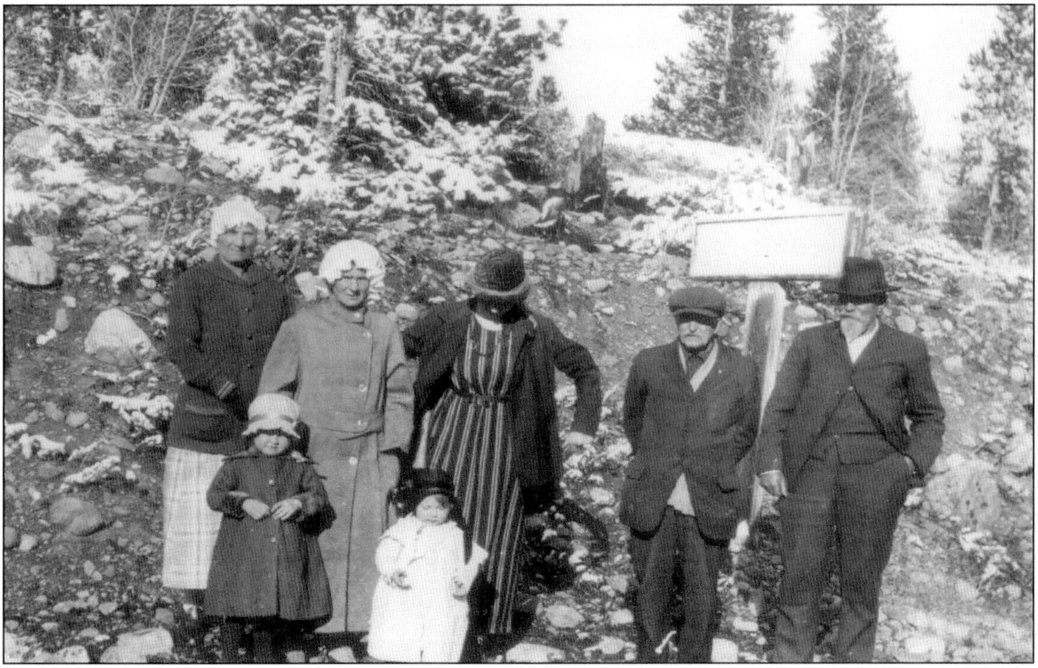

Ethnic Origins. A variety of ethnic groups migrated to Frisco and the Ten Mile Canyon. The logging industry near Wheeler drew Swedish and Norwegian families. The mines employed many from Great Britain, especially those from Cornwall and Wales. The Irish, by far the largest group arriving in the area, and the Germans owned many businesses and saloons in Frisco and the towns of the Ten Mile Canyon.

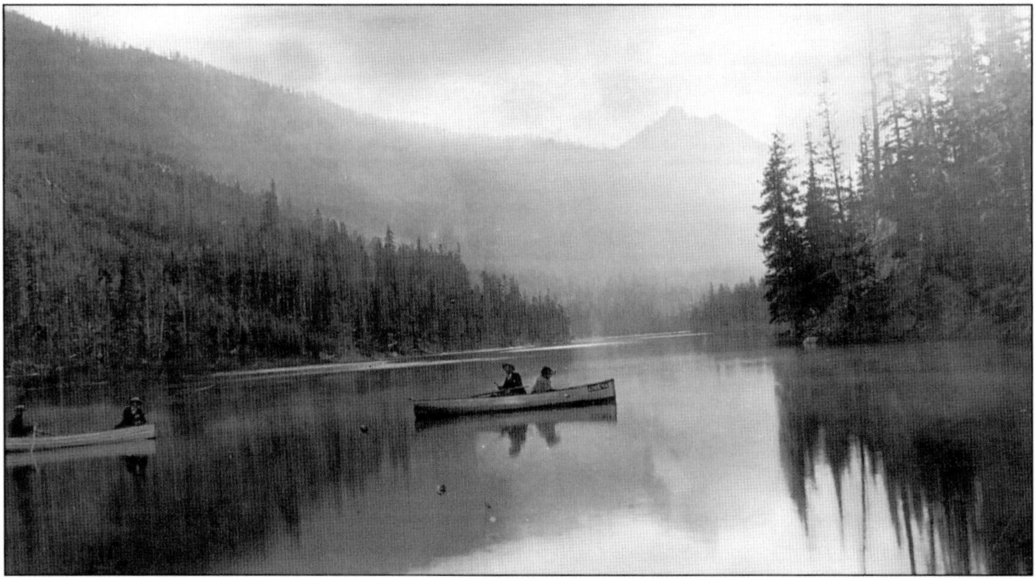

UNEVA LAKE. On January 2, 1906, the Colorado Southern Rio Grande Development Company purchased the Uneva Lake property with plans to develop a fishing resort. Uneva, a natural glacial lake covering 57 acres, is found west of Ten Mile Creek at an elevation of 9,616 feet. Peak 1 (12,522 feet) and Tenmile Peak (12,805 feet) rise east of the lake.

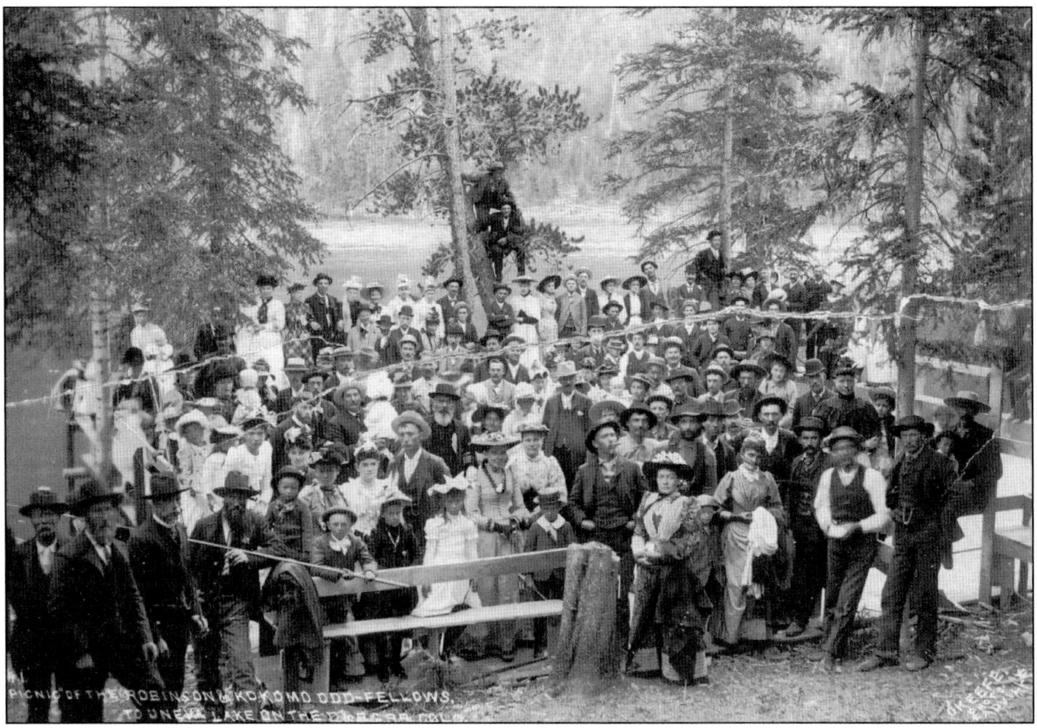

ODD FELLOWS AT UNEVA LAKE. Members of the Odd Fellows lodges in Robinson and Kokomo gathered for this photograph at Uneva Lake. The Odd Fellows and their sister organization, the Rebekahs, enrolled members in various lodges throughout the county. While caring for members remained a primary function of the groups, many of their activities were social in nature.

Three

Towns of the Ten Mile Canyon

Gone But Not Forgotten

Following the discovery of silver in the Ten Mile Canyon, several towns were founded to provide supplies for the mines and homes for mine employees and their families. Carbonateville, Robinson, Kokomo, Recen, Wheeler Junction, and Curtin all existed for as long as their reason for being remained. Land speculators laid out many of the town sites in the Ten Mile Canyon with wide streets and blocks of building lots—enough for thousands of people. Photographs show similarities between the towns, including false-front wooden buildings facing trash-littered streets and yards, streets lined with wooden sidewalks to keep people's feet away from mud and litter, and houses interspersed among the businesses. The town marshal in Recen attempted to rid the town of the sewage, dead animals, and garbage. Fines for non-compliance were high. For sewage, offenders had to pay $2–$5 for each 48 hours the problem persisted; for garbage and dead animals, the fine was $5–$50 per offense.

Residents of the Ten Mile Canyon feared fires. Recen hired a fire marshal to inspect buildings, chimneys, and stoves. If a fire marshal found a problem, he ordered immediate repairs and could levy fines of five dollars per day. Town ordinances prohibited selling gunpowder after the lamps were lit unless store owners exercised extreme caution. Merchants could not store over 100 pounds of gunpowder at a time. No more than three barrels of kerosene or other explosive oils were permitted in an area. Ordinances prohibited the sale of petroleum products after the evening lights were lit. If the marshal discovered a merchant concealing these substances to evade the ordinance, he levied a fine of $5–$100 dollars per offense. When voters approved a water system for firefighting, domestic purposes, and irrigation, the town board appropriated $3,000 from the 1898 budget. Even with all the precautions, disastrous fires struck Robinson in 1916, Wheeler Junction in 1882, and Kokomo in 1881.

The silver bust of the 1890s took its toll on the towns of the Ten Mile Canyon. Unemployment rose. Families moved away. Once-thriving towns faced bleak times. These towns live on in diaries, newspaper articles, pictures, and in stories passed from generation to generation—gone but not forgotten.

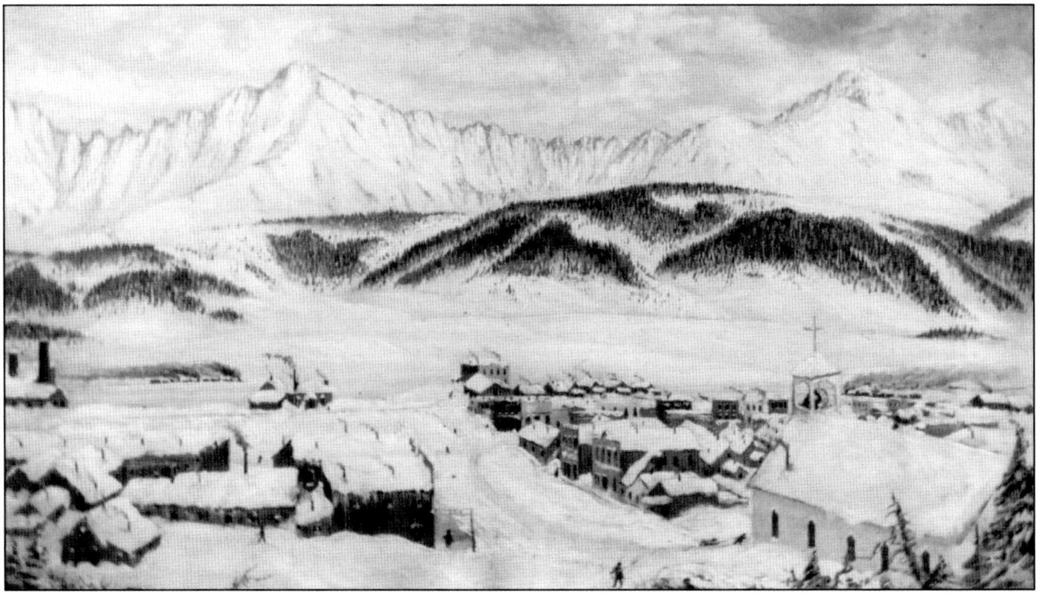

Robinson in 1879, Looking East. Named for George B. Robinson, a Leadville merchant, Robinson offered views of Fletcher Peak and Little Bartlett Mountain to the east, Chalk Mountain to the south, and Sheep Mountain to the west. By 1887, the town had a bank, an assay office, hotels, a grocery store, dance halls, saloons, a theatre, and an opera house. The community church looked out over the entire town. (Used with permission from the Bill Fountain Collection.)

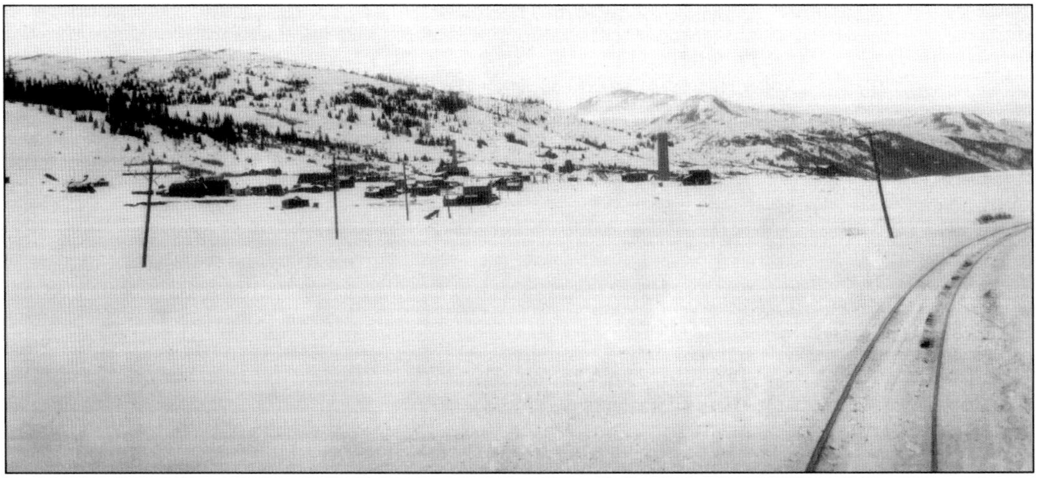

A Snowy Winter in Robinson. Robinson, located two miles south of Kokomo and 94 feet higher, endured heavy winter snow. At one time the largest town in the Ten Mile Canyon, Robinson had six smelters, four sawmills, and a newspaper called the *Summit County Times*. The smokestacks in this photograph indicate the location of two of those smelters. Numerous mines sent their ore to the smelters for processing. (Used with permission of the Colorado Railroad Museum.)

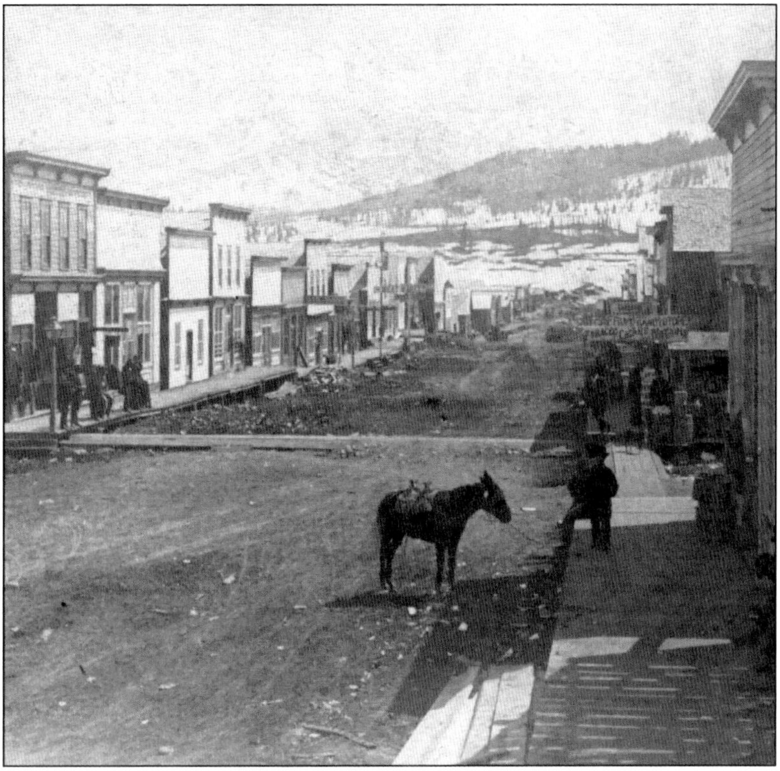

Main Street, Robinson. Also called Robinson's Camp, Ten Mile City, Summit, and Summit City, Robinson grew rapidly because of its proximity to the rich Robinson Mine. The town housed the hard rock or lode miners who worked in the mine. Structures with false fronts lined the main street of the planned community. A boardwalk allowed people to cross from one side of the street to the other. (Used with permission from the Ed and Nancy Bathke Collection.)

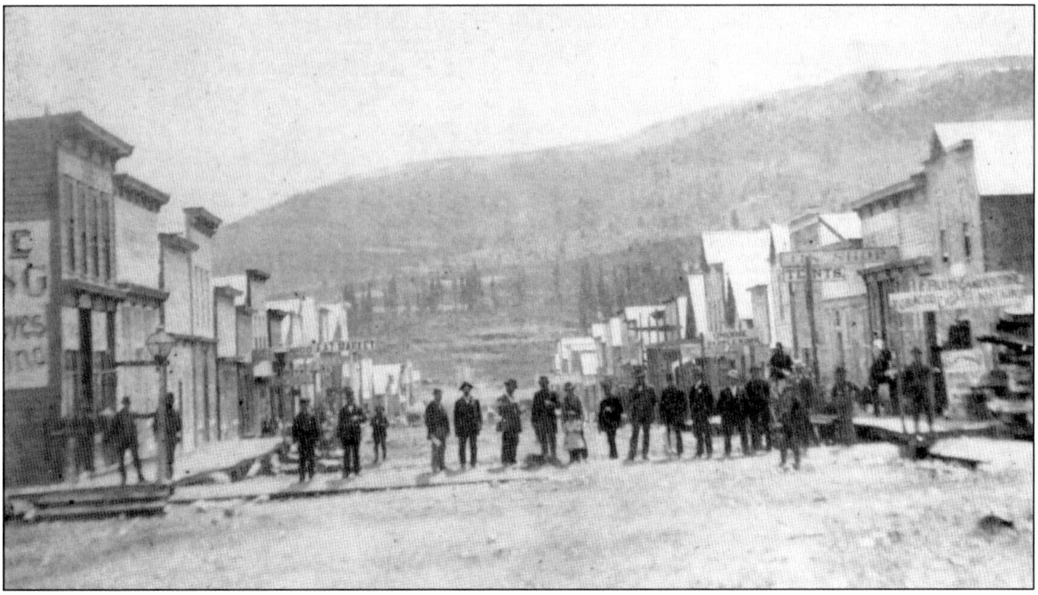

Robinson's Fluctuating Population. Men dominated the population of Robinson. Here, they pose on a boardwalk crossing the main street. The yearly *Colorado State Business Directory* estimated population and advertised businesses in Robinson. The 1881 directory listed businesses but gave no population estimate. In 1882, the directory estimated a population of 500. In 1883, the population estimate was 800; in 1884 and 1885, 400; and in 1887, 300. By 1889, the population had dropped to 250. (Used with permission from the Ed and Nancy Bathke Collection.)

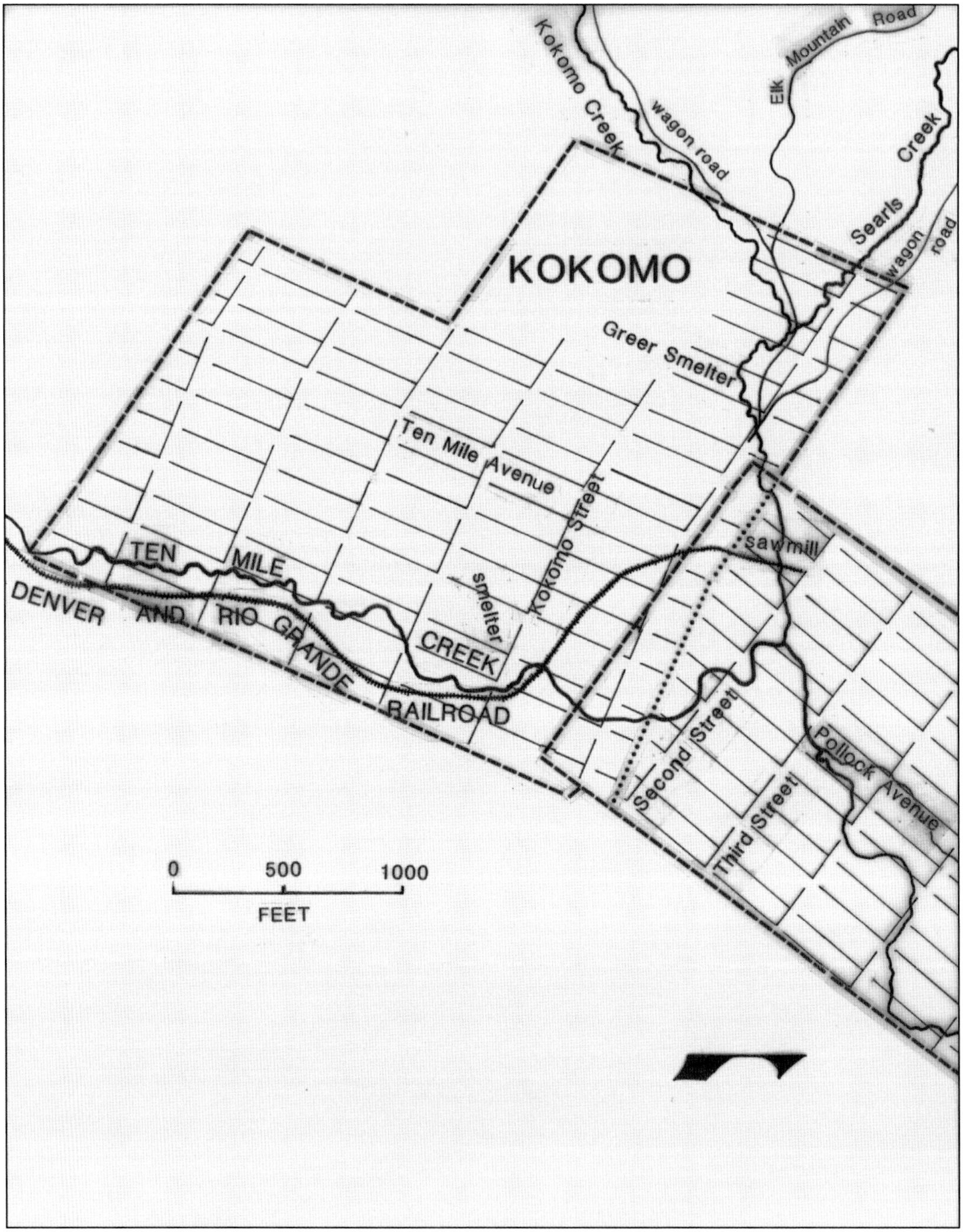

KOKOMO. In 1879, Amos C. Smith and others in the Ten Mile Land and Mining Company laid out a town across from McNulty Gulch on East Sheep and Elk Mountains. Dubbed Kokomo—probably because Smith came from Kokomo, Indiana—it became a supply center for miners in the upper (southern) Ten Mile. On May 17, 1879, the town incorporated and chose Smith as its first mayor. (Map drawn by author.)

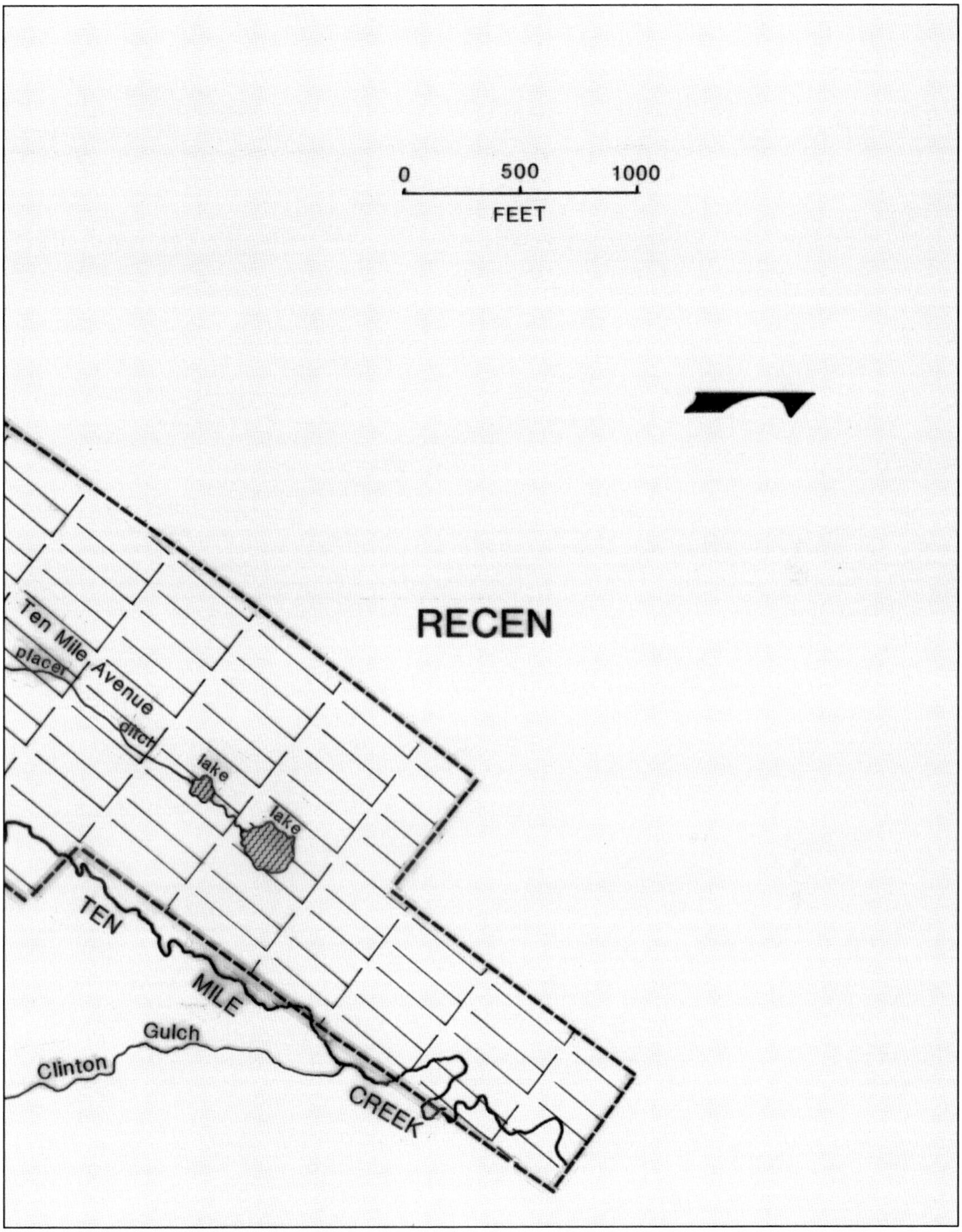

RECEN. In Recen, another planned settlement, lots measured 25 feet wide and 100 feet deep. Main streets were 60 feet wide, side streets 50 feet. The company offered free lots to those burned out by an 1881 fire in neighboring Kokomo. It required only that the new owners erect a $300 building in 30 days. (Map drawn by author.)

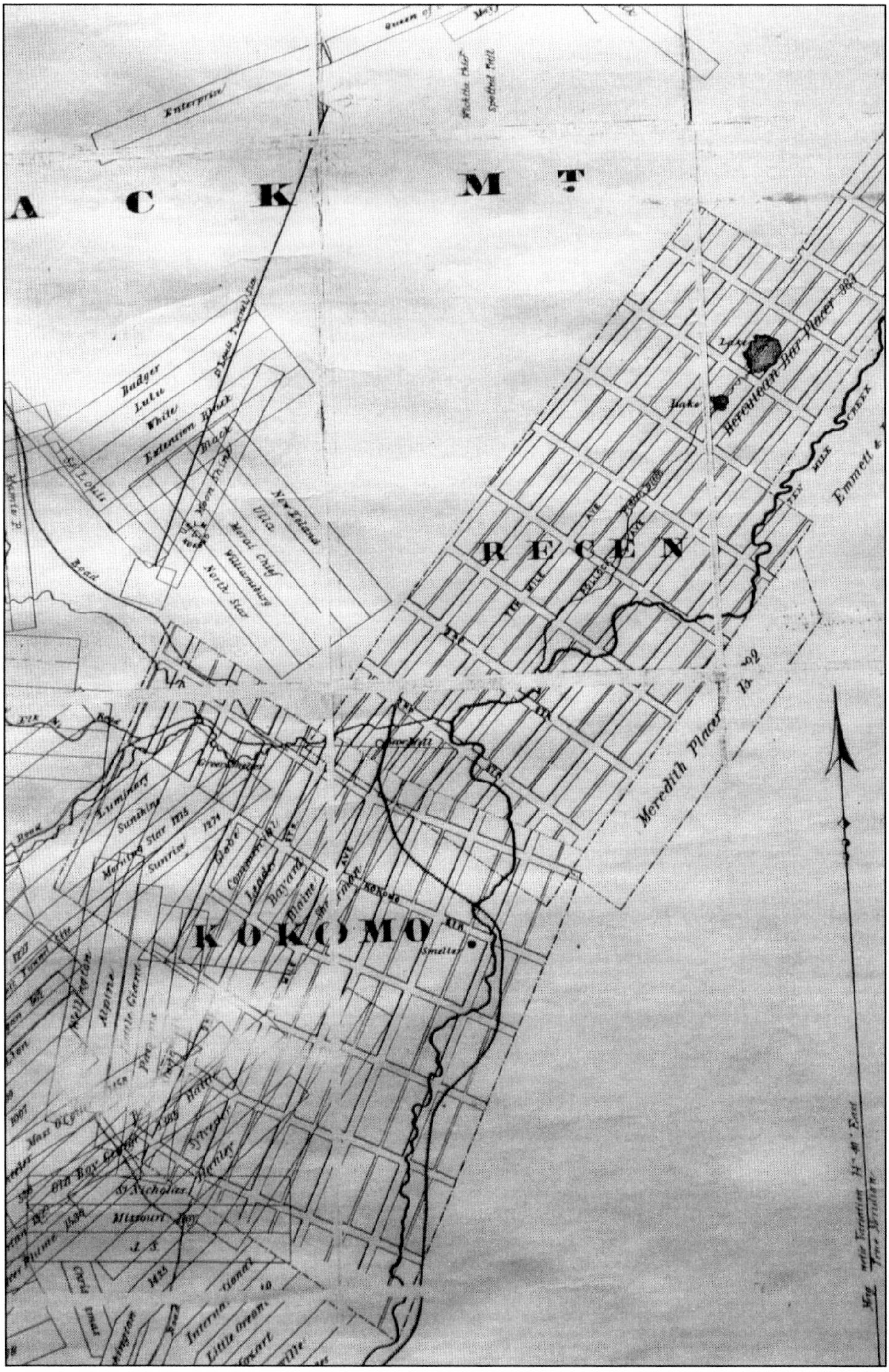

Kokomo-Recen. Speculators platted these towns amid the mining claims to the west of the Ten Mile Creek. Lots sold swiftly, with many purchased by business owners hoping to supply the needs of the residents and nearby mines. While Kokomo grew toward the north, Recen, to the north, grew southward. Poor roads proved the biggest obstacle for the town and its businesses.

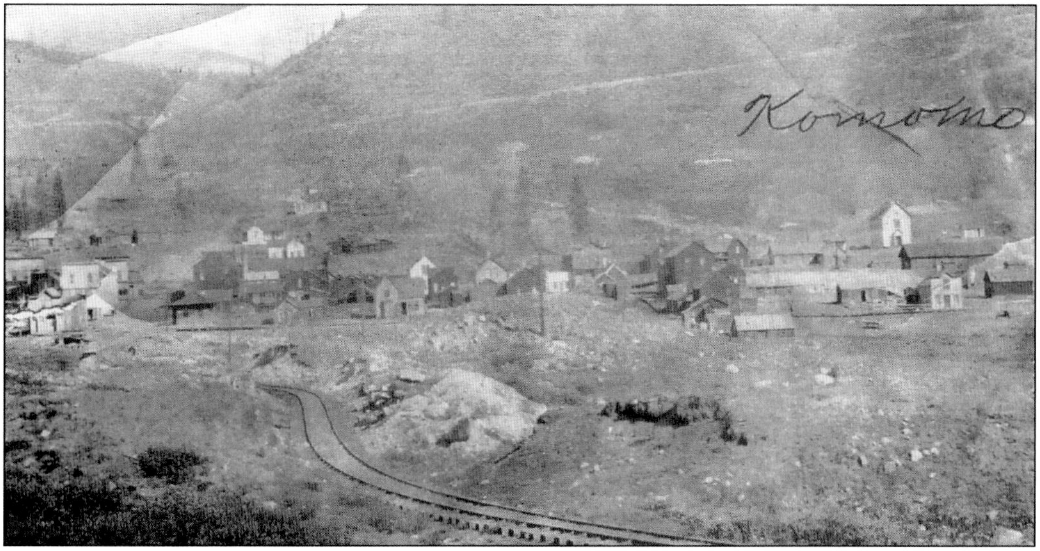

KOKOMO OVERLOOK. The schoolhouse overlooked the business district of Kokomo. Prior to the arrival of the railroad in 1880, goods, mail, and passengers arrived by pack trains, stagecoaches, and wagons. The tracks in the foreground led to the Denver, Leadville & Gunnison (later Colorado & Southern) depot built in 1895. Between 1913 and 1918, the company moved the depot to a site near the left edge of the photograph.

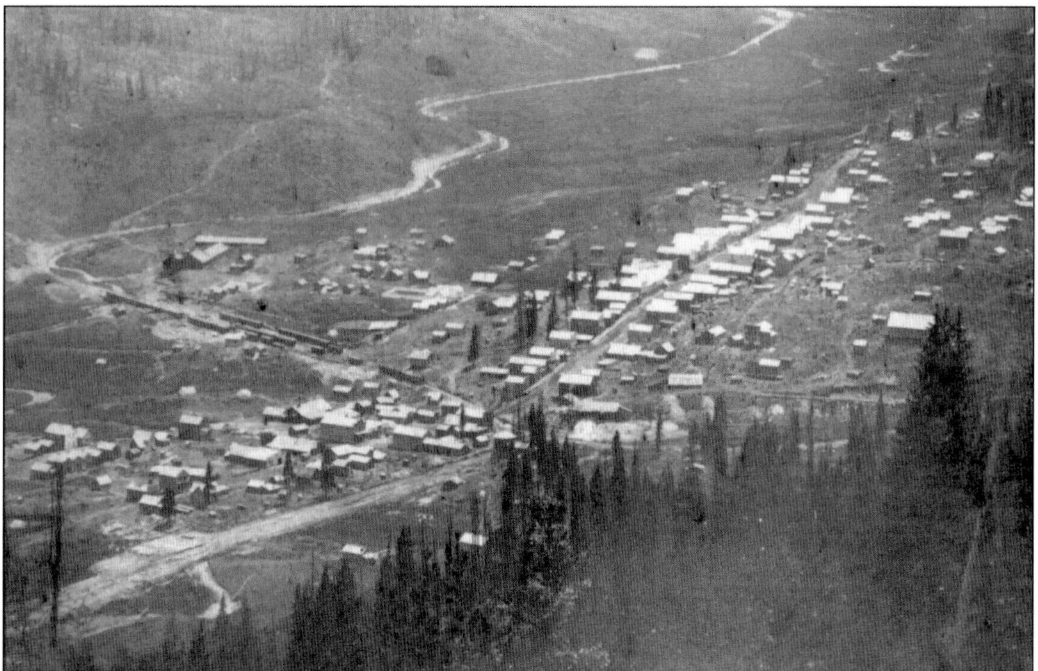

OVERVIEW OF KOKOMO IN 1885. Despite precautions, Kokomo suffered a devastating fire on October 13, 1881, that left 80 families homeless. Many buildings burned, including a hotel, bank, dance hall, mint, post office, three saloons, two law offices, two fruit stores, and the town newspaper office. Only by tearing down buildings could the fire be contained. Residents rebuilt the town in just a few years. (Used with permission from the Ed and Nancy Bathke Collection.)

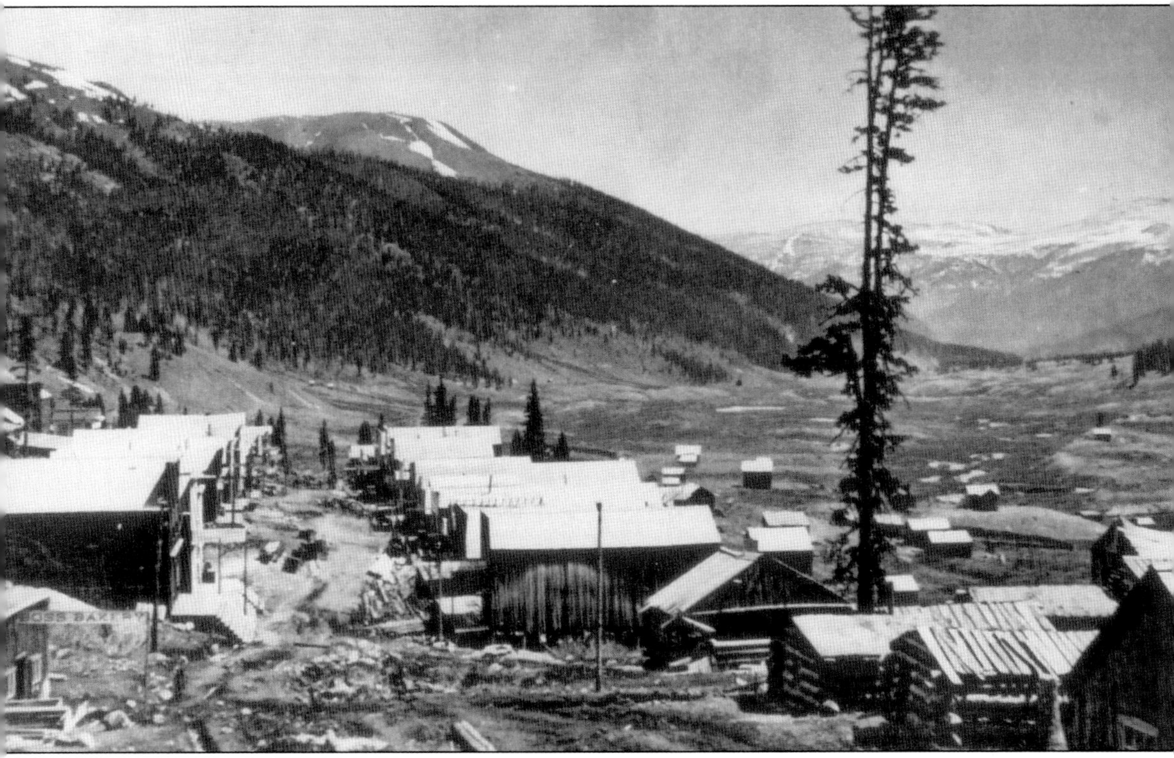

TEN MILE AVENUE IN KOKOMO. The town company offered free lots to anyone who would build on them. Homes were interspersed among the businesses along the main street. Because of its size and booming economy, Kokomo supported specialty shops including two sign- and house-painting companies, two confectioneries, several bakeries, four drugstores, and five men's clothing stores.

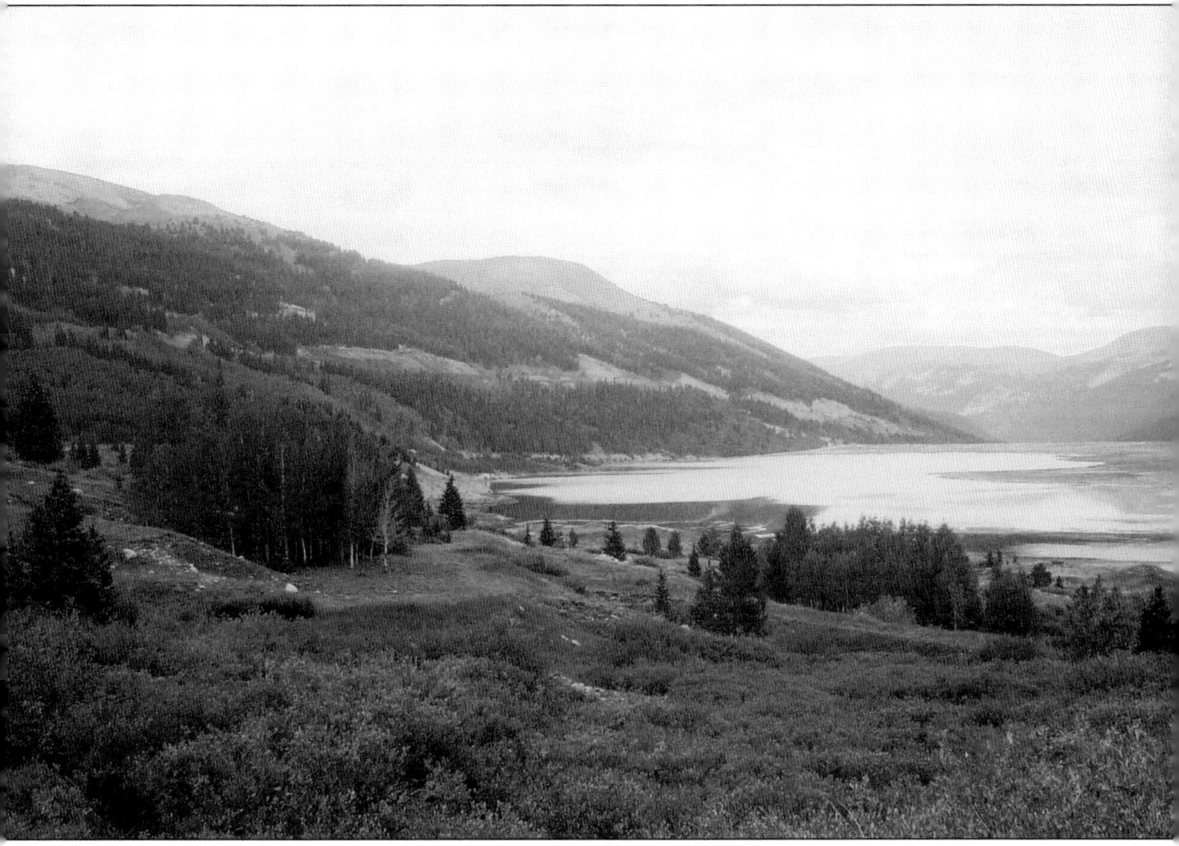

KOKOMO—A CENTURY LATER. By 2006, vegetation had reclaimed the parts of the Kokomo site not buried by the tailings pond of the Climax molybdenum mine. When the mine closed because of low worldwide prices for molybdenum, the pond stopped its slow encroachment on the site and vegetation returned. If the mine reopens, the tailings will eventually cover all of Kokomo. (Used with permission from the Bill Fountain Collection.)

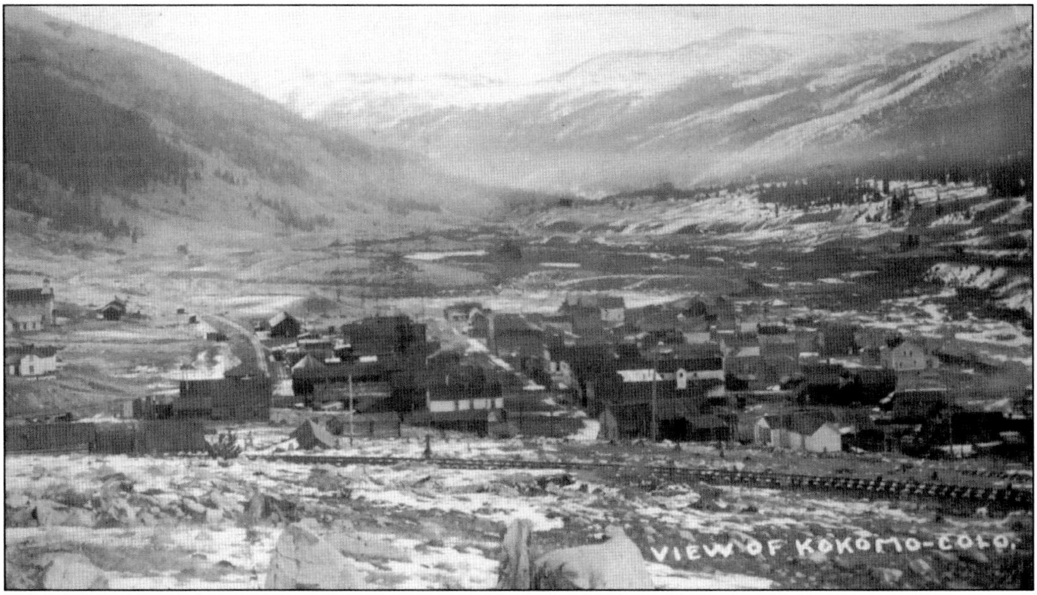

VIEW OF KOKOMO. Kokomo and Recen flourished while Carbonateville withered and died; the short walking distance to the richest mines from Kokomo and Recen doomed the more distant Carbonateville. Workers, feeling little loyalty to a particular town, moved quickly, following the trails to the new and rich strikes on Elk Mountain, Sheep Mountain, and Jacque Peak. See page 109 for a view of the Kokomo town site in 2009. Note the identical rocks in the foreground. (Used with permission of the Lake County Public Library, Colorado Mountain History Collection.)

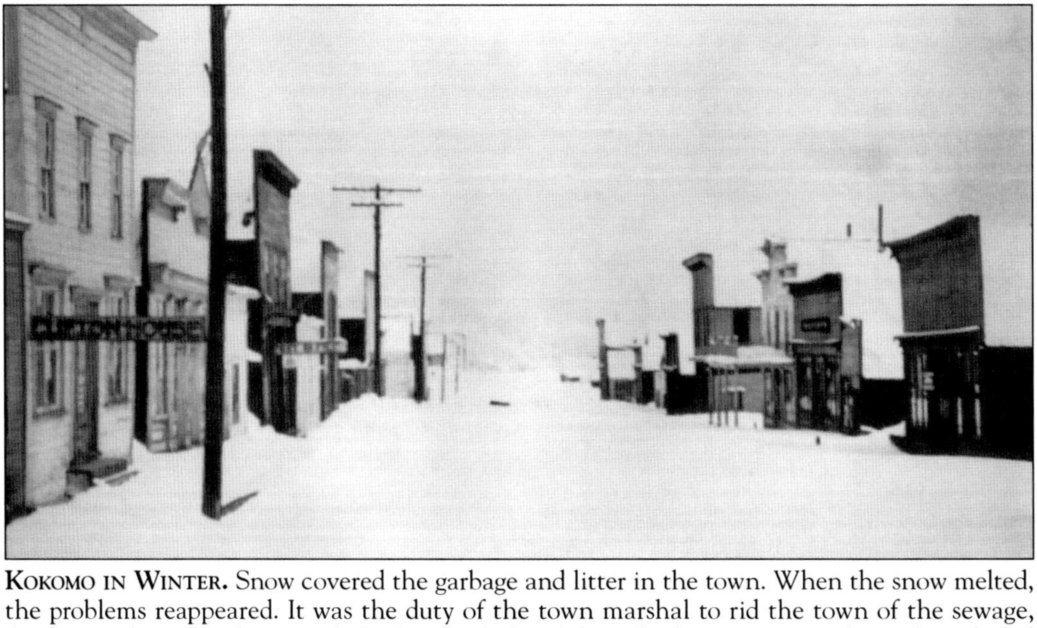

KOKOMO IN WINTER. Snow covered the garbage and litter in the town. When the snow melted, the problems reappeared. It was the duty of the town marshal to rid the town of the sewage, dead animals, and garbage. To help the marshal with his job, the newspaper editor often chided merchants and others who did not do their part to keep the town looking neat.

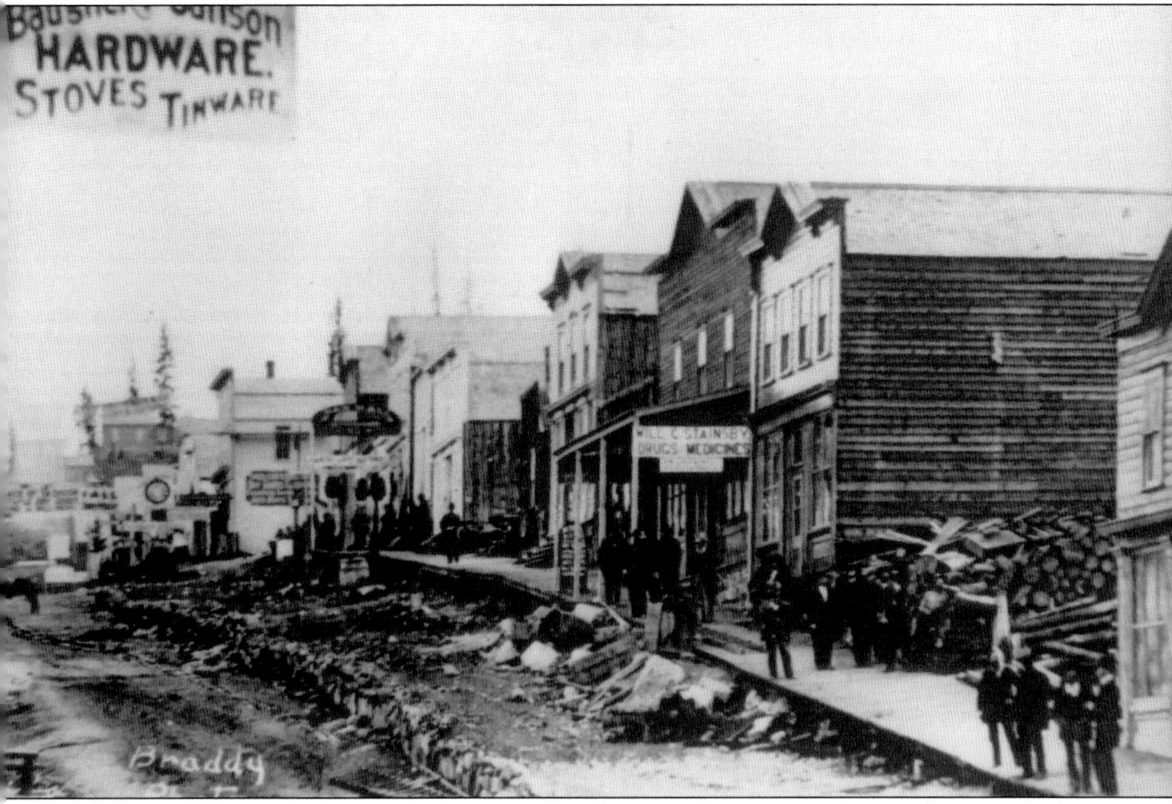

KOKOMO'S MAIN STREET. The town served as a supply center for miners in the southern Ten Mile Canyon. Some of the signs on the false-front wooden buildings identified places such as the Palace of Fashion, GAR (Grand Army of the Republic) Hall, a clothing house, a fancy staple dry goods merchant, and a dressmaker. Each merchant was responsible for keeping one half of the street in front of his or her business free of litter.

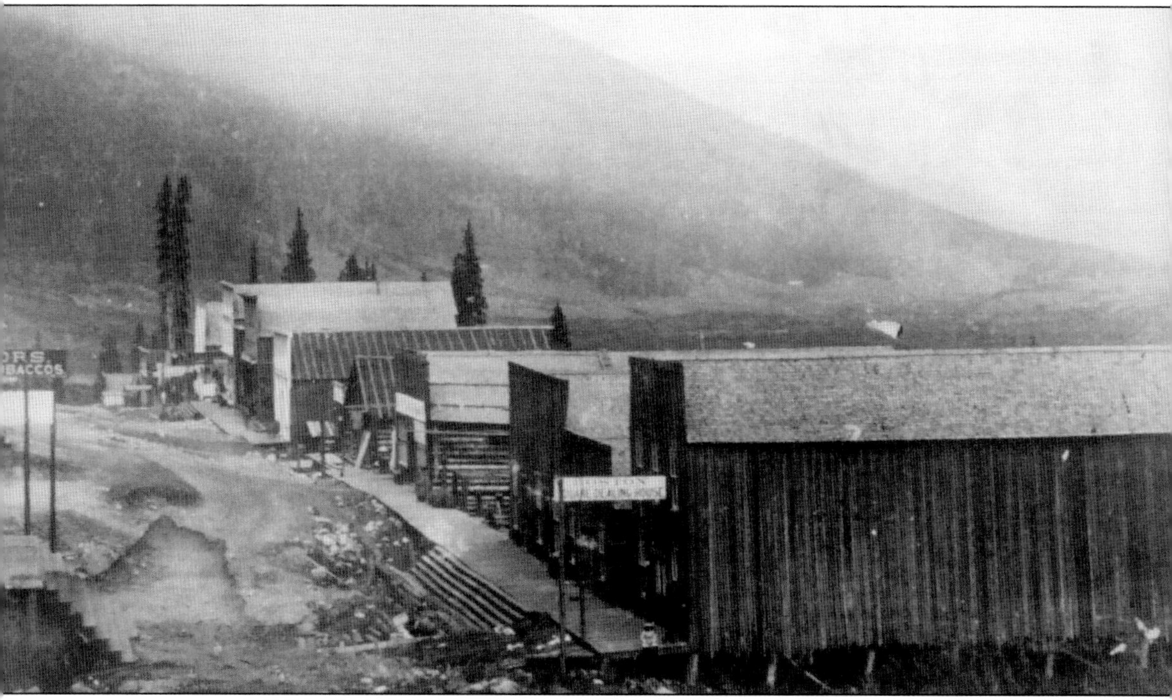

Hotels in Kokomo. The Grand Central Hotel, Boston House, Clifton House, and Mountain House were among several hotels lining Ten Mile Avenue in 1879 and the early 1880s. Saloon and hotel proprietors advertised cigars, tobacco, and whiskey. Inside, men enjoyed games of chance such as euchre, seven-up, cribbage, faro, monte, roulette, and keno while drinking rotgut as often as real whiskey.

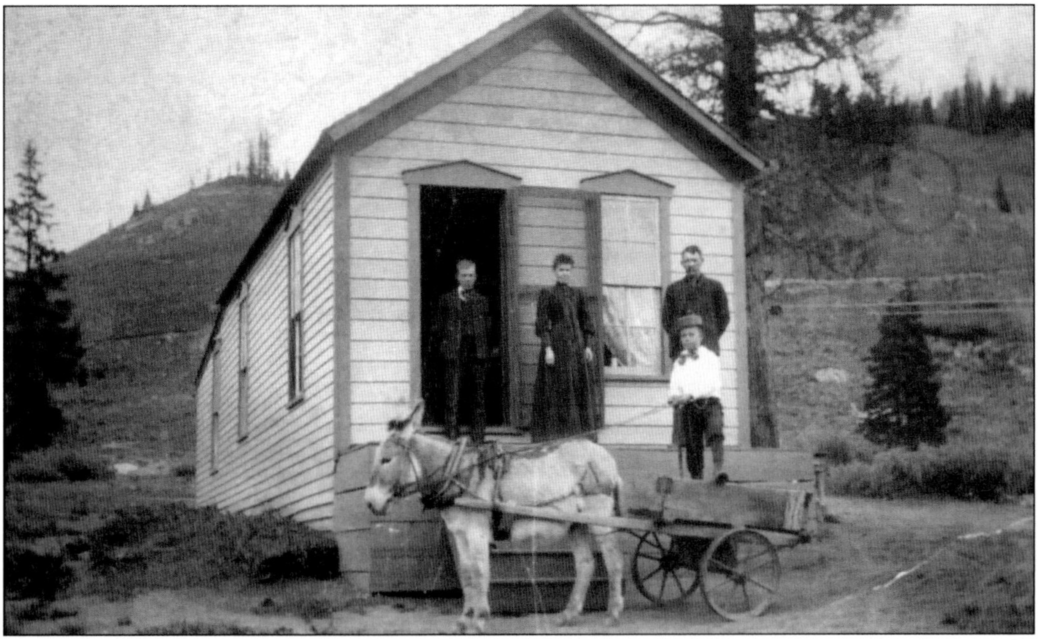

Turner House in Kokomo. Dressed for the photograph, the family stands in front of one of the better-constructed homes in Kokomo. Sawmills in the area provided sawn lumber for homes like this one. The young boy carried goods back home from the grocery and hardware stores in town with his burro-pulled cart. Perhaps he offered friends a ride as well.

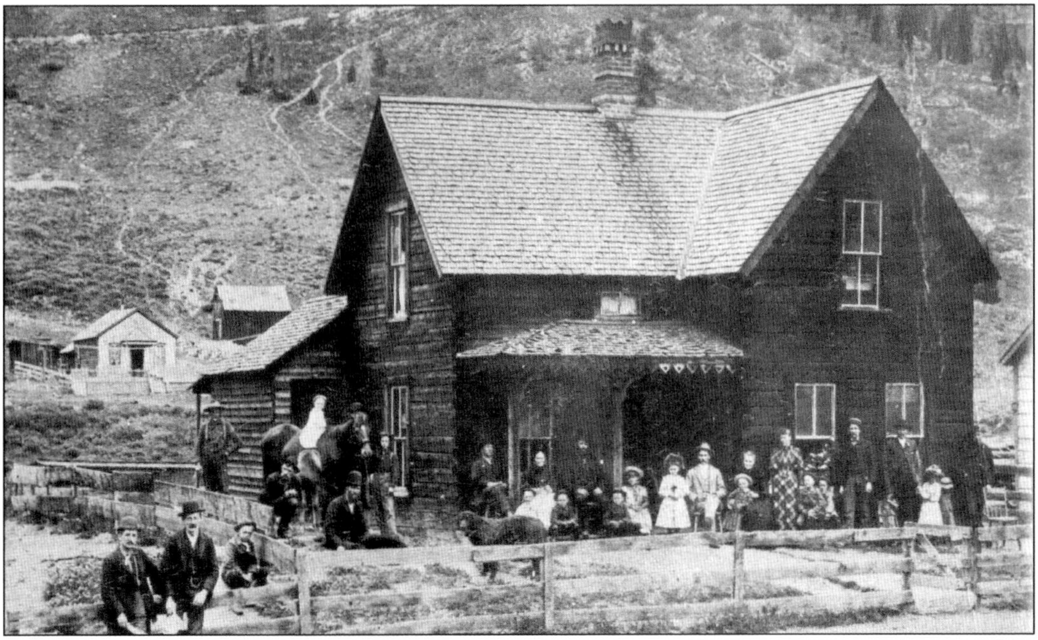

Kokomo Residents in 1894. The population dropped from a high of 2,500 in 1881 (estimated by the *Colorado State Business Directory*) to 800 in 1883 and to 300 by 1885. In 1887, the directory listed a population of 100. The boom and bust cycle hit Kokomo hard. After the silver panic of 1893, families like this might have faced financial difficulties and moved on to more promising mining areas. (Used with permission from the Bill Fountain Collection.)

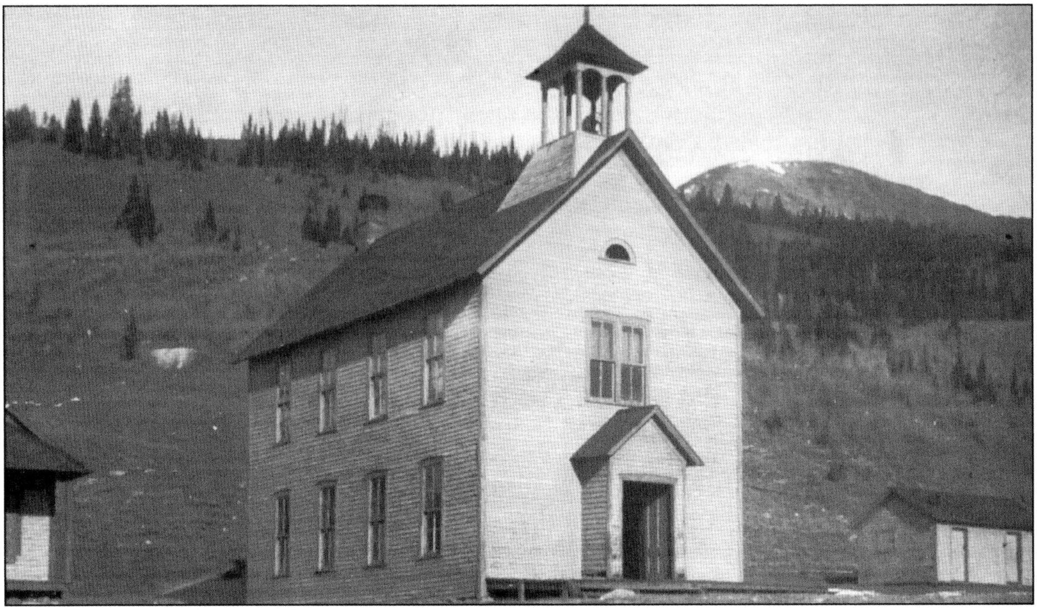

Kokomo Schoolhouse. In this building, teachers taught children in grades one through eight. Although male teachers taught in the county, many teachers were women. Teaching was considered an extension of their roles as mothers and they would not be deterred by low wages. School boards often required teachers to perform additional tasks outside of their official duties, such as carrying water, chopping wood, lighting lamps, and keeping the wood fires burning.

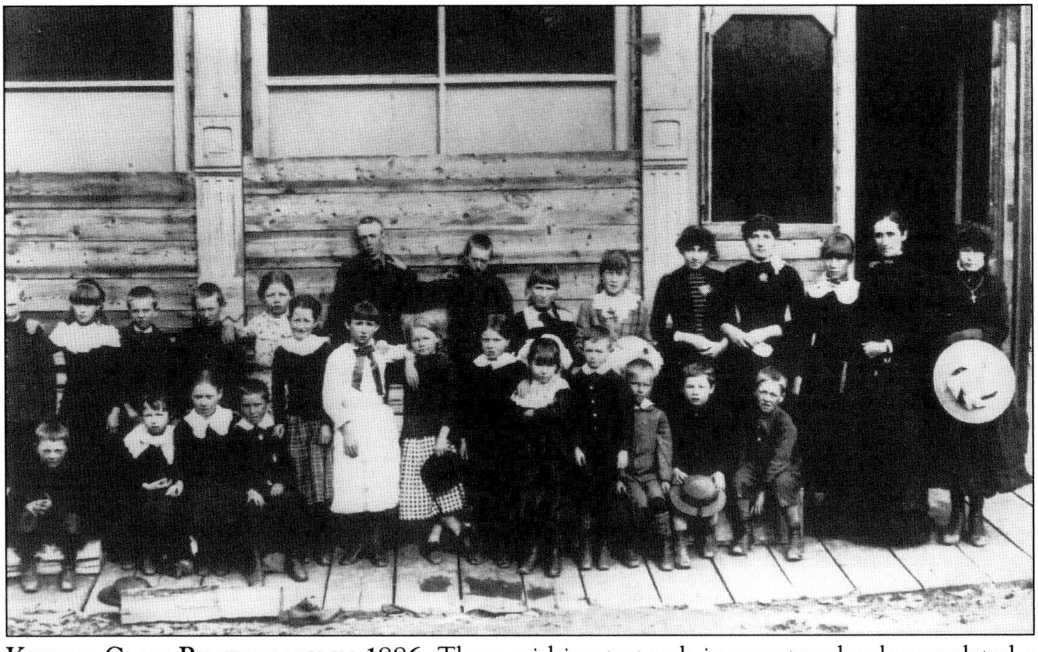

Kokomo Class Photograph in 1886. Those wishing to teach in county schools completed a teacher's examination offered four times each year at the school superintendent's office. The test contained questions on science; grammar; the classics; mathematics; geography; and the history of the world, United States, and Colorado. The *Summit County Journal* published the names and scores of those who took the examination.

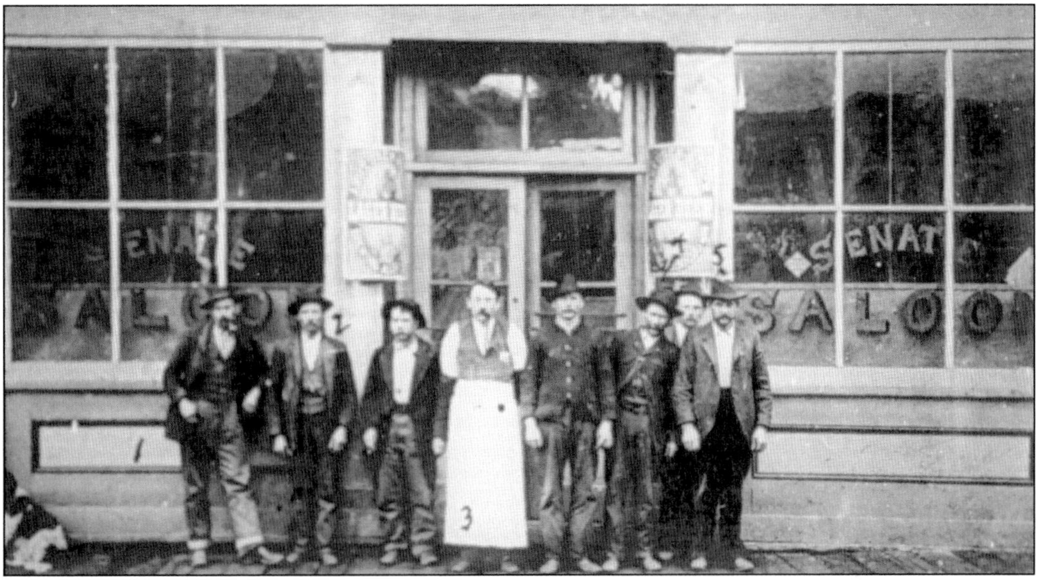

The Senate Saloon. This saloon, owned by Sumner Whitney (center, wearing large apron), was located in Recen on Ten Mile Avenue between First and Second Streets. Here, according to the signage, patrons drank Anheuser-Busch beer. Sumner served as a county deputy marshal. When he was killed in a shootout with Pug Ryan's gang, his wife operated the saloon—a rare occupation for a woman.

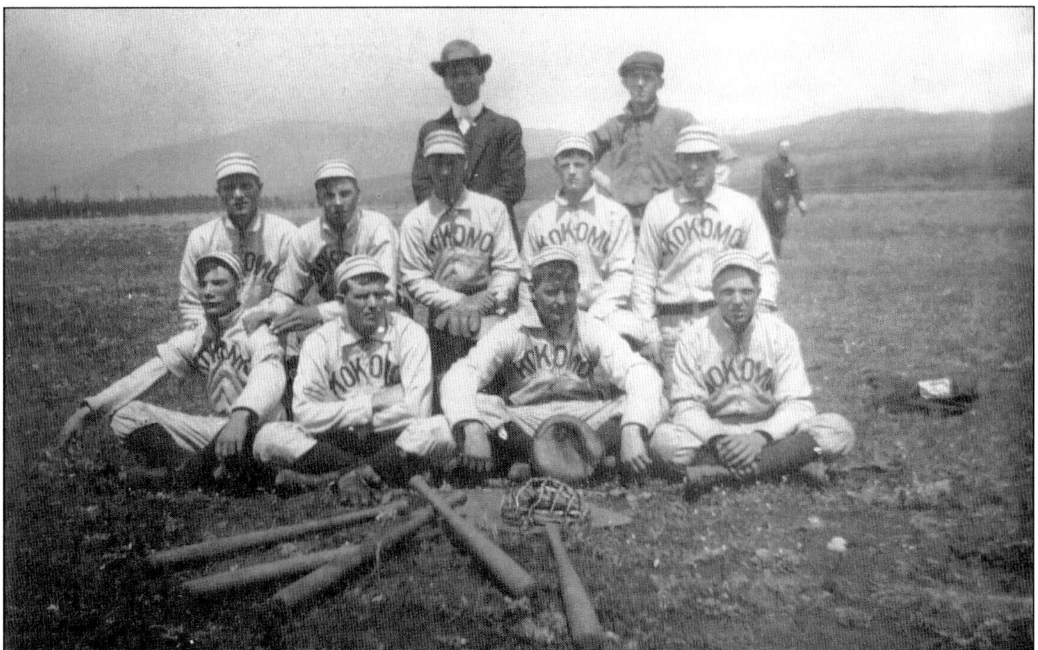

Kokomo Baseball Team in 1906. Baseball teams drew many spectators to their games. Teams from Dillon, Montezuma, Breckenridge, Slate Creek, Frisco, and Kokomo traveled throughout the county and across county boundaries for games. The *Summit County Journal* reported on each one in detail, with headlines screaming, "Dillon Crushes Kokomo," "Slate Creek Mauls Frisco," and "Montezuma Murders Alma."

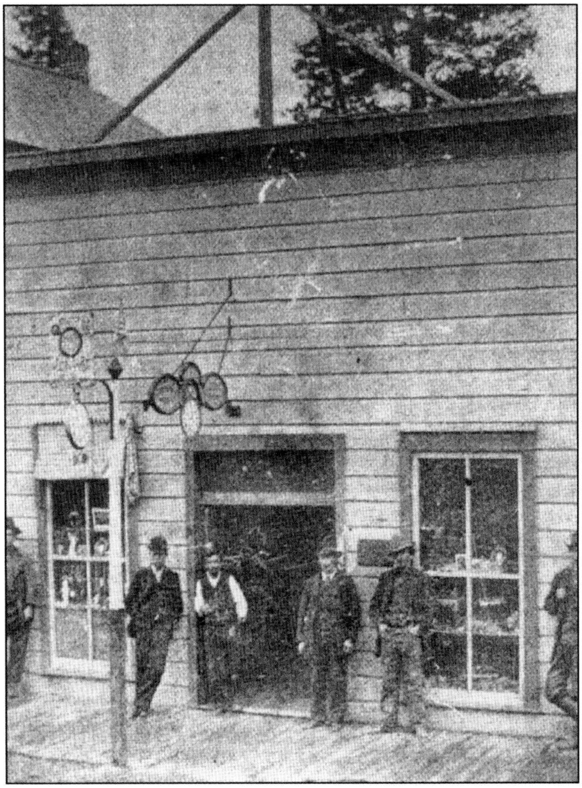

RECEN WATCHMAKER IN 1881. Watchmakers could be found in most large mining towns. The presence of a watchmaker indicated the importance of clocks and watches to town residents. The Sanborn Fire Insurance Company map for Kokomo, drawn in 1886, shows a watchmaker on Ten Mile Avenue south of Second Street and a half block north of the Denver & Rio Grande tracks. (Used with permission from the Bill Fountain Collection.)

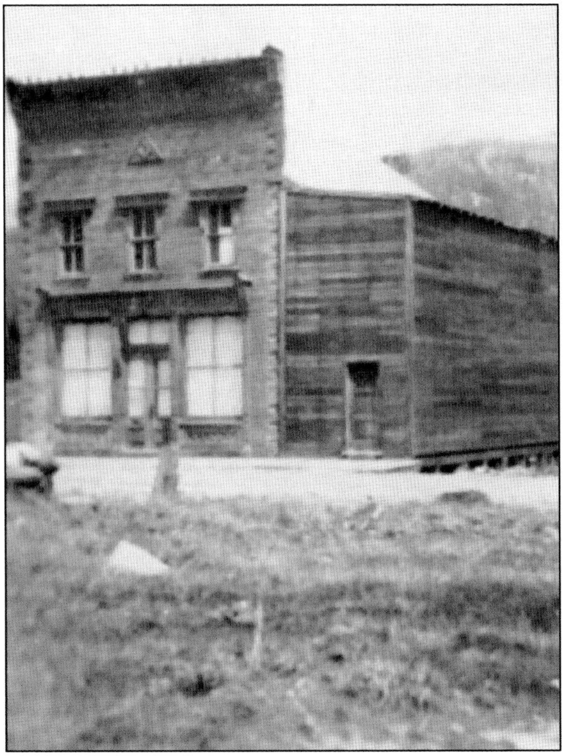

THE MASONIC LODGE IN KOKOMO. The original lodge building, constructed in 1881, burned six months after it was built when fire destroyed most of the town. This building, constructed in 1882 by Henry Nelson, housed Corinthian Lodge No. 42 of Kokomo, established September 19, 1881. Fraternal organizations such as the Masons and Odd Fellows welcomed new members to the community and provided comfort at times of death and illness.

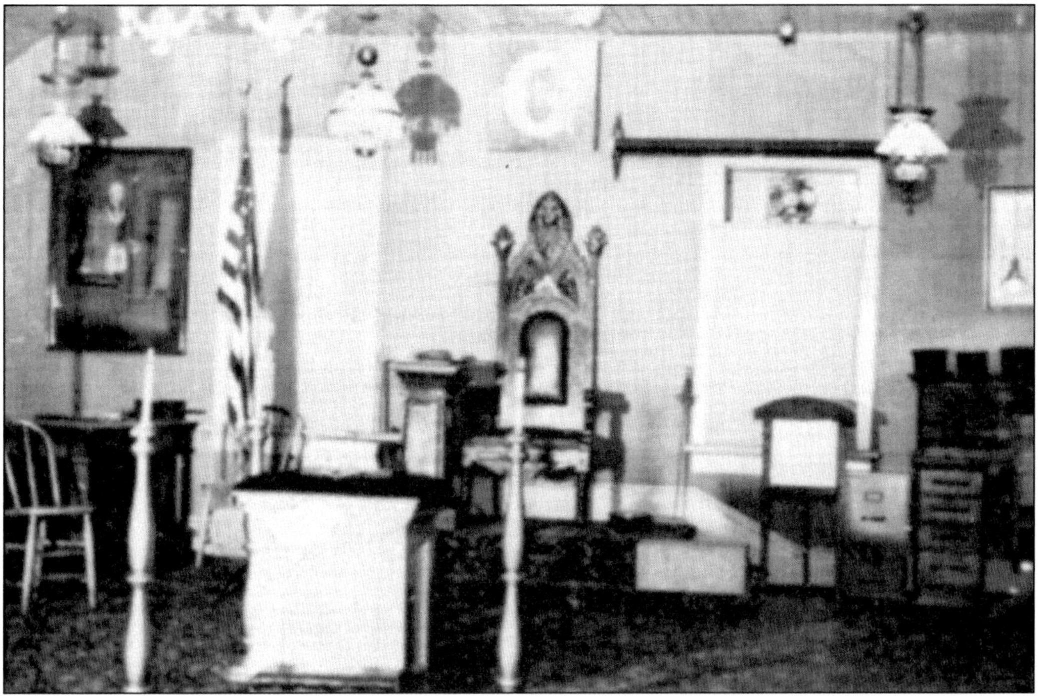

Interior of Masonic Lodge No. 42. The ornately decorated room contained many prized possessions of the lodge. Members salvaged the cottage organ, dated December 9, 1879, from the Robinson church. Railroad pictures on the walls previously hung in the Kokomo depot. When the lodge consolidated with the Leadville lodge, the furnishings became part of the Kokomo room in the Leadville lodge building.

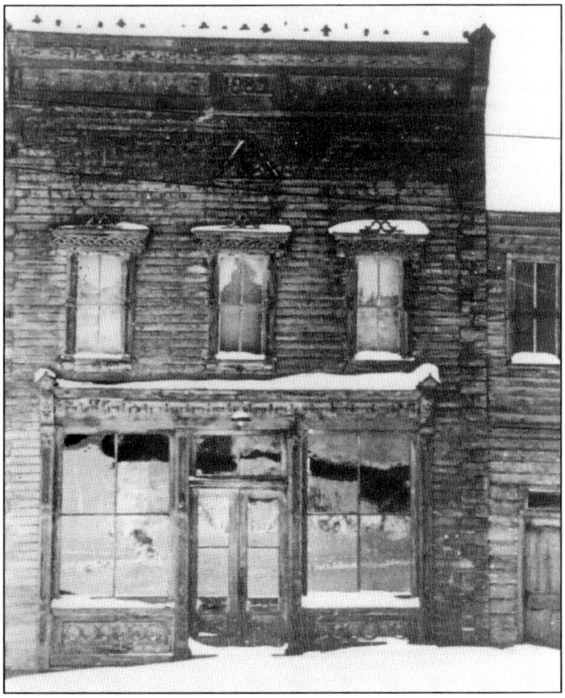

Masonic Hall in Ruins. At one time, this building—at an elevation of 10,618 feet—held the distinction of being the highest Masonic lodge in the world. The Masons used the building continuously until 1966. By the time the owners of the Climax molybdenum mine purchased the town site of Kokomo and began to tear down the remaining buildings, the former lodge sat in ruins.

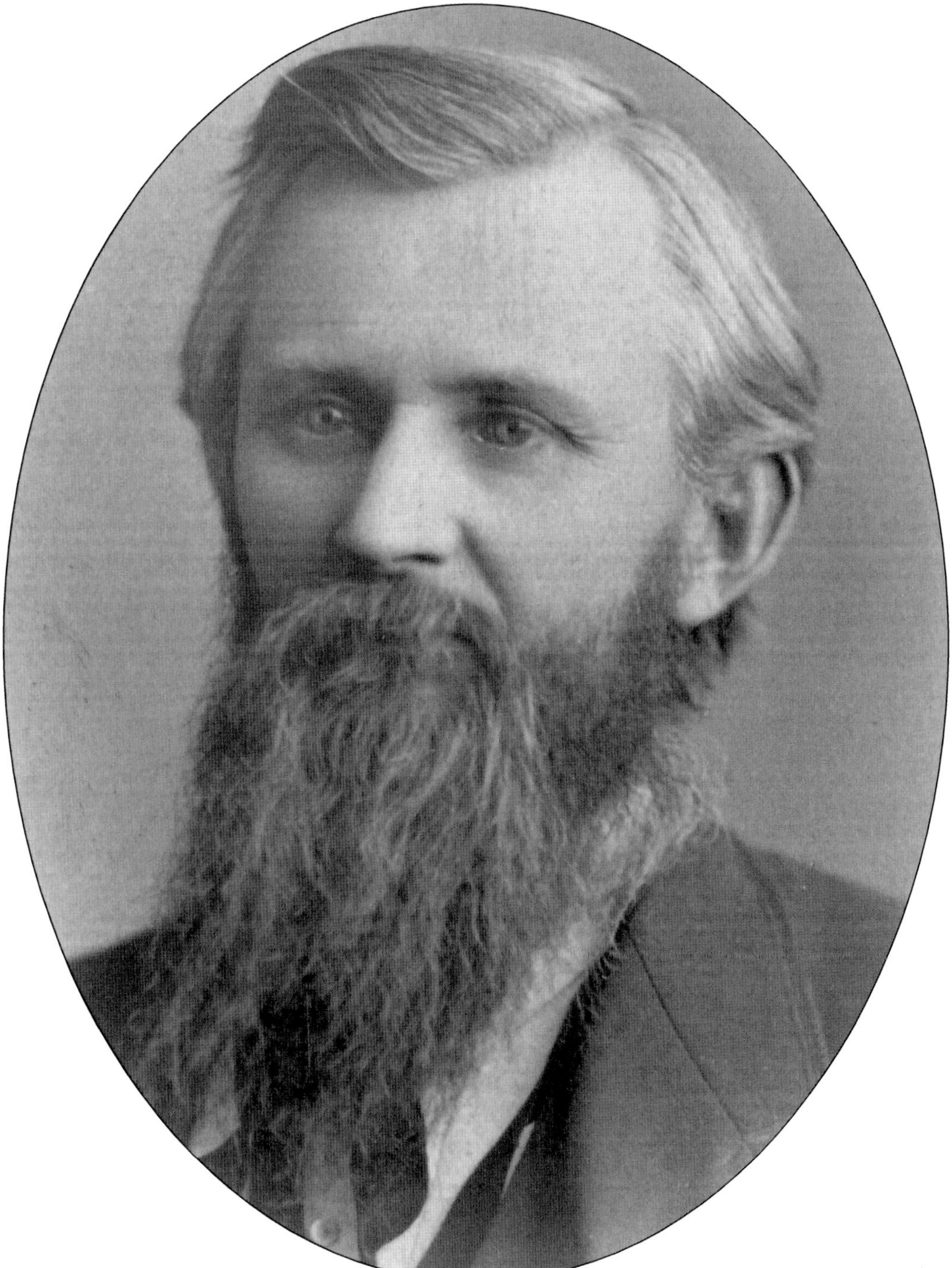

John S. Wheeler. Wheeler, an entrepreneur, built a sawmill at the confluence of the West Ten Mile and Ten Mile Creeks in 1878 to supply lumber for the mines, Kokomo smelter, and railroad that he knew would come. Sheep grazed in the rich pastures on his ranch. The town of Wheeler Junction grew from these early activities, with extensive logging attracting many Swedes and Norwegians to the area. (Courtesy History Colorado.)

Four

Mining in the Ten Mile Canyon

All That Glitters Is Not Gold

The interplay of geology, geography, and climate made mining difficult in the Ten Mile Canyon. The geologic processes that injected minerals into the rocks of the canyon deposited more silver, copper, lead, and zinc than gold. The glaciers that created the spectacular U-shaped valleys and cirques lining the canyon did not erode free gold from the mineralized veins. Melting snow did not deposit vast amounts of gold in streams for prospectors to find. The harsh, long winters—with deep snow, low temperatures, and strong winds—combined with altitudes over 10,000 feet to present unrelenting challenges. The mountains ringing the canyon caused problems with isolation that mining companies found difficult to overcome.

The earliest attempts at gold mining occurred when prospectors worked the streams in McNulty Gulch. Tents and crude log cabins appeared quickly. Supplies came over high mountain passes. After the initial boom of 1860–1861, most men left when their claims produced little gold. They knew the veins contained silver, but mining it required technology and capital they did not have. The transportation network needed to get the ore to mills and smelters did not exist. The mineral wealth did not lend itself to men working individual claims.

After many failed attempts, the silver rush began in 1879. Improved technology and money from investors allowed the ore to be mined profitably. Although claims covered Elk, Sheep, Red, and Copper Mountains and Jacque Peak, the lack of communication and transportation networks still hindered operations. With the building of the nearby towns, miners had adequate shelter, but supplies still came over roads that were snow-covered in winter, muddy in spring, and dusty in summer and fall.

In three years, the Ten Mile Canyon changed from a wilderness to a world of ceaseless activity littered with the remains of hard rock or lode mining. As time passed, lessees began leasing portions of mines—a sure sign of declining production. Optimism changed to pessimism. This cycle of boom and bust, hope and discouragement, continued into the 1890s, when silver prices plunged. Mines and mills closed, and even though many eventually reopened, the economy continued its downward turn into the next century.

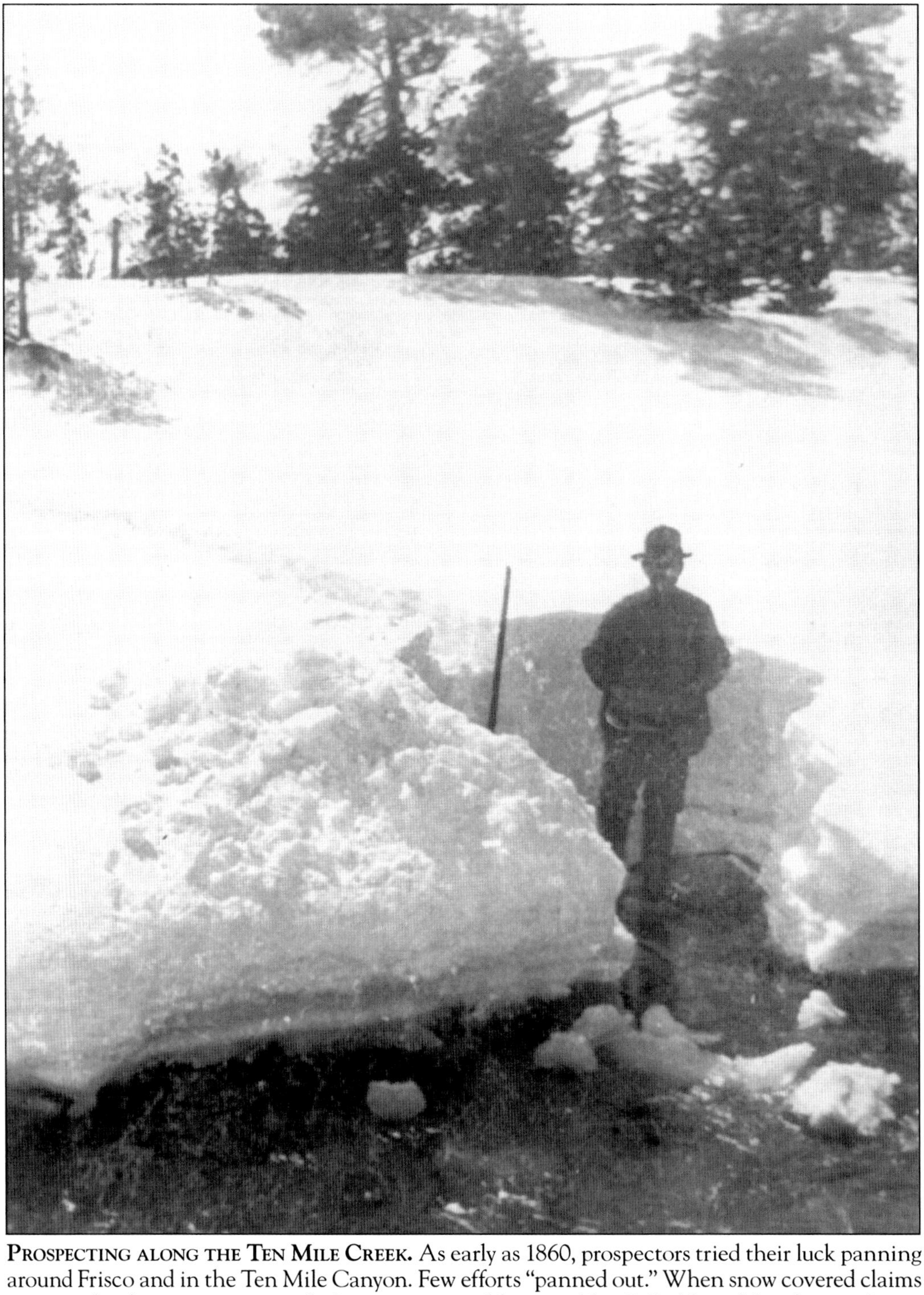

Prospecting along the Ten Mile Creek. As early as 1860, prospectors tried their luck panning around Frisco and in the Ten Mile Canyon. Few efforts "panned out." When snow covered claims to great depths, panning ceased. As soon as possible, men like C.O. (Oscar) Lindquist, shown here, shoveled their way through the snow to search for the nuggets, working in freezing water for hours each day.

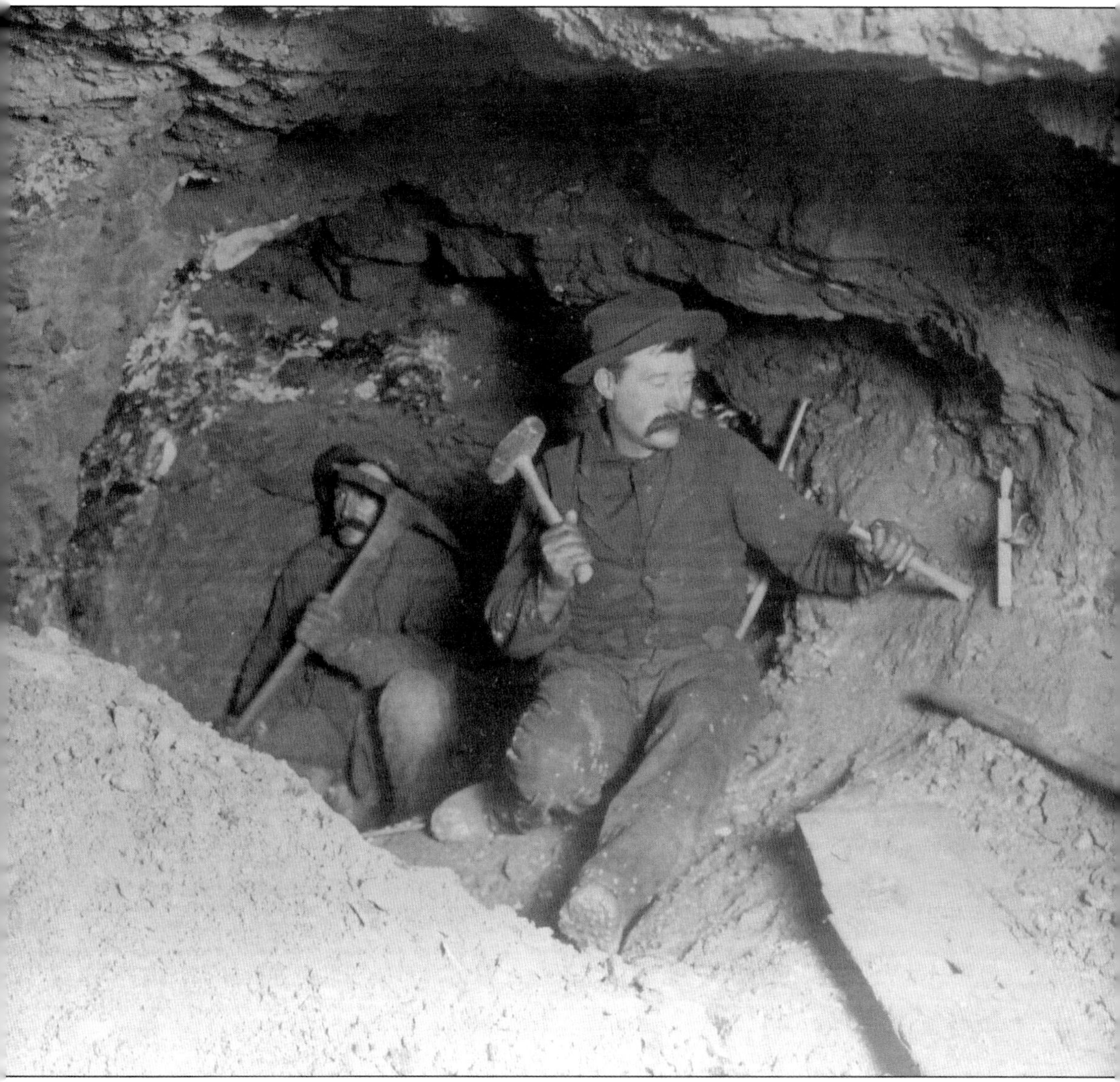

Single Jacking. In a confined space, a miner used a drilling technique called single jacking. Holding the drill steel with one hand, he wielded a four-pound hammer with the other, striking the steel 50 times per minute. Miner's candles provided light and iron candleholders jammed into rock or timber supported the candles. Often, the miners had to purchase their own candles at a cost of five cents apiece. (Used with permission from the Ed and Nancy Bathke Collection.)

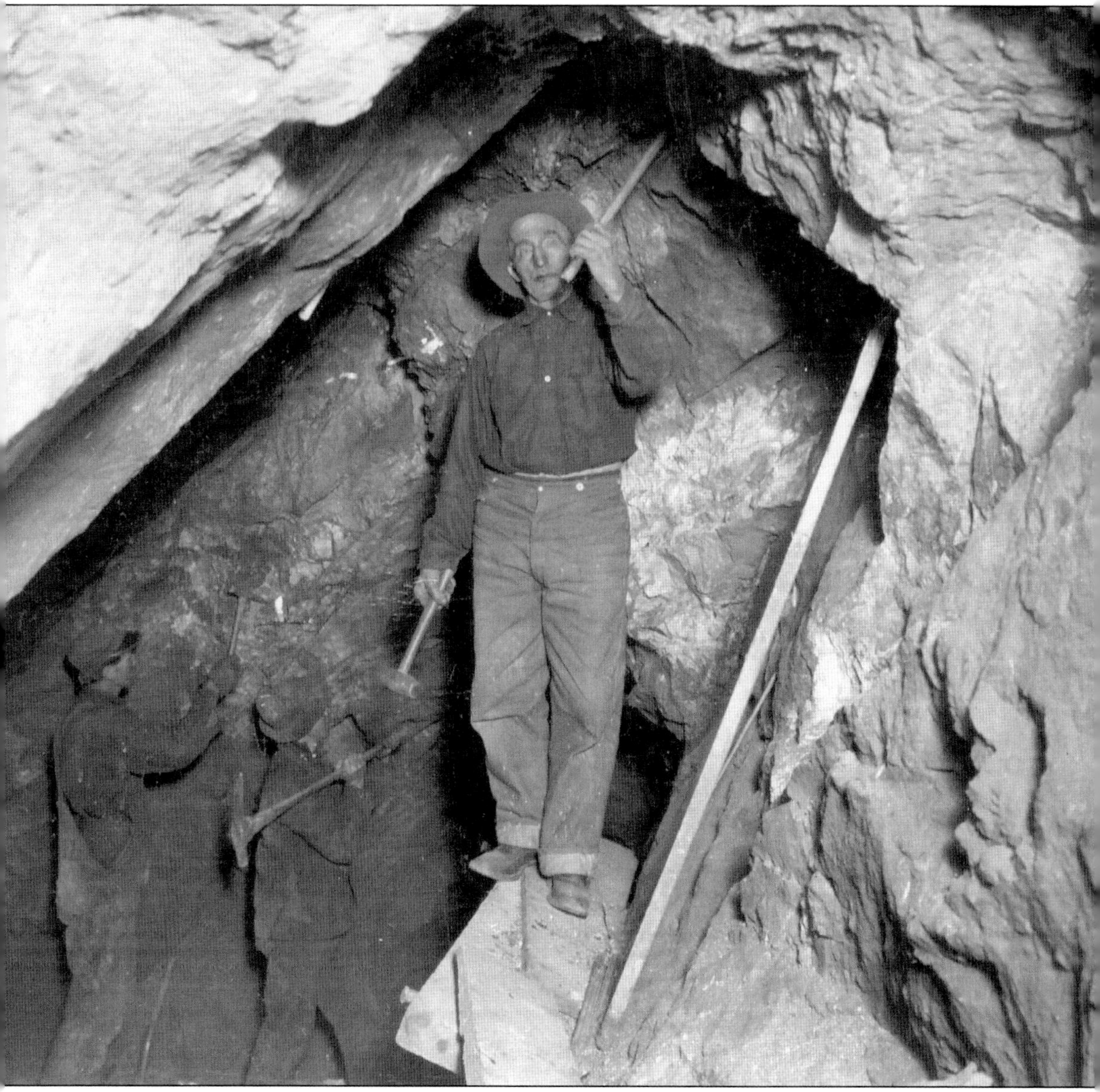

DOUBLE JACKING. If space permitted, two men used the double jacking method, as shown in the background of this photograph. One man swung the eight-pound sledge 25 times per minute; the second rotated the steel. The men changed positions when the steel needed sharpening, or every 15 minutes. When necessary, miners stood on boxes, tree trunks wedged between rock walls, or boulders to work an overhead vein. (Used with permission from the Ed and Nancy Bathke Collection.)

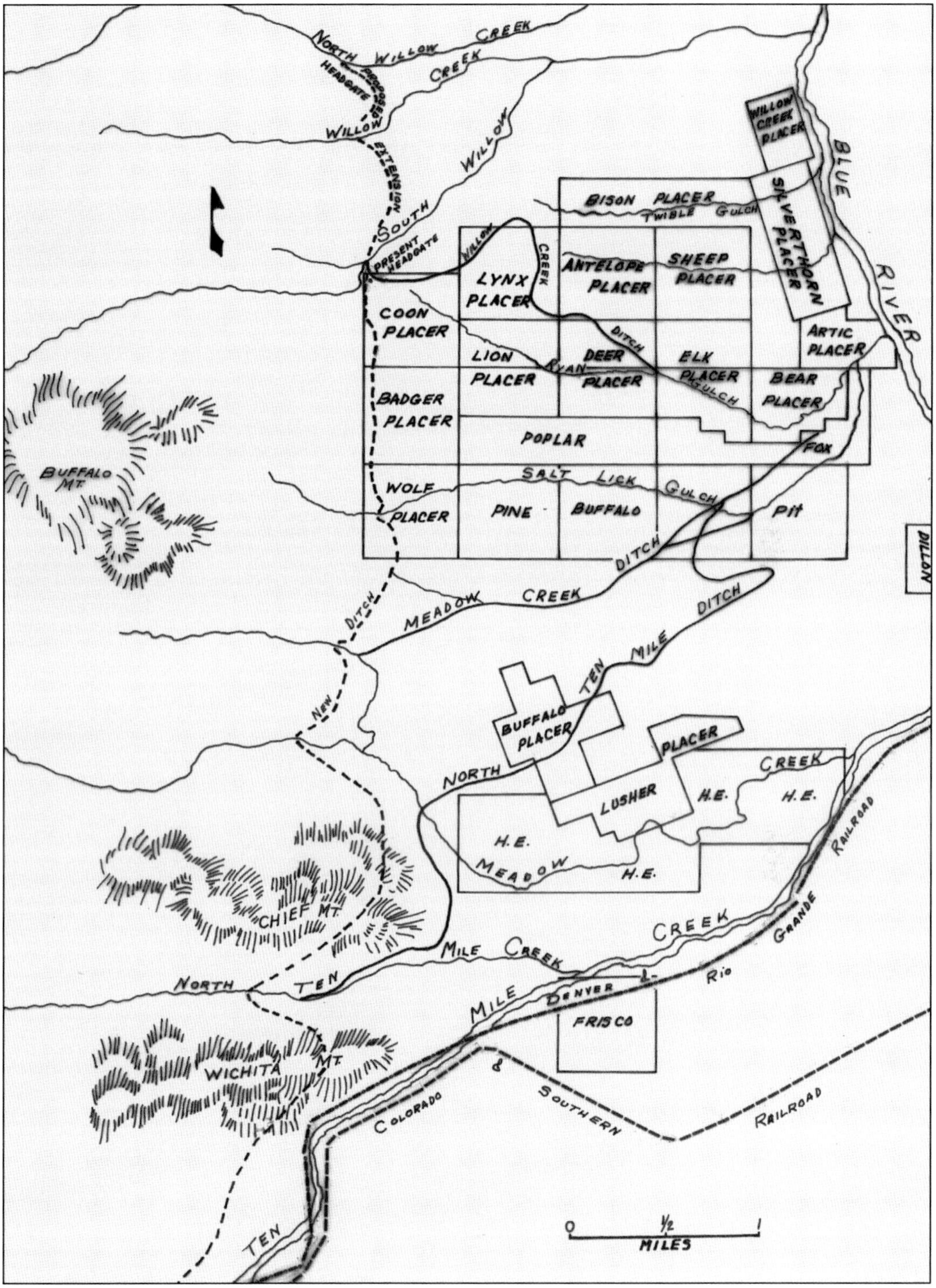

UNDATED MAP OF MINING CLAIMS NORTH OF FRISCO. Placer claims on the flanks of Buffalo Mountain north of Frisco tell of the variety of wildlife inhabiting the forests around the town. Streams flowing through the claims, as well as flumes and ditches, brought the water needed for the hydraulic methods employed by the miners. (Map drawn by author.)

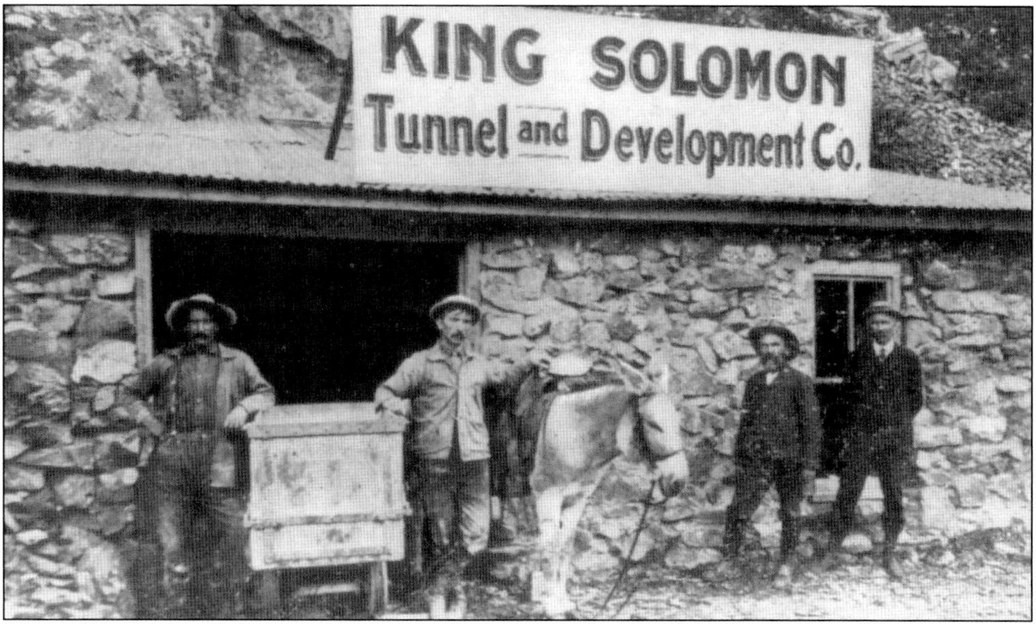

King Solomon Tunnel and Development Company. The King Solomon Mine, located just south of Frisco on the eastern wall of the Ten Mile Canyon, produced both gold and silver. A tunnel that stretched well over 3,000 feet in length cut across many mineralized veins. The mine continued shipping ore as late as the first decade of the 1900s. (Courtesy Denver Public Library, Western History Collection, X-62432.)

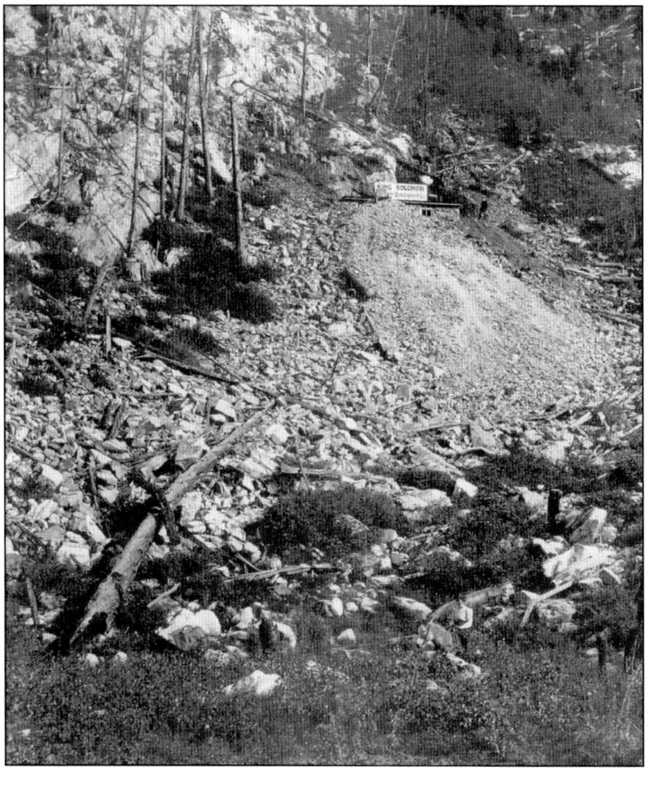

Deep Tunnel Theory. King Solomon founder Col. James H. Myers believed, as many miners did, that deeper tunnels produced richer ore. Because the mineralized fluids rose from below, people thought that the richest ores solidified at greater depths. Myers found East Coast investors who agreed with him and financed a plan to dig a long and deep tunnel at the King Solomon Mine in the hopes that they would all be rewarded with very rich ore.

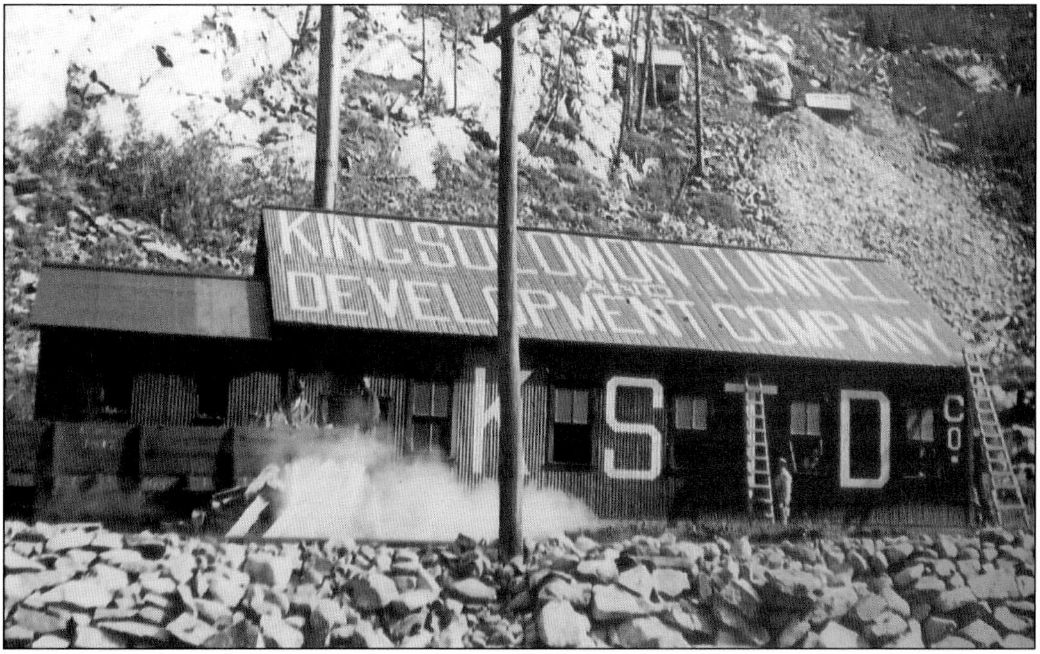

Power Plant. To power the machinery needed at the mine, the company installed a compressor and boiler costing $15,000 in a building constructed on a very narrow ledge of level land. The Colorado & Southern Railroad tracks ran directly in front of the power plant. Men painted the information on the roof to advertise King Solomon to potential investors who might be passengers on the train. (Used with permission from the collection of Bob Schoppe and the Denver, South Park & Pacific Historical Society.)

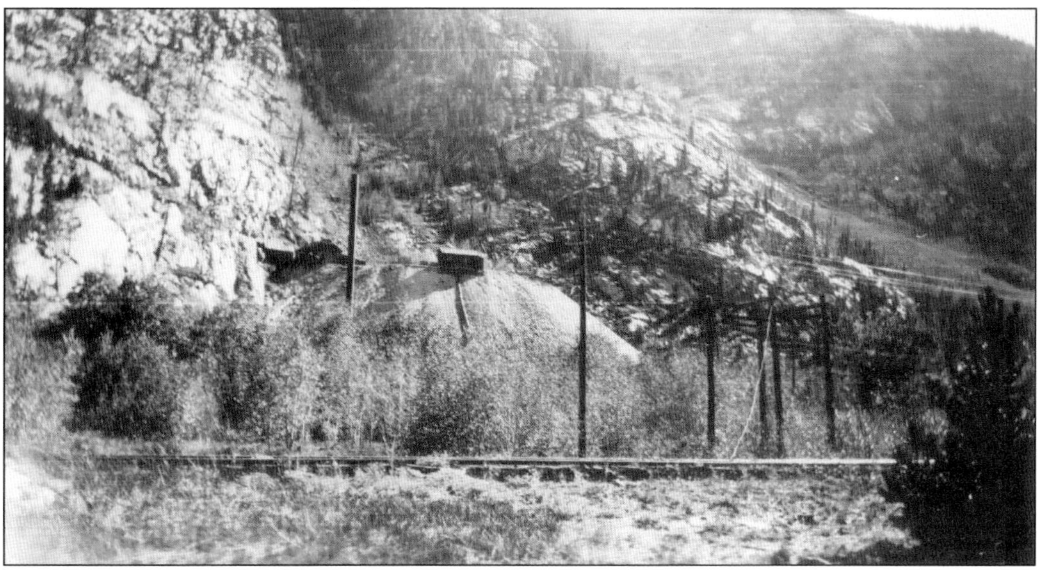

Mine Dump of the King Solomon Mine. The mine dump, filled with waste rock blasted from the numerous tunnels of the King Solomon Mine, dwarfed the power plant and its 100-foot-tall smokestack. The Denver, South Park & Pacific tracks brought supplies and the heavy equipment needed for the mining operation. Workers constructed the buildings on a narrow ledge of level land next to an avalanche chute.

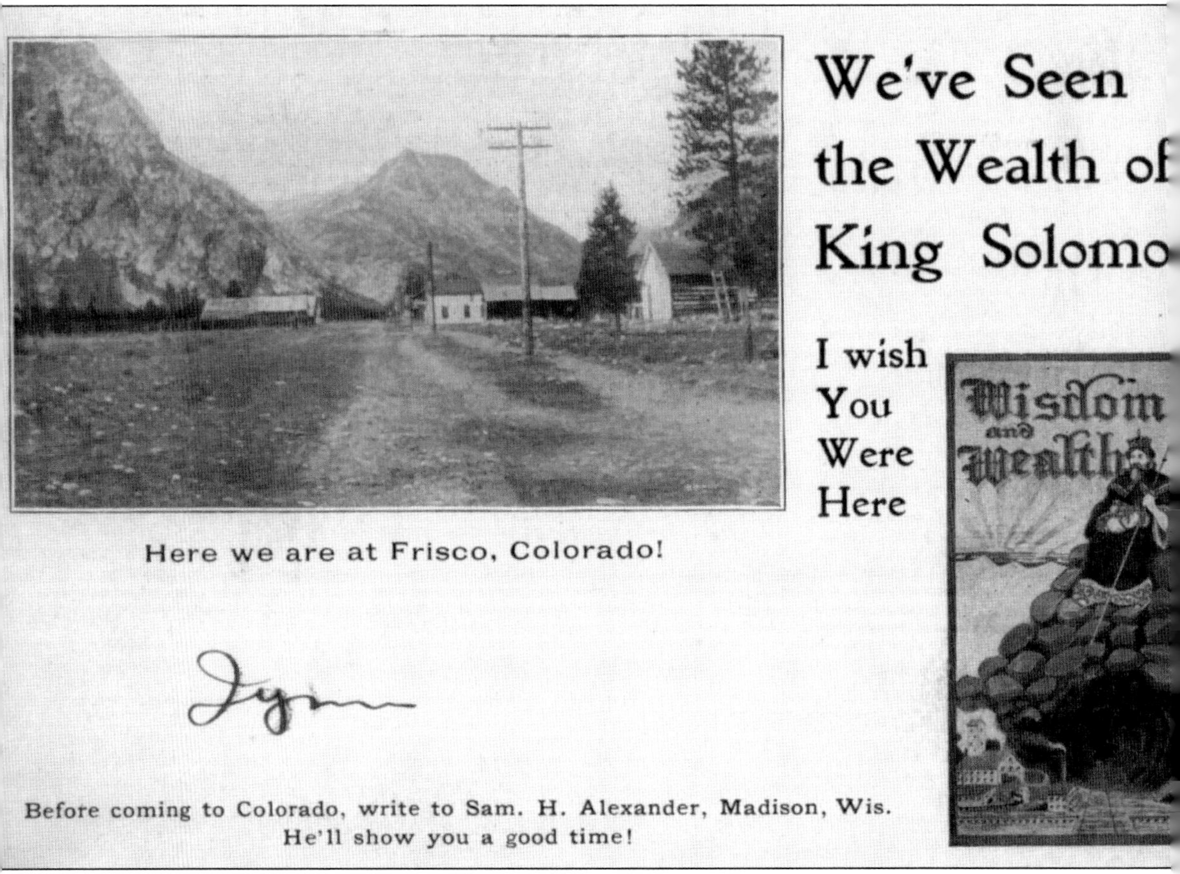

MINE ADVERTISEMENT. Mining companies worked constantly to assure firm financial backing for their enterprises. Along with a formal prospectus, companies prepared postal cards such as this to attract the attention of potential investors. This card equated the wisdom of investing with future wealth and introduced the town of Frisco. Note that an interested person wrote to Madison, Wisconsin, for further information and a promised "good time." (Used with permission from the Ed and Nancy Bathke Collection.)

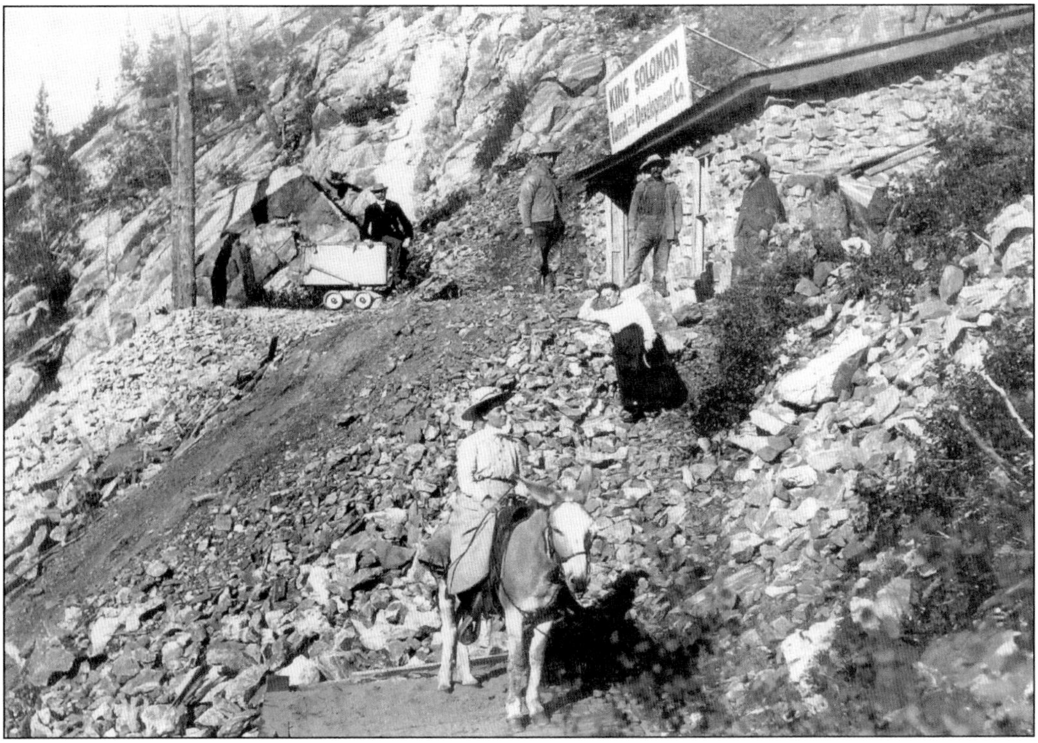

VISITORS TO THE KING SOLOMON MINE. To assure future investment in his ventures, Colonel Myers invited many to visit the operation. As one of the biggest boosters of mining in the Ten Mile Canyon, he traveled extensively in search of those willing to finance his projects. He wrote numerous letters and articles explaining his deep tunnel theory to those who would listen.

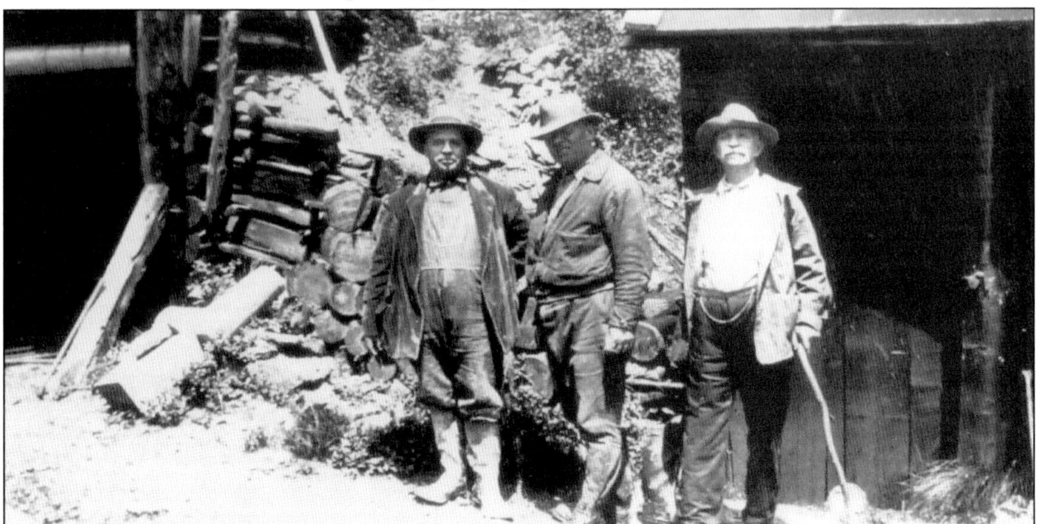

THE SQUARE DEAL MINE. Although he was a master at promoting his own mining interests, Colonel Myers openly criticized those he felt cheated their investors. The Square Deal Mine in the north Ten Mile attracted his attention and ire. Calling it the Crooked Deal, he offered a reward to anyone who could prove that the mine had produced a pound of ore for which the owners received payment.

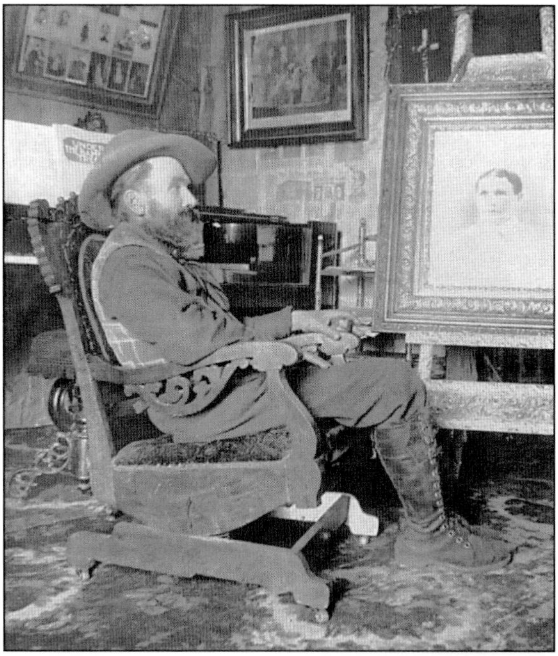

James Havens Myers Jr. Known by the nickname Dimp, Myers served as mine superintendent while the tunneling at the King Solomon Mine progressed. At times, three shifts of men worked around the clock hoping to meet the goal of 100 feet per month. While supervising work at the King Solomon, Myers also held the title of superintendent of the Mint Mining Company on Ophir Mountain, southeast of Frisco.

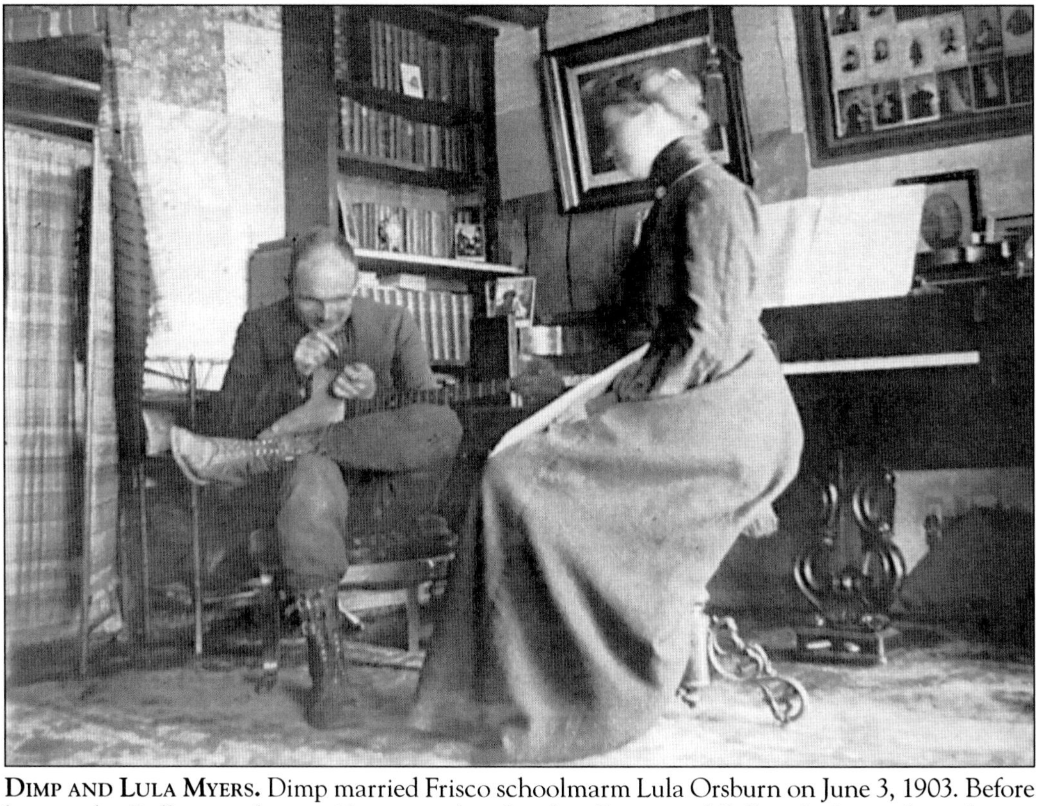

Dimp and Lula Myers. Dimp married Frisco schoolmarm Lula Orsburn on June 3, 1903. Before buying the Delker ranch near Keystone, they lived in Frisco and Dillon. Lula taught only one semester in the Frisco schoolhouse before being fired because she chose not to return the romantic interests of several "old" men on the school board. She already had her eyes set on Dimp.

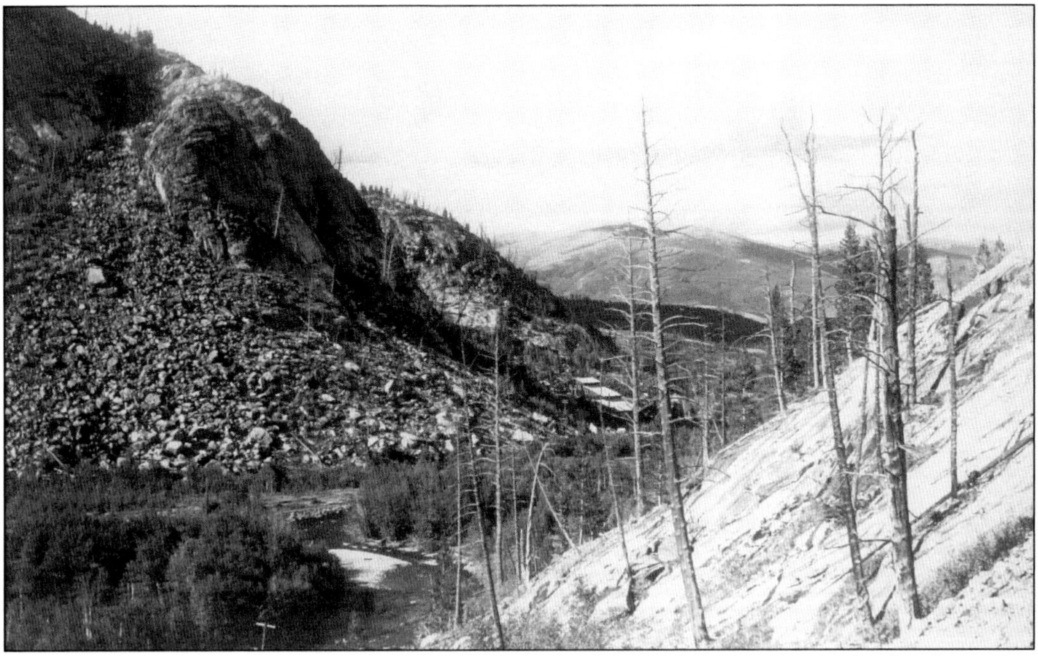

The Excelsior Mine and Mill. Located on the west side of the canyon, south of Mile Marker 201 on I-70, the Excelsior Mine produced silver, gold, lead, and copper. In the early 1900s, the mine, owned by Frank Wiborg, had a huge concentrating mill next to the Denver & Rio Grande track and nearby power plant. The mine realized greater profits from the ore produced because concentrating the ore eliminated worthless waste rock.

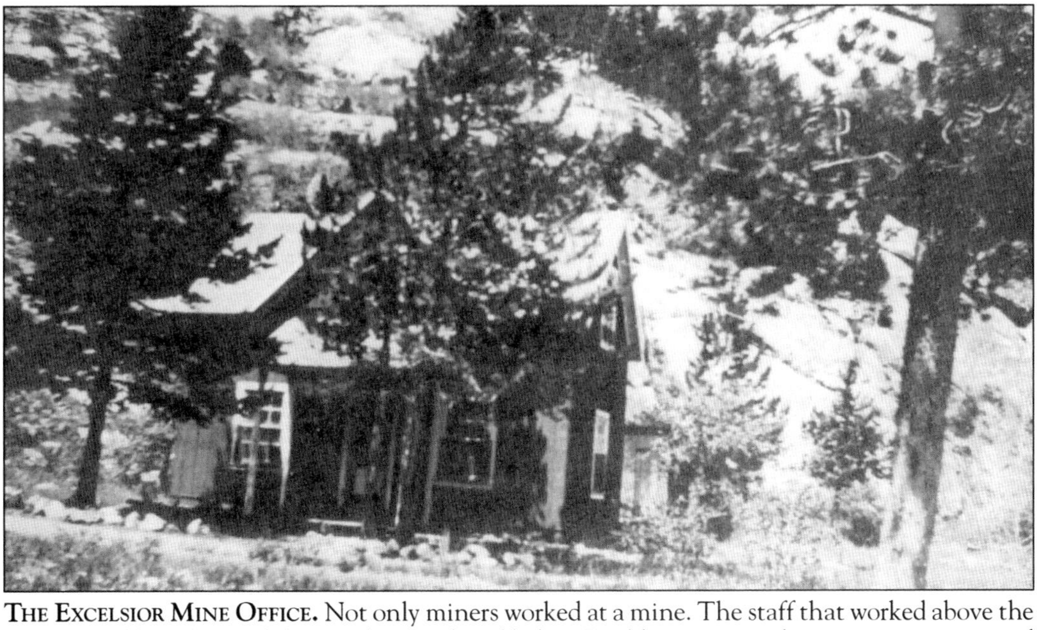

The Excelsior Mine Office. Not only miners worked at a mine. The staff that worked above the ground could easily equal the number employed below. Bookkeepers, supply agents, managers, and superintendents spent their days insuring that those working below ground had the equipment and supplies necessary to keep operations running smoothly. In addition to their ski jumping activities, Peter Prestrud and Eyvind Flood worked at the Excelsior Mine.

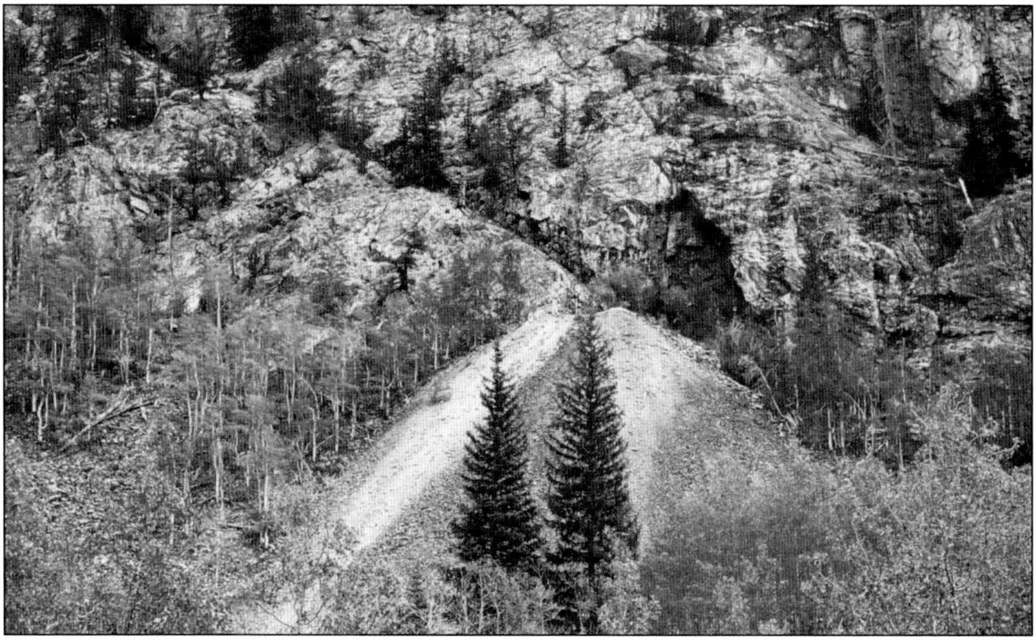

Adit on Mount Royal. Mine prospectors looked for fault lines as places to explore for valuable ore because the movement along faults trapped mineralized fluids. Here, an adit—the horizontal opening to a mine—entered the east face of the canyon along a very visible fault line. The colors on the mine dump indicate that miners found minerals as they tunneled deeper into Mount Royal. (Photograph by author.)

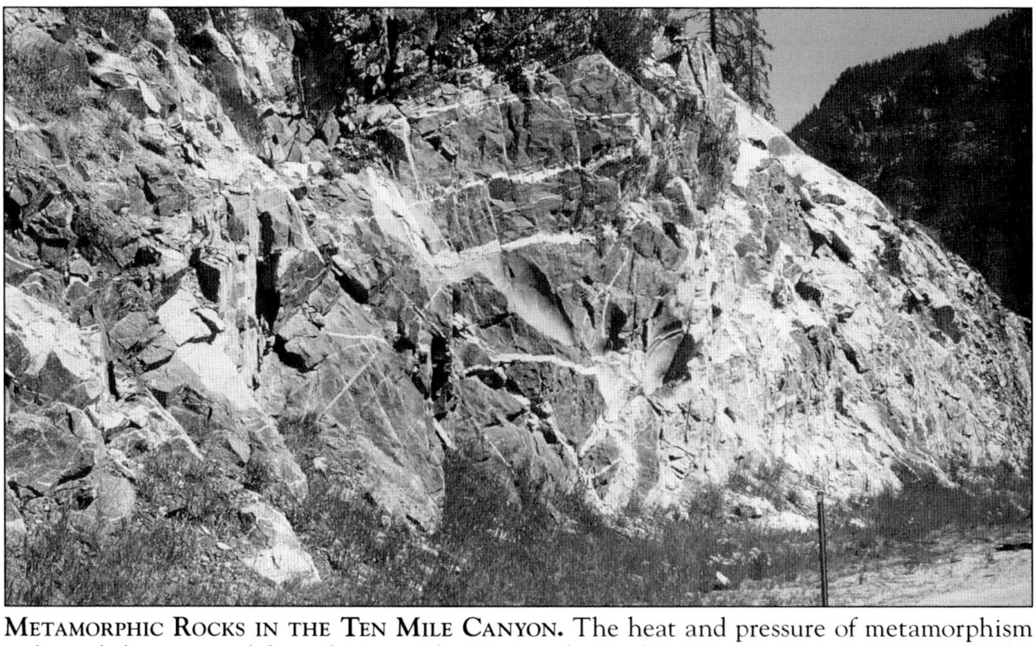

Metamorphic Rocks in the Ten Mile Canyon. The heat and pressure of metamorphism indicated the potential for rich ore to the practiced eye of a prospector. Movement along the many faults in the canyon further concentrated the bodies of ore. Therefore, prospectors looked at the heavy veining in the gneiss, schist, and migmatite in the Ten Mile Canyon as worthy of additional exploration. (Photograph by author.)

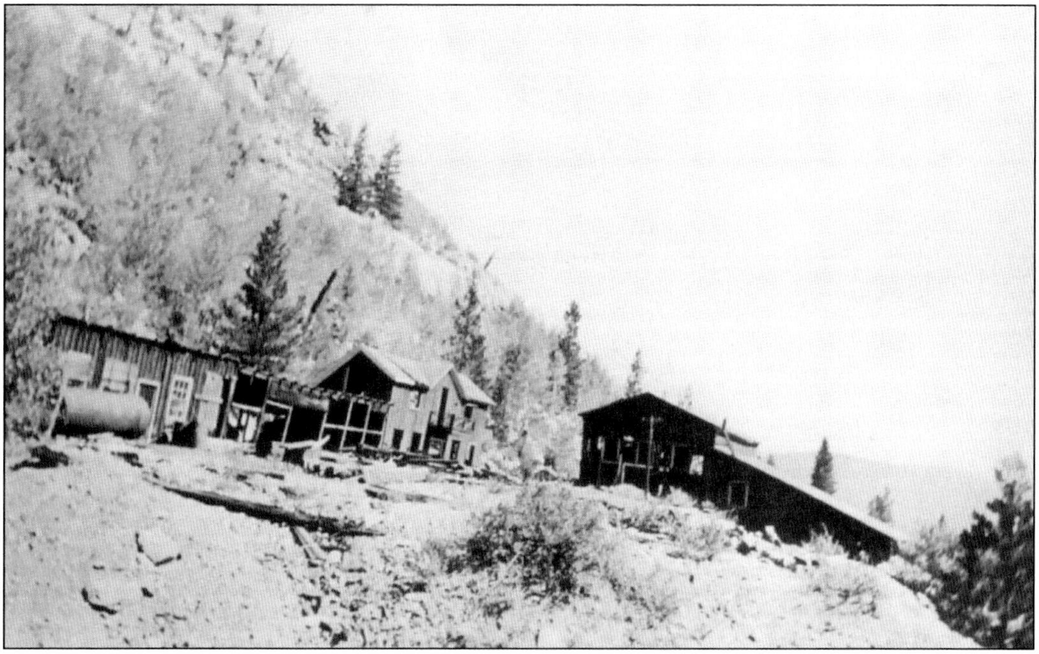

GRAVITY IN THE MILLING PROCESS. When building mills, men took advantage of gravity. Ore entered at the top of the mill. Each step in the process occurred at a lower level. The milled, concentrated ore exited at the lowest level. After the silver crash of 1893, Frisco residents stripped the mining buildings of materials needed for home construction in town.

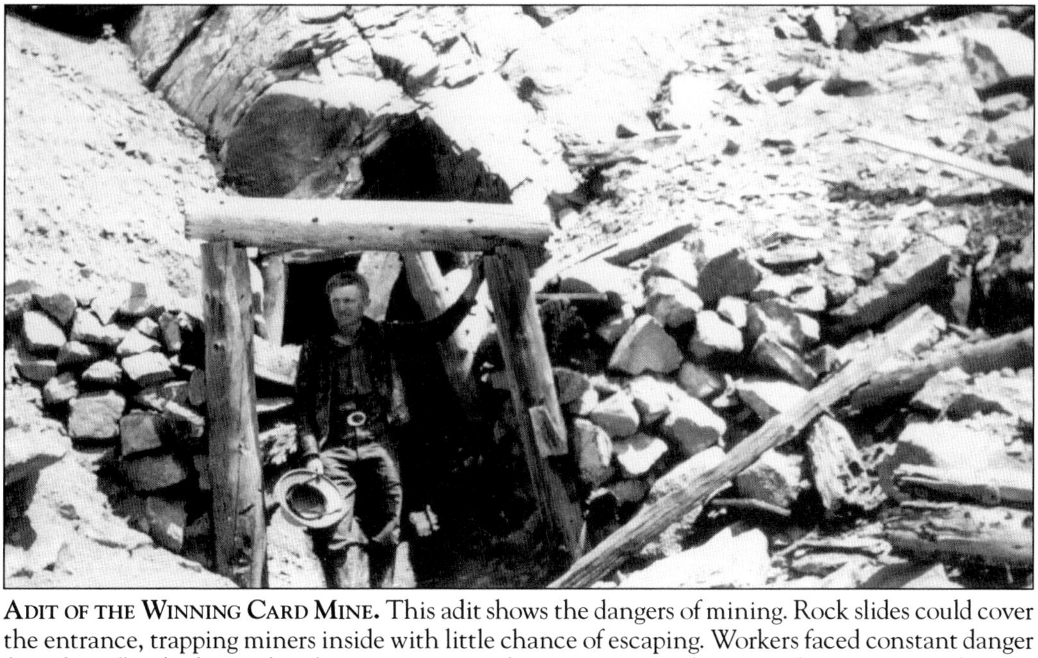

ADIT OF THE WINNING CARD MINE. This adit shows the dangers of mining. Rock slides could cover the entrance, trapping miners inside with little chance of escaping. Workers faced constant danger from fires, floods, dropped tools, unsanitary conditions, poor ventilation, and premature explosions. Silicosis, or white lung disease, was common among those who worked below ground.

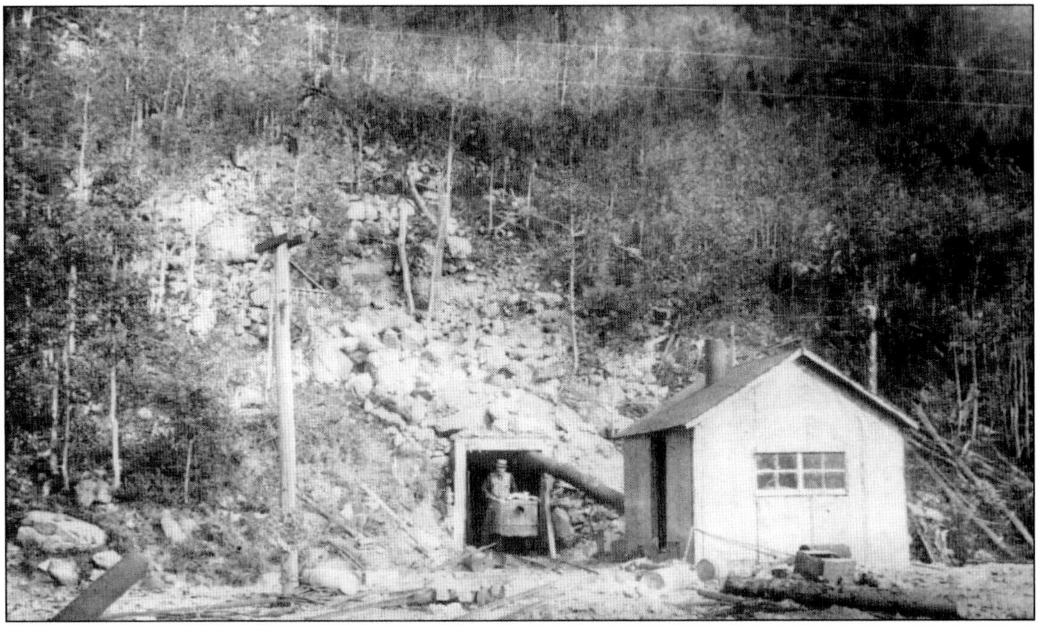

TRAMMER IN PORTAL OF ADIT. A trammer pushing an ore cart stands in the portal of an unidentified mine. Next to the track rests a timber cart that could be lifted onto the tracks and pushed into the adit. The pipe carried compressed air into the mine. The use of compressed air and the power lines indicate this photograph was taken around the turn of the 20th century.

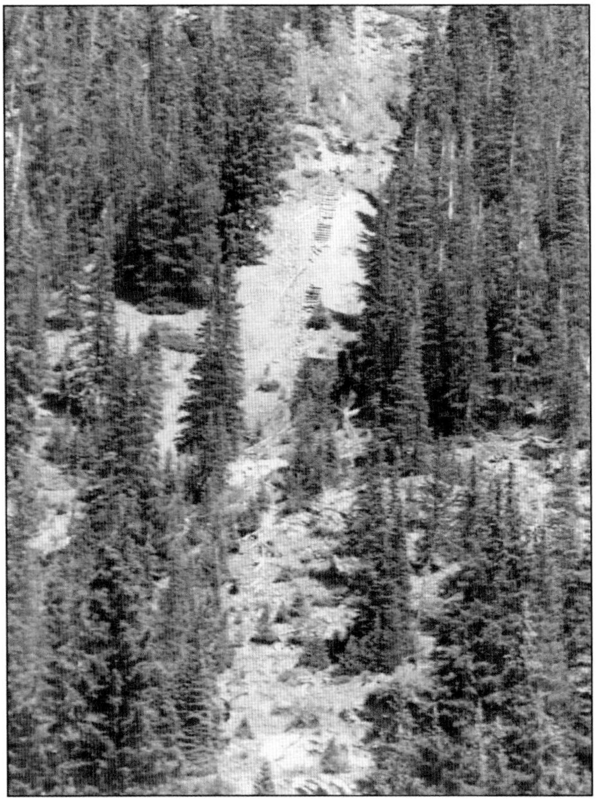

TRAMS. The steep western walls of the Ten Mile range afforded little room for buildings. To overcome these difficulties, men built trams to carry ore down to storage facilities. In some cases, trams carried men and supplies up to adits and tunnels high on the western wall of the canyon. Lift towers climbed precipitous heights to get to the mines much as ski lifts carry skiers today.

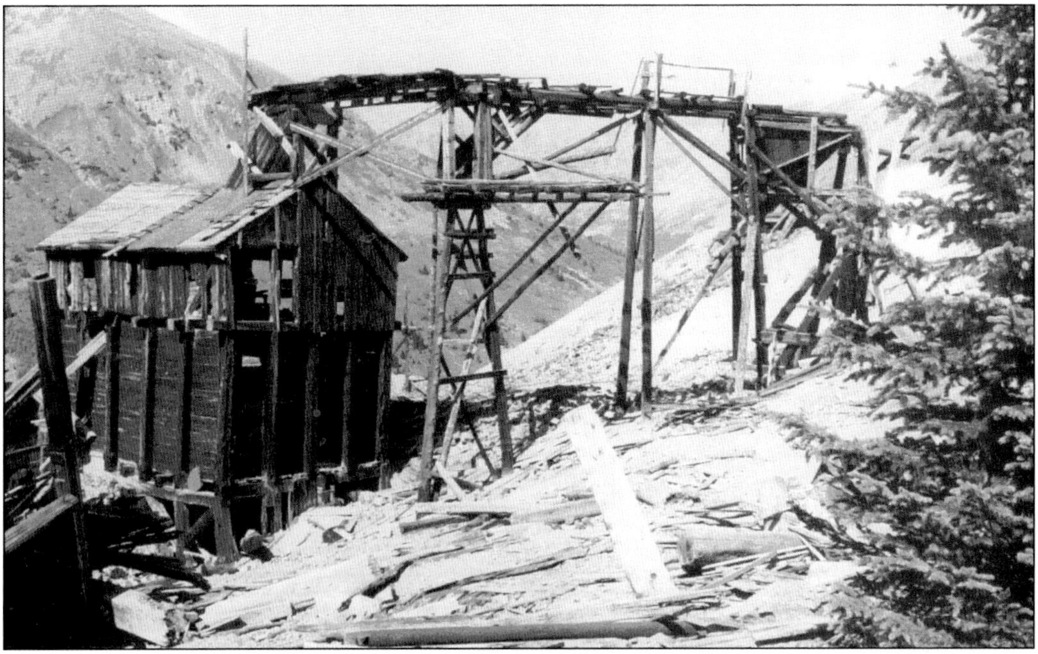

Engineering Skill. The lumber used to construct mining structures far up on the slopes of the Ten Mile Canyon had to be transported to the mine sites, where little level ground was available for buildings and other structures. Any storage bins or elevated tracks for ore carts had to withstand high winds, heavy snow, soaking rain, and unstable, weathered rock.

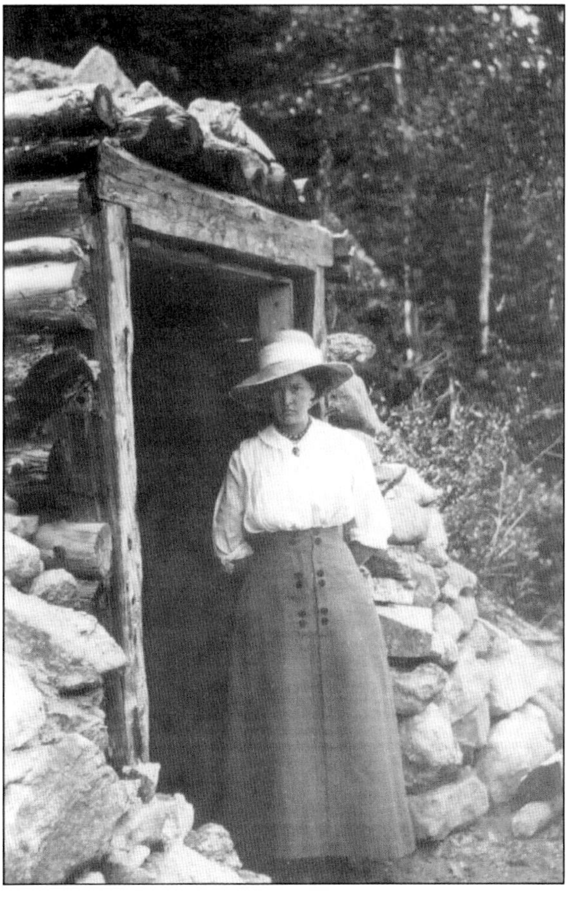

As Close as She Will Get. Because of the many dangers involved in mining, miners tended to be very superstitious. An inverted horseshoe mounted on the wall brought good luck. Whistling scared away the rich ore. Cornish miners would not touch a mining tool if a topside executive stood nearby. The biggest superstition of all kept women out of the mines, alleging they brought bad luck.

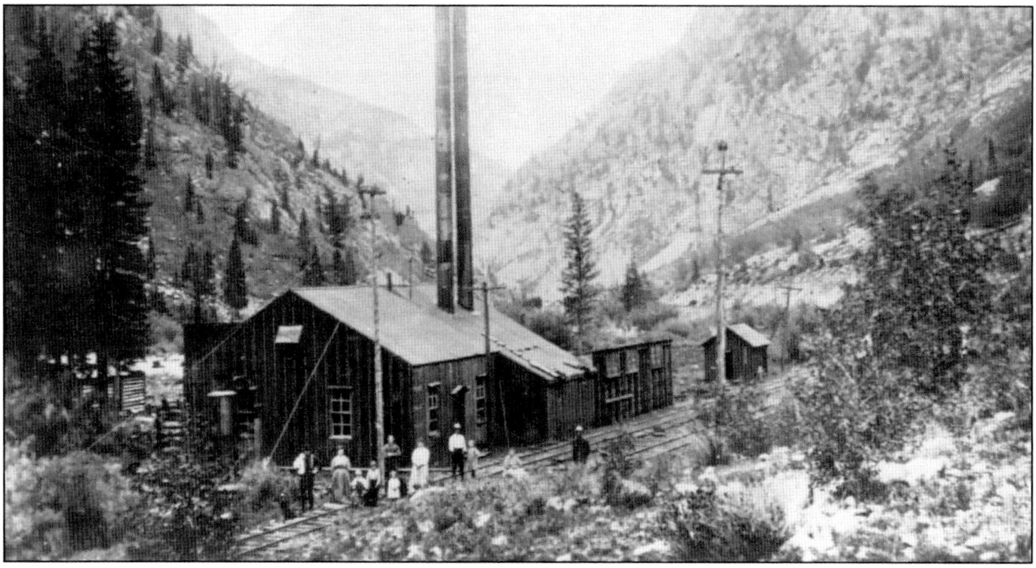

Power Plant at Curtin. Many power plants lined the railroad tracks in the Ten Mile Canyon. The plants burned coal delivered by the trains in order to provide the power necessary to operate mining equipment, deliver compressed air for the pneumatic drills, and, in some cases, pump in fresh air to overcome poor ventilation in the mines. Members of the Giberson and Ruth families posed for this photograph.

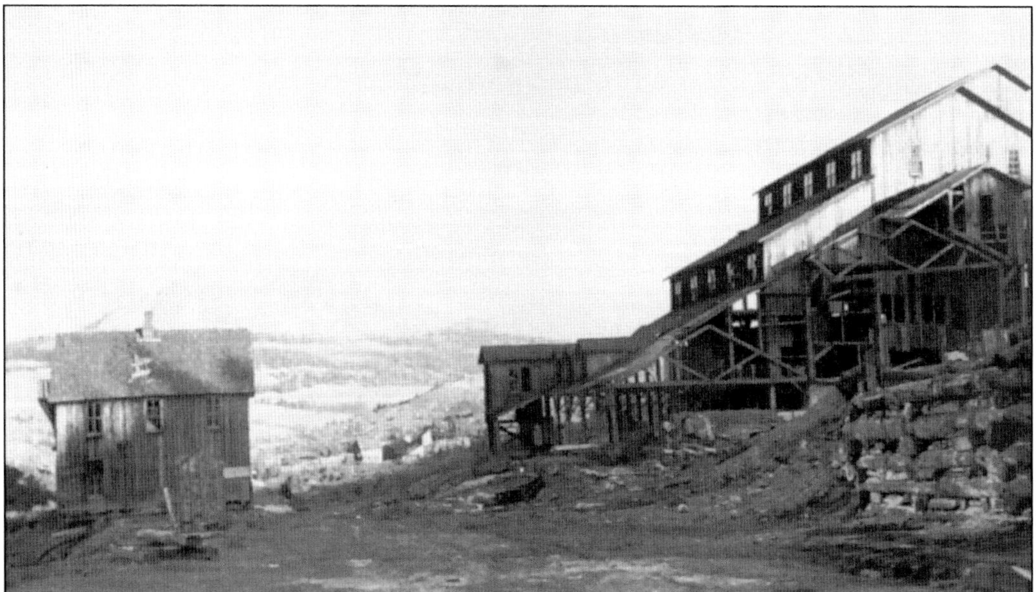

Kimberly Mill in Kokomo. One of several mills operating in Kokomo during the 1890s and early 1900s, the Kimberly Mill concentrated ore from many mines. Mills were either custom or integrated mills. A custom mill processed ore from a variety of small mines that could not afford their own mills. Integrated mills handled the ore from a group of mines all owned by the same mining company.

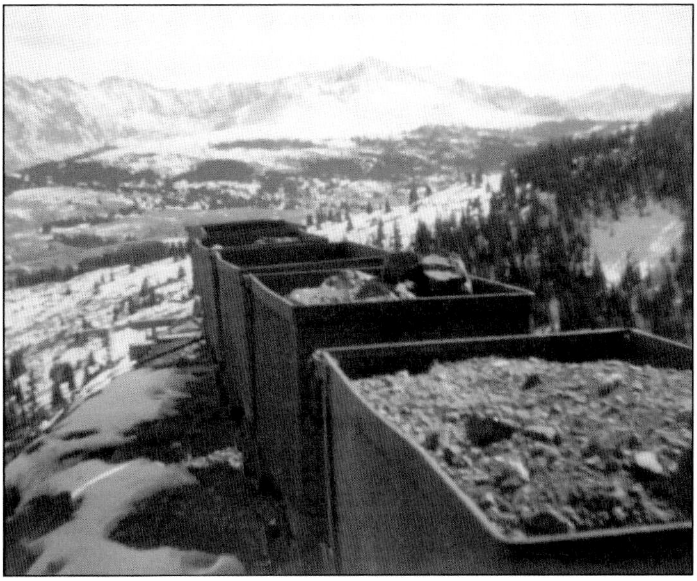

Ore Cars at Kimberly Mill. After the assay process determined the worth of the ore, it underwent further processing: milling, concentrating, and smelting. Two of these steps occurred at a concentrating mill. Men and machines worked together to pulverize the ore in these cars through a variety of physical and chemical processes. They then discarded the unused portion of the ore in the mine dump and prepared the concentrate for smelting.

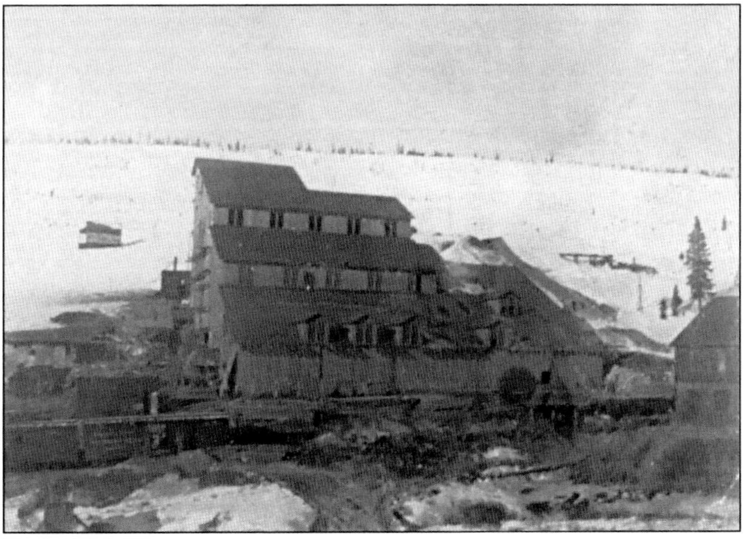

The Kimberly-Wilfley Mill. Reflecting the addition of Arthur Redman Wilfley as an investor, the renamed mill rarely operated at a profit. The problems at the mill resulted from the falling silver prices occurring throughout the state. During World War I, prices rose enough so that the mill operated at a profit, but the lack of railroads and adequate roads for trucks to carry ore hindered production.

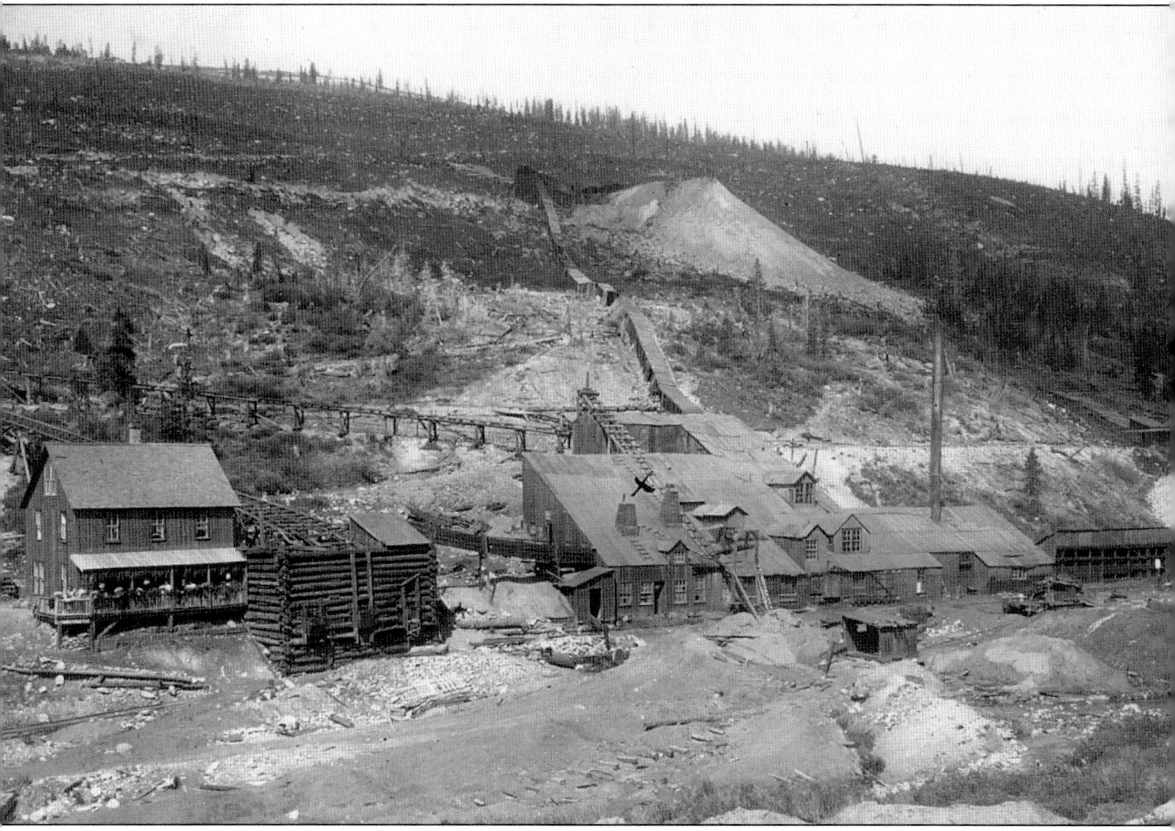

WILFLEY MILL AND SMELTER. Here, Arthur Redman Wilfley began his experiments with new techniques and equipment in hopes of processing the low-grade ore of the southern Ten Mile. A covered conveyor and raised track carried ore to the mill. The smokestack indicates the location of the smelter. A boardinghouse for the workers sits to the left of the log building. The mill was destroyed by fire in October 1891. (Used with permission from the Bill Eloe Collection.)

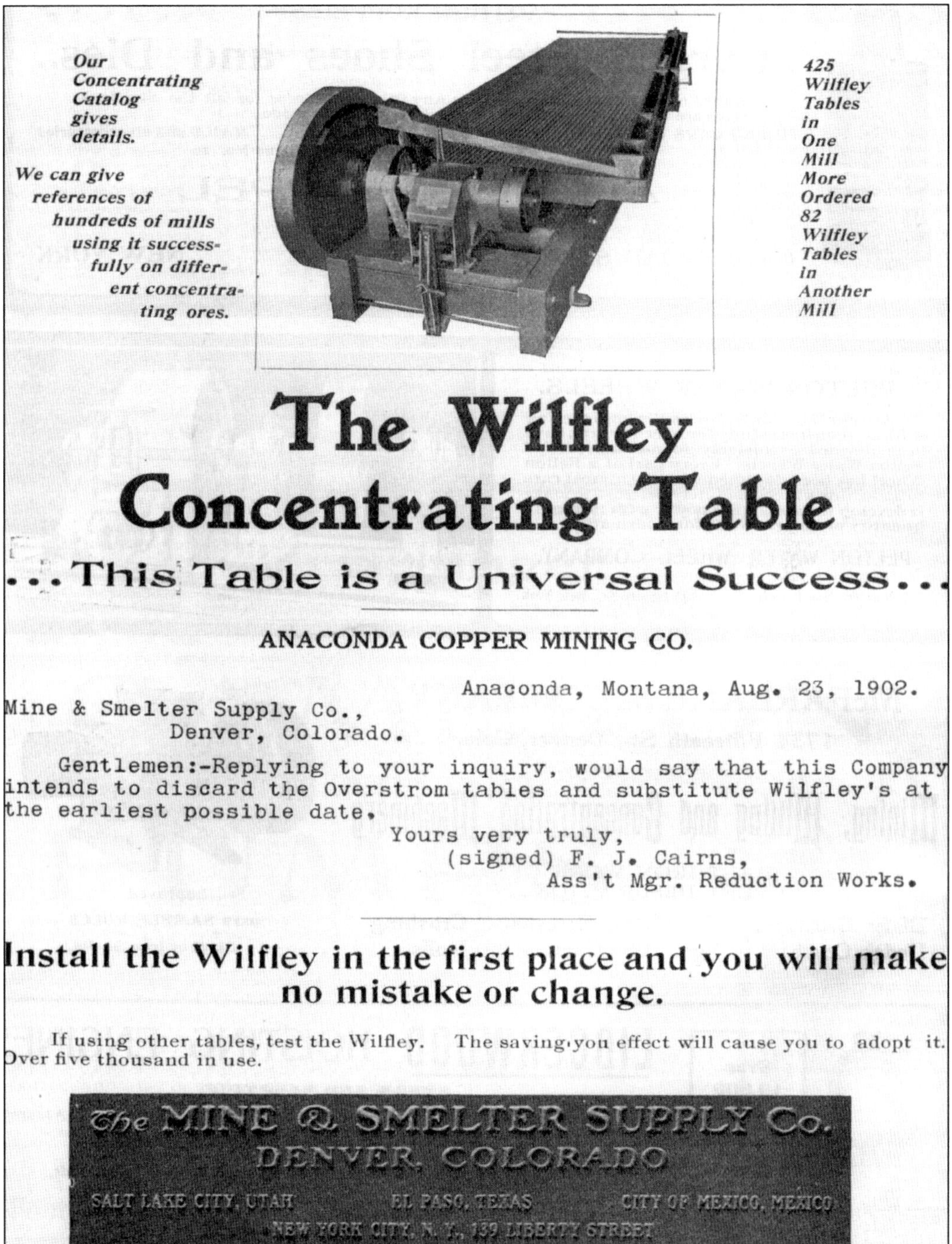

The Wilfley Concentrating Table. In the 1890s, Arthur Redman Wilfley developed his highly successful, transversely inclined vibrating table that concentrated the low-grade ores of the Ten Mile Canyon that contained silver, lead, copper, iron, zinc, and gold. The 12-foot-by-5-foot tables cost $450 and sold throughout the county and state. This advertisement appeared in the October 2, 1902, edition of the *Mining Reporter*, published in Denver. (Used with permission from the Ed and Nancy Bathke Collection.)

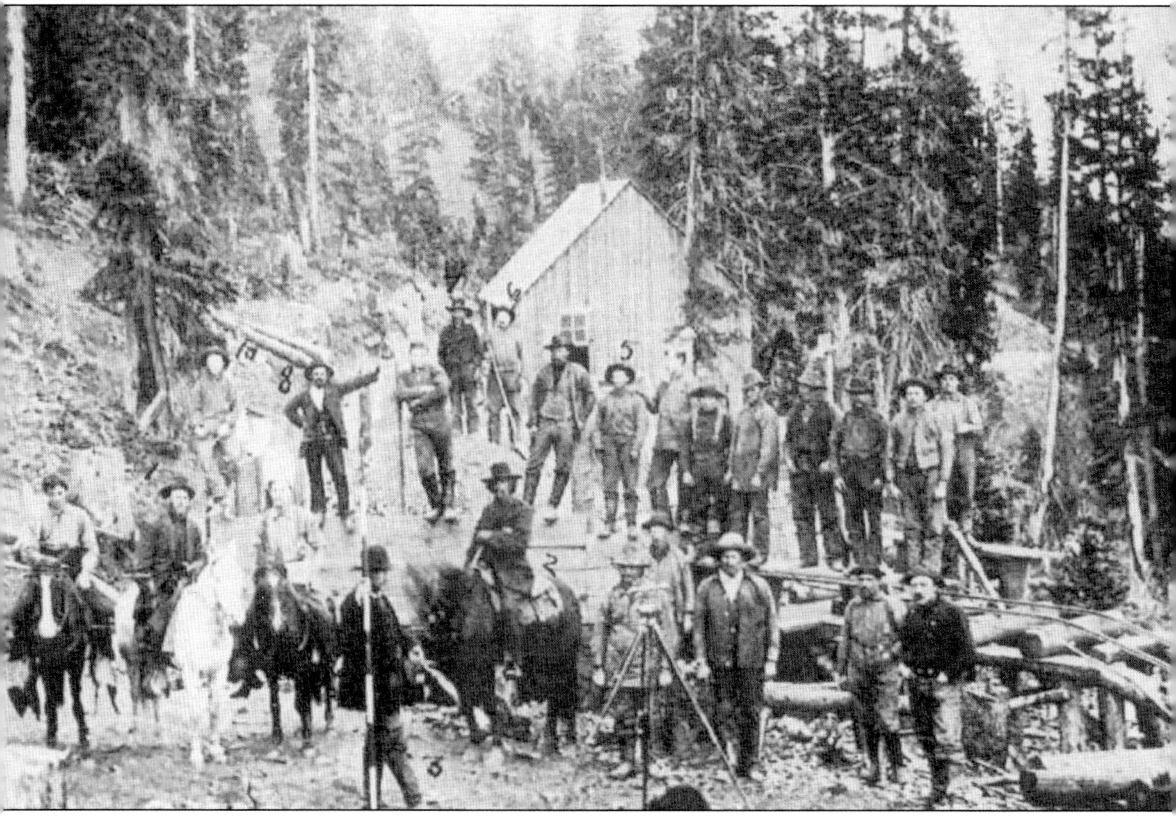

Queen of the West Mine. Located north of Kokomo on Jacque Peak, the Queen of the West Mine, which produced silver-galena ore, was discovered by Daniel Recen in 1881. With additional financial backing from William Graff, the mine became the largest on Jacque Peak. A boardinghouse sheltered the 40 men who worked ten-hour days. Like other mines, it endured yearly cycles of hope and discouragement. (Used with permission from the Bill Fountain Collection.)

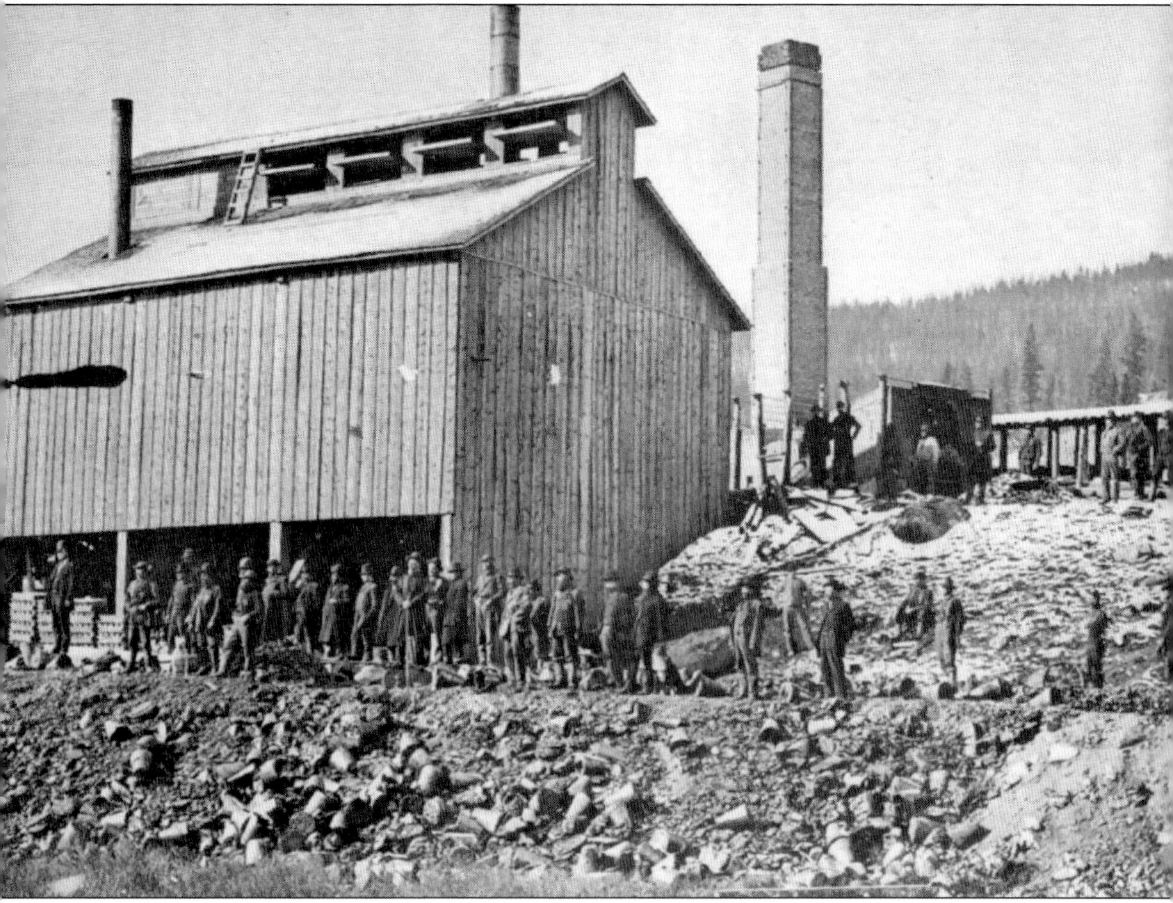

KOKOMO REDUCTION WORKS. Very quickly, mine operators realized that by reducing the amount of worthless ore carried by wagons and trains, profits would rise. Smelters completed the operation. The Kokomo Reduction Works became the White Quail Smelter. Silver bars prepared by the smelter rest on the loading dock to the right of the workers posing for the picture. In 1881, the smelter produced 950 tons of silver bullion, worth $475,000. (Used with permission from the collection of Bob Schoppe and the Denver, South Park & Pacific Historical Society.)

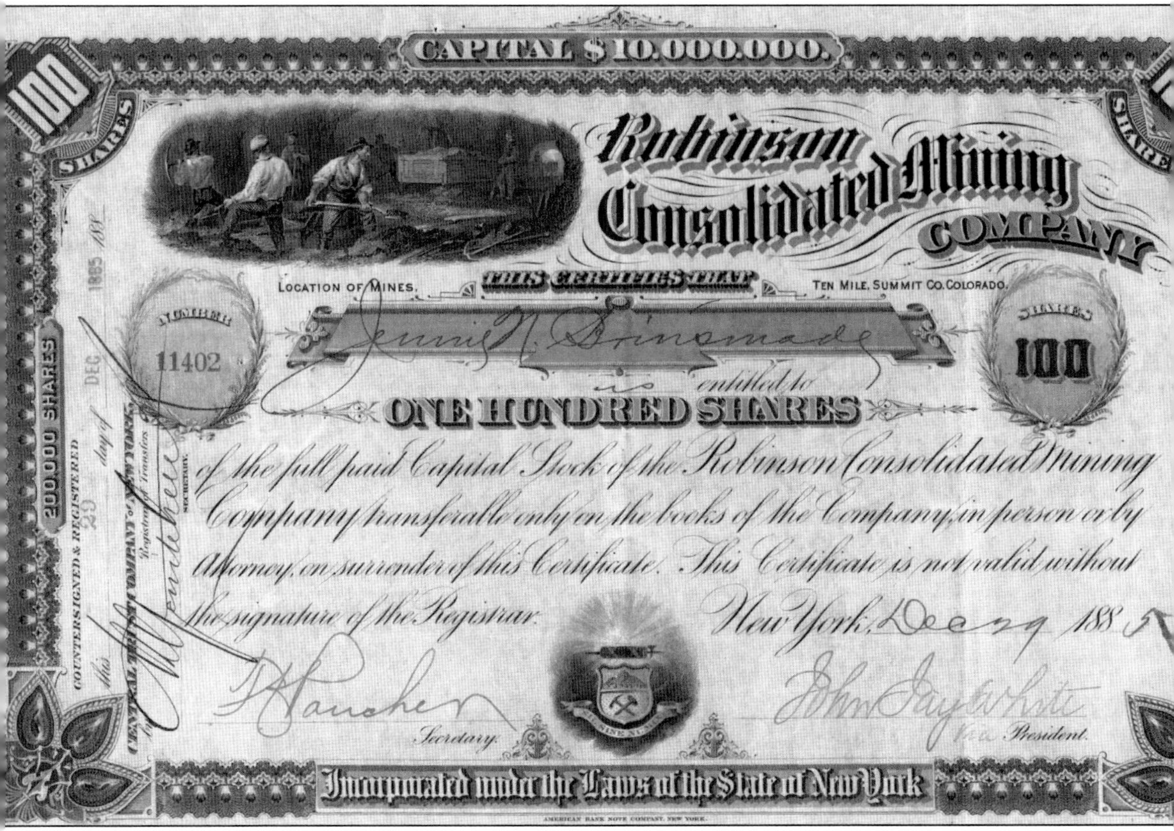

Robinson Consolidated Mining Company Certificate. This company grew to become the largest in the mining district, producing silver ore of good smelting quality because the ore contained 50 percent lead. Railroad cars carried the ore to refineries in Omaha, St. Louis, and Chicago, where the silver could be profitably separated from the lead. Production from the mine dropped each winter, which hurt efforts to entice investors to support the operation financially. (Used with permission from the collection of Bob Schoppe and the Denver, South Park & Pacific Historical Society.)

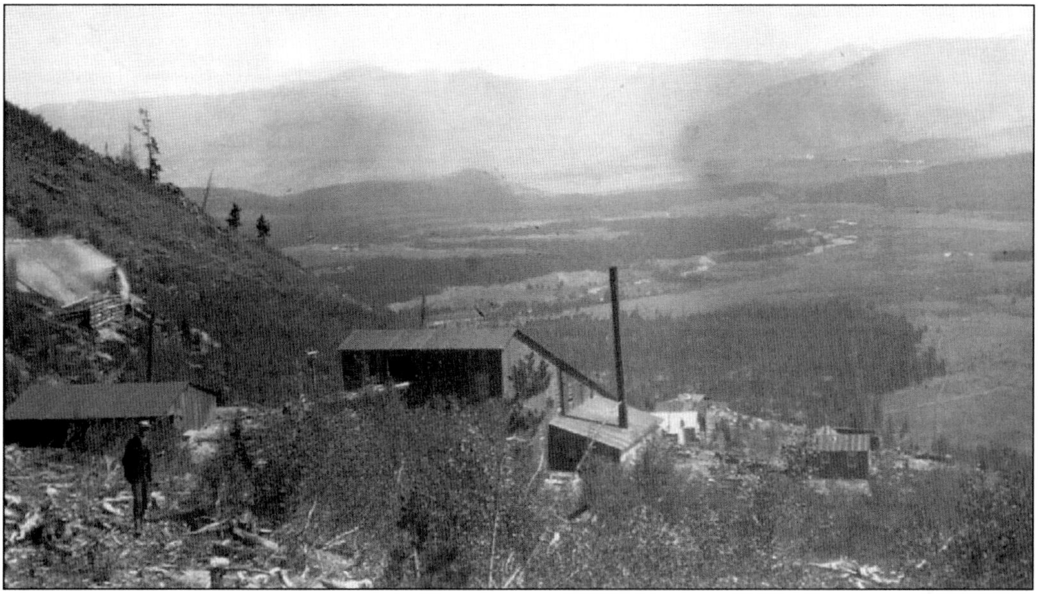

MASONTOWN. In its heyday, the town sitting at about 10,000 feet on Mount Royal probably had several hundred residents. A 20-stamp mill, powered by water from Miner's Creek, concentrated the ore produced by the mine. Originally called the Victoria Mine, the complex consisted of numerous claims owned by the Masontown Mining and Milling Company. Old Dillon appears in the distance at right.

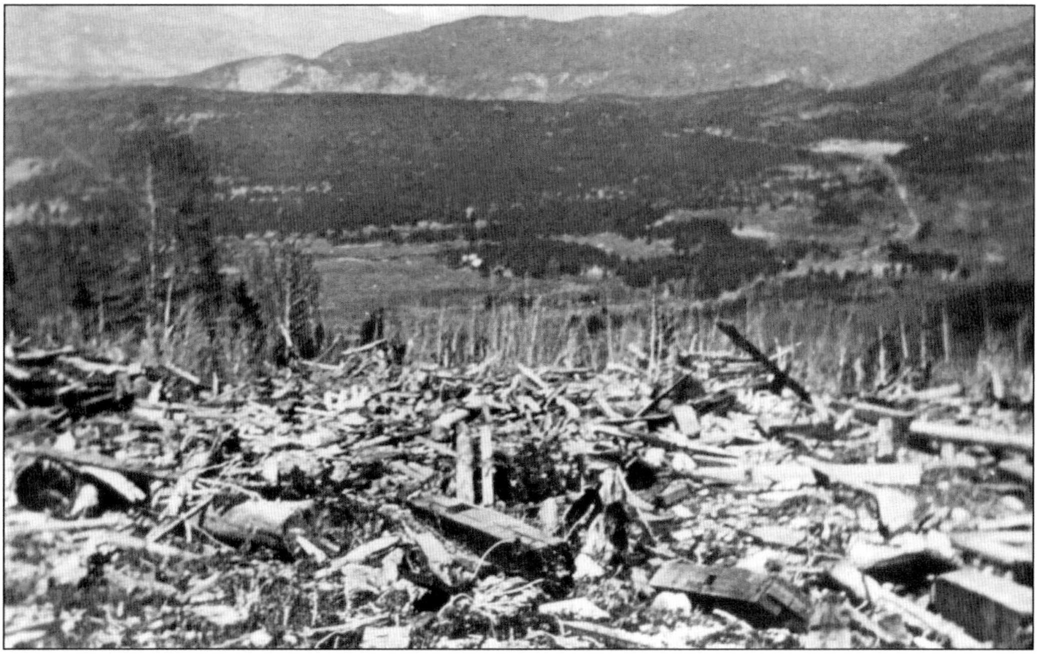

MASONTOWN SLIDE. In March 1926, a snow slide roared down the well-used avalanche scar visible on Mount Royal and demolished what remained of Masontown. When financial backers did not realize the returns they had expected, they invested their money elsewhere. Without financial resources, mining ended around 1910 and the town became a ghost town. There was little left for the snow slide to bury.

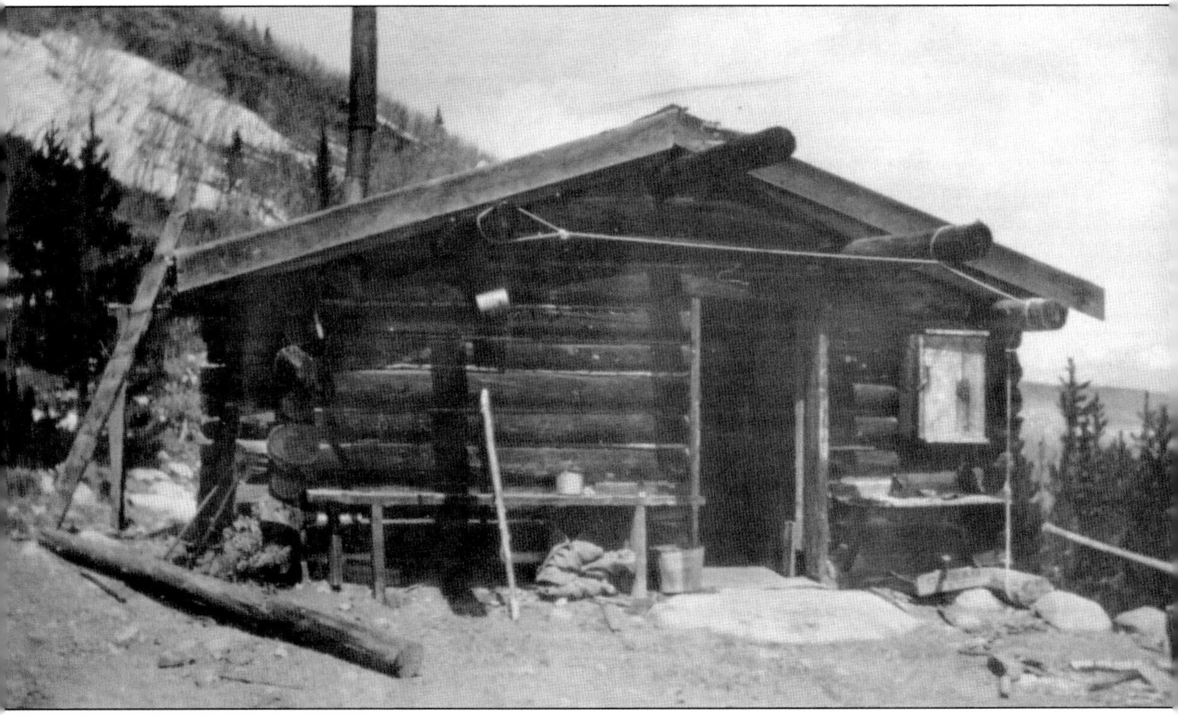

HOME, SWEET HOME. Workers at Masontown lived in the boardinghouse provided by the company or in cabins like this one. Generally, workers preferred living in company-owned boardinghouses where food and lodging were available for a small cost per week. Meals featured meat, eggs, baked goods, stews, vegetables, and fruit. The men favored beef above other meats and preferred fresh fruit and vegetables, but often endured canned varieties.

Five

Roads and Railroads
The Transportation Network

The economic development of Frisco and the Ten Mile Canyon depended upon cheap, efficient transportation. An adequate network of roads and railroads meant the difference between growth and stagnation for towns and mines.

As soon as companies confirmed the mineral wealth of the Ten Mile Canyon, roads became a priority. Snow, mud, rockslides, and avalanches hindered the monumental task of building and maintaining roads.

The huge tonnage of goods entering and ore leaving the canyon demanded railroads, although the true destination for both railroads was Leadville and not Frisco, Dickey, or Kokomo. Two narrow-gauge railroads served the county: the Denver & Rio Grande and the Denver, South Park & Pacific. Their fortunes rested on mining; when it died, so did the railroads, although it must be recognized that the railroads had a stranglehold on the mining economy from the beginning due to high transportation costs.

William Jackson Palmer, president of the Denver & Rio Grande, felt that a population engaged in mining generated the highest profits by far for a railroad. His company began serving Robinson in December 1880, Wheeler in September 1881, and Dillon in November 1882. The Denver, South Park & Pacific laid track over Boreas Pass and reached Dickey at the end of 1882. There, the line split, with the main line turning toward Frisco and a branch heading north to Dillon. Both companies competed for the business of Frisco and the towns and mines of the Ten Mile Canyon.

As mines closed and profits withered, the railroads curtailed service. The Denver & Rio Grande stopped all service in the early 1920s. The Denver, South Park & Pacific, now owned by the Colorado & Southern, removed its tracks in 1937 and 1938.

The railroads brought many changes. They made the low-grade ores of the Ten Mile Canyon more profitable, changed the diets of the residents by bringing fresh fruits and vegetables to stores and markets, carried agricultural products from Summit County to restaurants as far away as New York City, and fostered tourism by offering Sunday afternoon excursions through the Ten Mile Canyon.

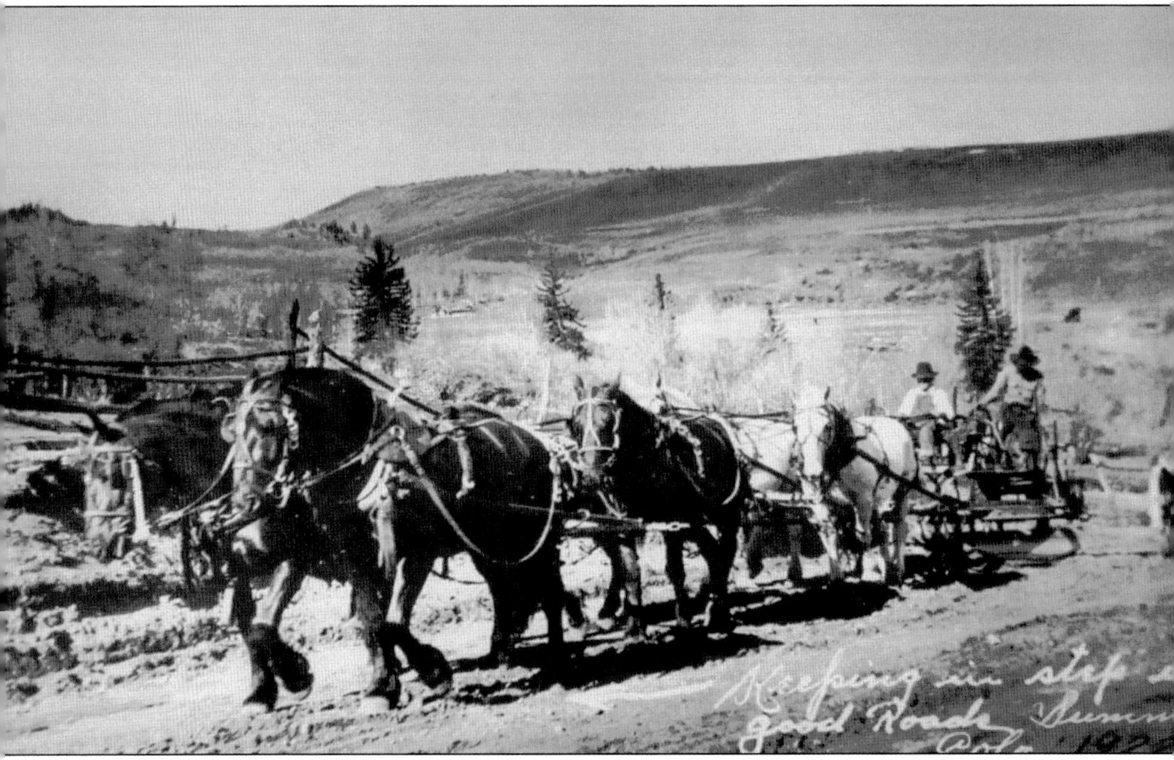

Wet in Spring, Dusty in Summer. In the 1880s, road building presented great difficulties. Trees had to be cut, boulders and stumps removed, and holes filled. Maintaining a road was a never-ending task. Storms washed out bridges and sent trees crashing onto roadways, wooden bridges burned easily, ice and snow made the roads treacherous for wagons and carriages in winter, and summer thunderstorms created muddy quagmires for drivers to negotiate.

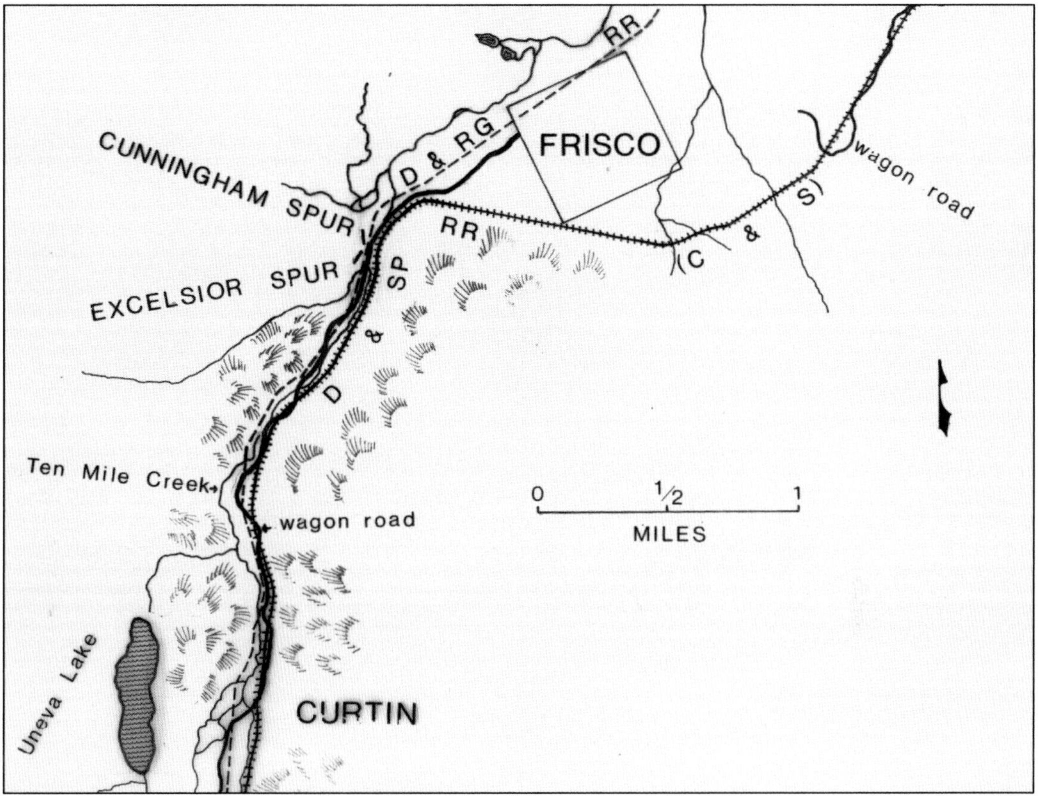

TRANSPORTATION NETWORK IN THE NORTHERN AND MIDDLE TEN MILE CANYON. Two railroad rights-of-way, a wagon road, and the meandering Ten Mile Creek lay side-by-side in the narrow canyon on this undated map. The railroads built spurs to serve mining and lumbering interests along the route. Top: Northern Ten Mile Canyon; Bottom: Middle Ten Mile Canyon. (Maps drawn by author.)

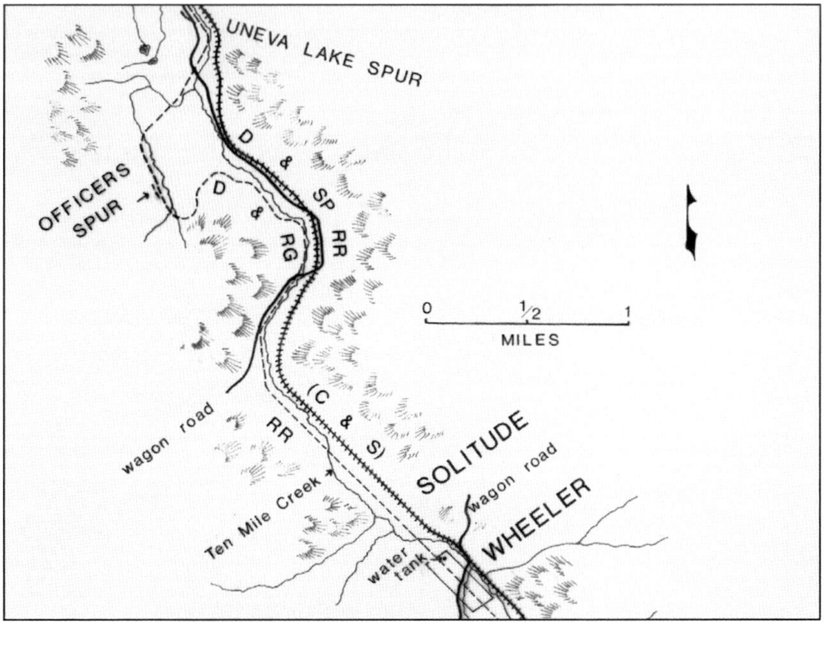

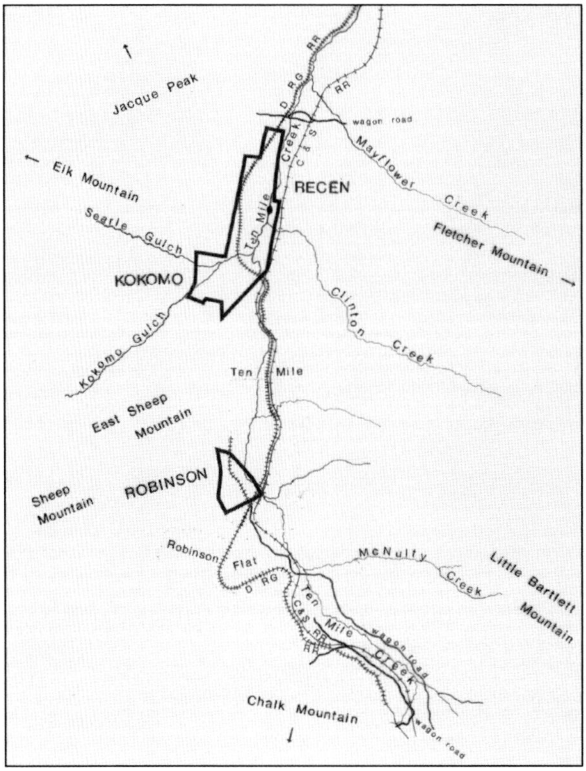

Transportation Network in the Southern Ten Mile Canyon. This map, a continuation of the previous two maps, shows Recen, Kokomo, and Robinson after 1898. By order of the US Circuit Court, which permitted an overhead crossing, the Denver, South Park & Pacific crossed the Denver & Rio Grande tracks on a trestle in the narrow canyon south of Kokomo. (Map drawn by author.)

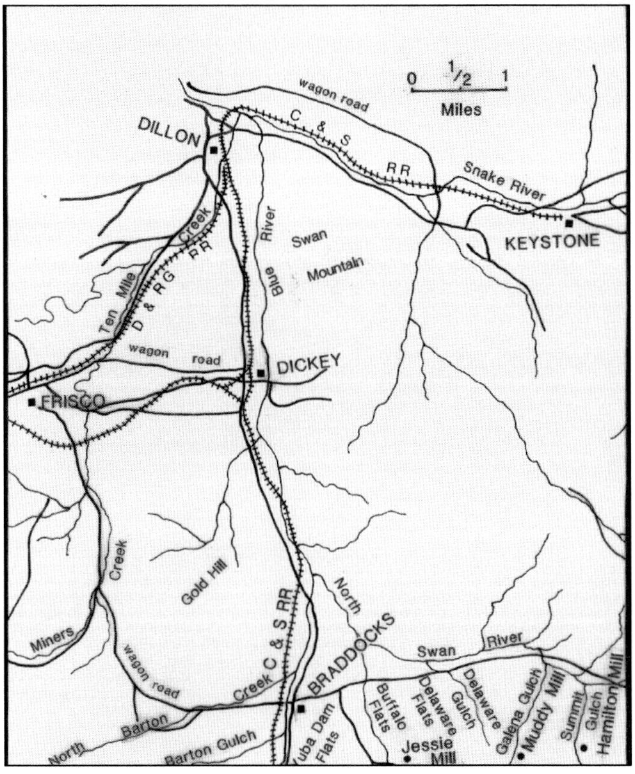

Saving Time and Track. Originally, the Denver, South Park & Pacific plans called for routing the line to Leadville through Dillon. By revising the plans so that the main and branch lines met at Dickey, two miles south of Dillon, the railroad saved four miles of track and shortened the distance to Leadville. The main line returned to the original survey through the Ten Mile Canyon near Frisco. (Map drawn by author.)

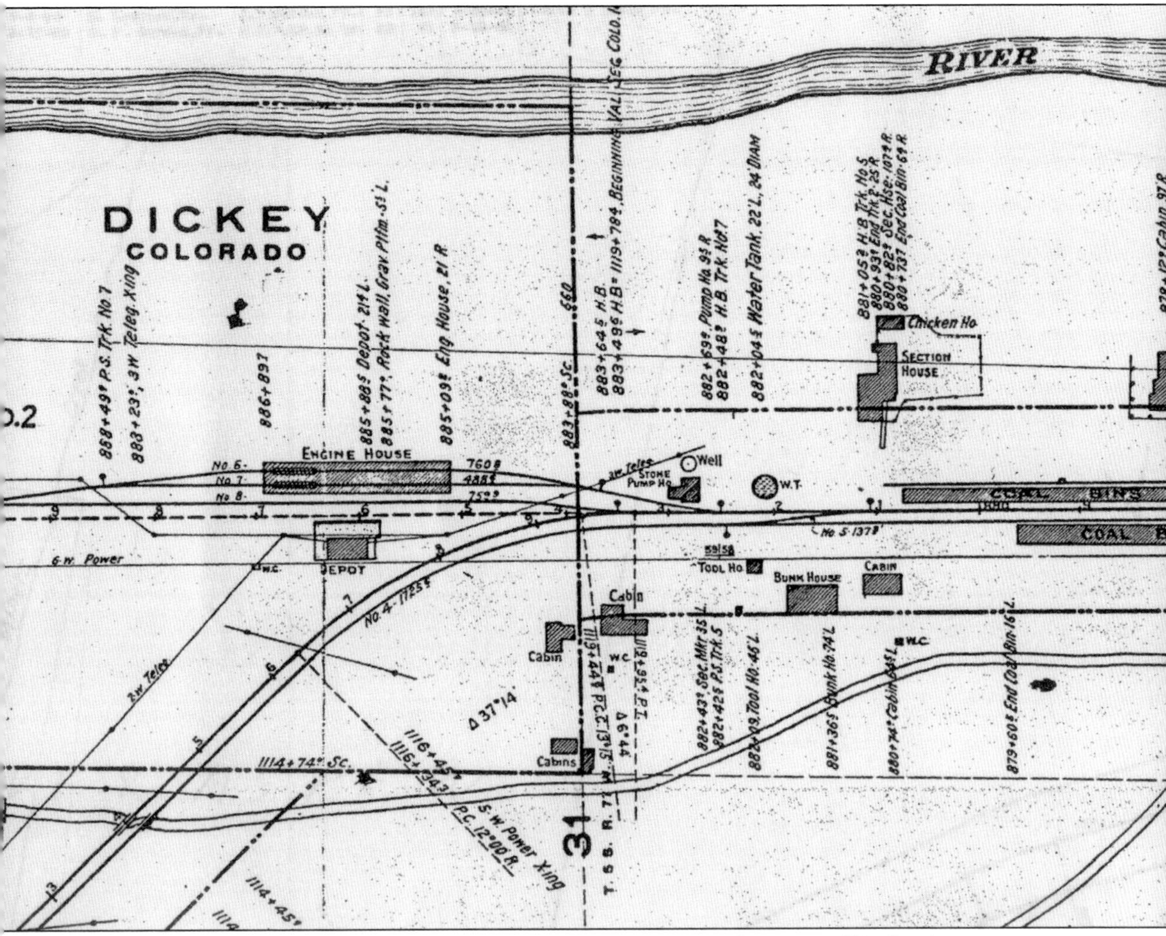

Map of Denver, South Park & Pacific Facilities at Dickey. Because of Dickey's importance, the facilities west of the Blue River were extensive. The two-stall engine house, well to supply the water tank, stone pump house, tool house, and coal chutes lined the track to the south. Cabins and a bunkhouse provided sleeping quarters for workers. The entire site is now under the water of Lake Dillon. (Used with permission from the collection of Bob Schoppe and the Denver, South Park & Pacific Historical Society.)

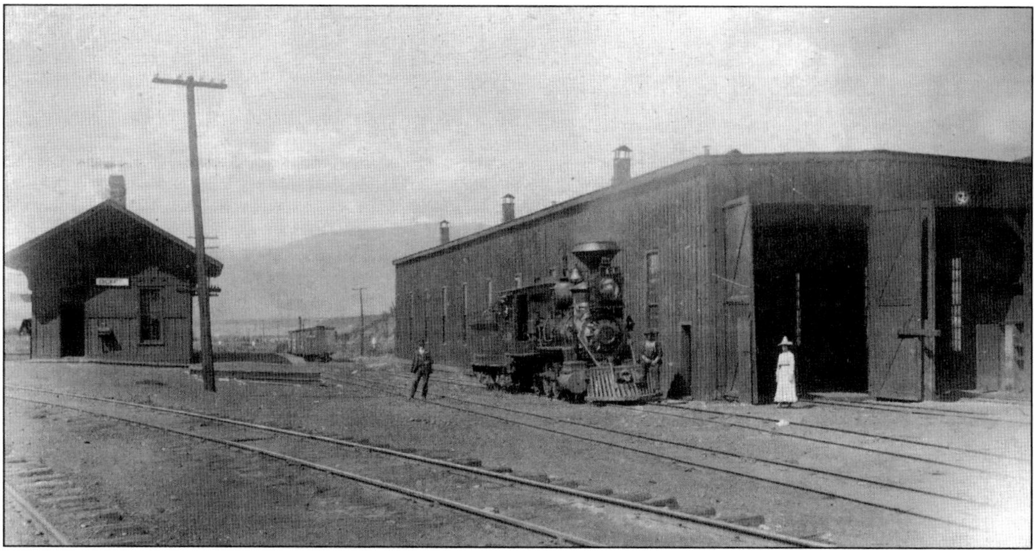

DICKEY ENGINE HOUSE. The engine house sat directly across the tracks from the depot. In the engine house, men serviced the locomotives, keeping them ready to help pull trains over Boreas and Fremont Passes. The track in the foreground led to Frisco; the track to Dillon ran between the buildings. The engine next to the engine house has a McConnel smokestack, also called a sunflower or pancake smokestack. (Used with permission from the Ed and Nancy Bathke Collection.)

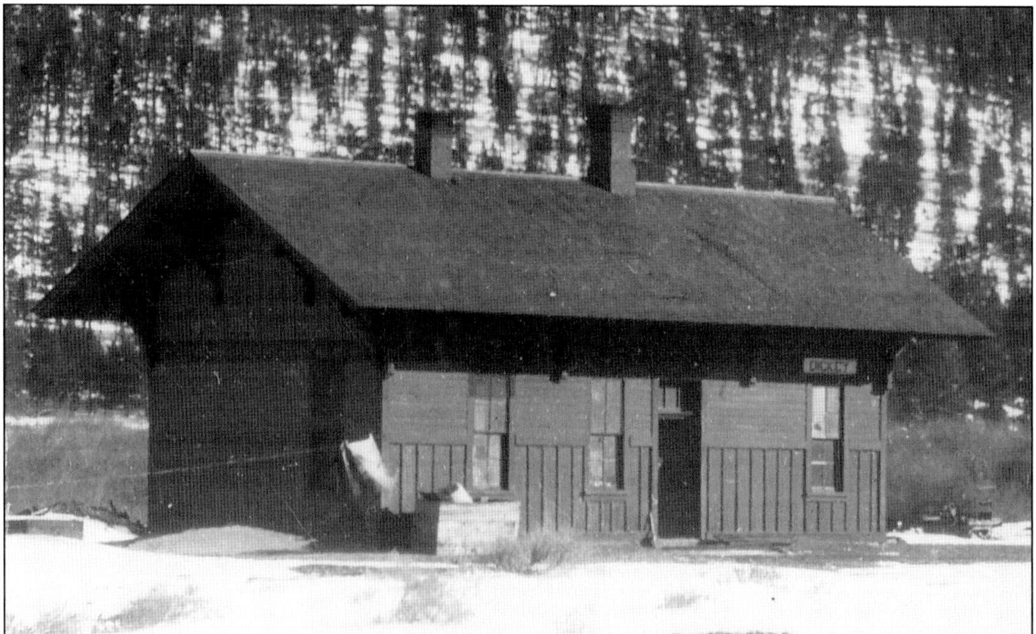

DICKEY DEPOT. According to the *Summit County Journal*, in December 1887, six fully loaded ore cars broke loose in Breckenridge and rolled along the track toward Dickey. Because of the 60-foot drop in elevation per mile between Breckenridge and Dickey, six miles away, the cars, moving too rapidly to negotiate the curve, jumped the track and flew through the air, destroying part of the depot. (Used with permission from the collection of Bob Schoppe and the Denver, South Park & Pacific Historical Society.)

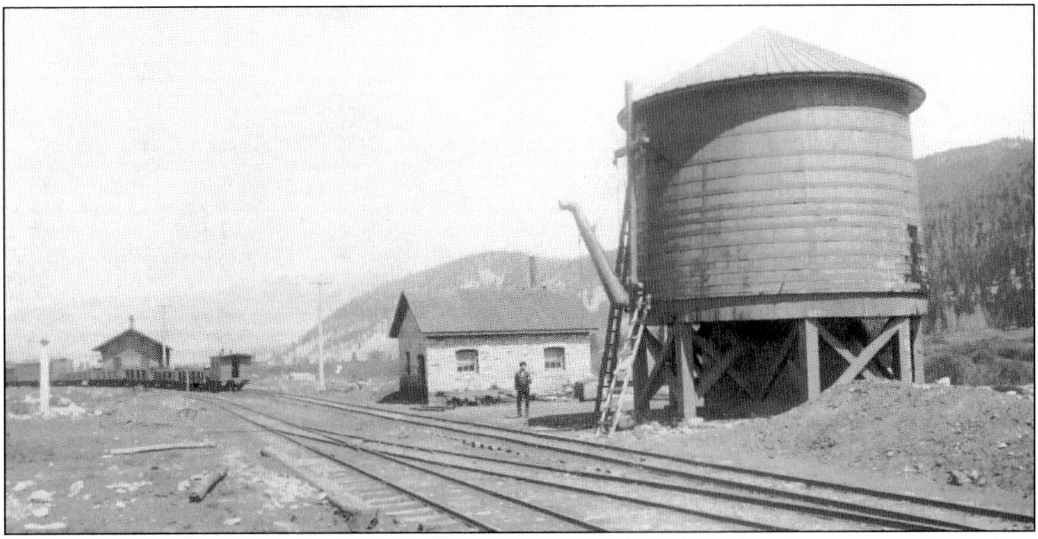

Dickey Pump House, Water Tank, and Depot. At Dickey, the railroad constructed a coaling station, depot, 47,500-gallon water tank, coal chute (in 1902), sidetracks for 188 cars, wye, and enginehouse (in 1902) with stalls to hold six helper engines. Dickey functioned as the junction between the Montezuma and Ten Mile mining districts, the switching point leading to Dillon and Keystone.

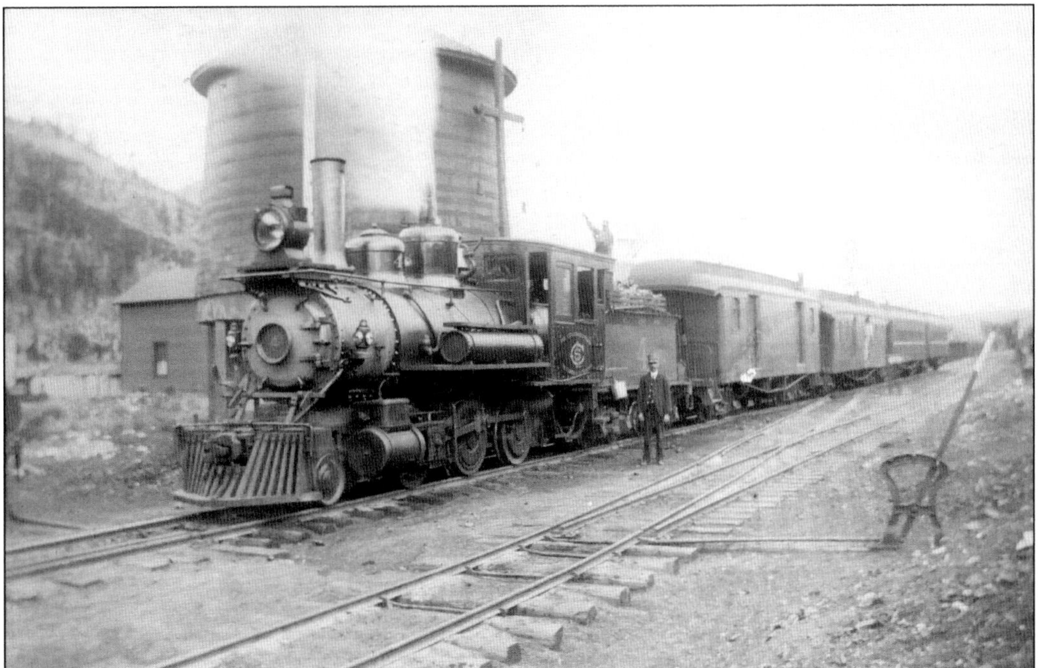

Tender with Water Tank at Dickey in 1903. Westbound Colorado & Southern engines took on water at Dickey and refilled at Solitude station, near Wheeler, before starting the climb to Kokomo, which was six miles away and 800 feet higher. After another refill at Kokomo, the engine arrived at Robinson, two miles farther and 94 feet higher. The elevation at Dickey was 9,004 feet; the elevation at Robinson 10,860 feet. (Used with permission from the Ed and Nancy Bathke Collection.)

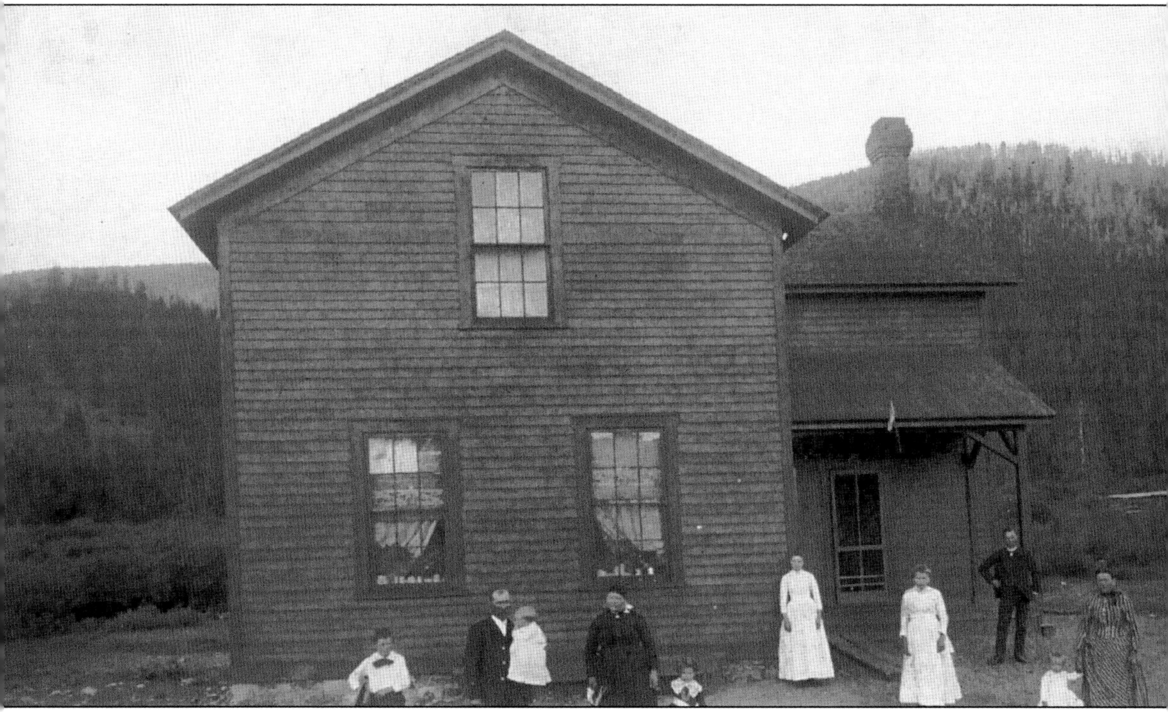

Dickey Section House. At intervals along the line, the Denver, South Park & Pacific built section houses to provide food and lodging for workers who maintained the tracks and other facilities. The two-story frame building sat between the coal bins and the Blue River. Next to the section house was the chicken house, visible at right in the photograph.

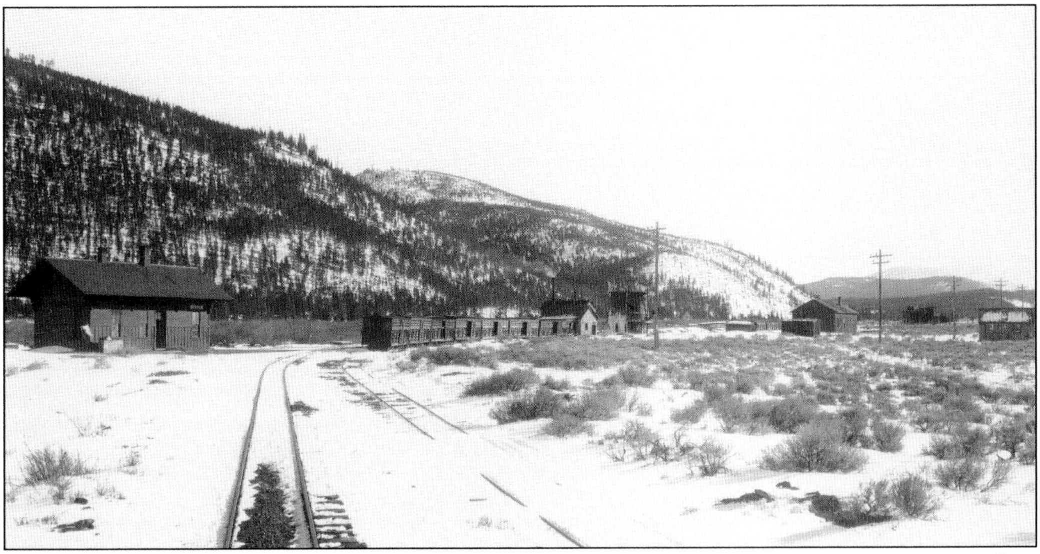

Dickey without the Engine House. Riders arriving in Dickey in 1928 from Frisco or Dillon saw the depot, pump house, water tank, toolshed, bunkhouse, and coal chute—but no engine house. That year, the railroad filed a petition with the Interstate Commerce Commission asking permission to abandon the line through Summit County. Residents countered that curtailing service would completely isolate them during long winters. The ICC denied the petition. (Used with permission of the Colorado Railroad Museum.)

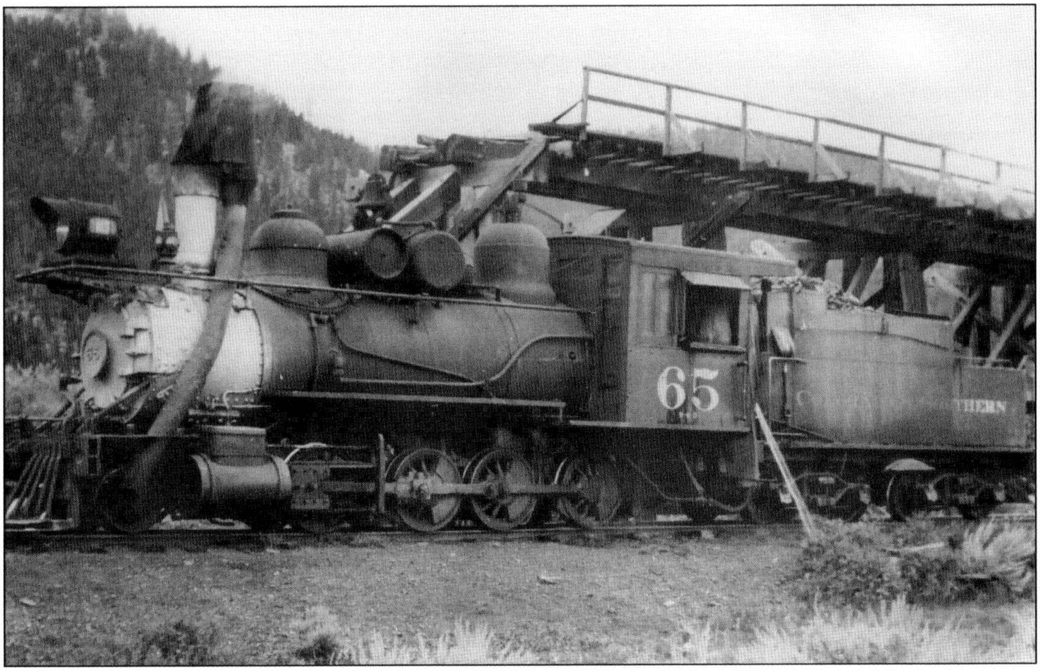

Engine 65 at Dickey, 1934. In 1900, avalanches blocked the tracks near Kokomo, stopping engine 65. The men walked to the section house in Curtin to wait for the rotary. Food ran low. Three meals a day soon became two and then one. The men slept in the coaches while they waited. Wood kept the engines running. When the men returned home, they had been in their same clothes for 10 days. (Used with permission from the Ed and Nancy Bathke Collection.)

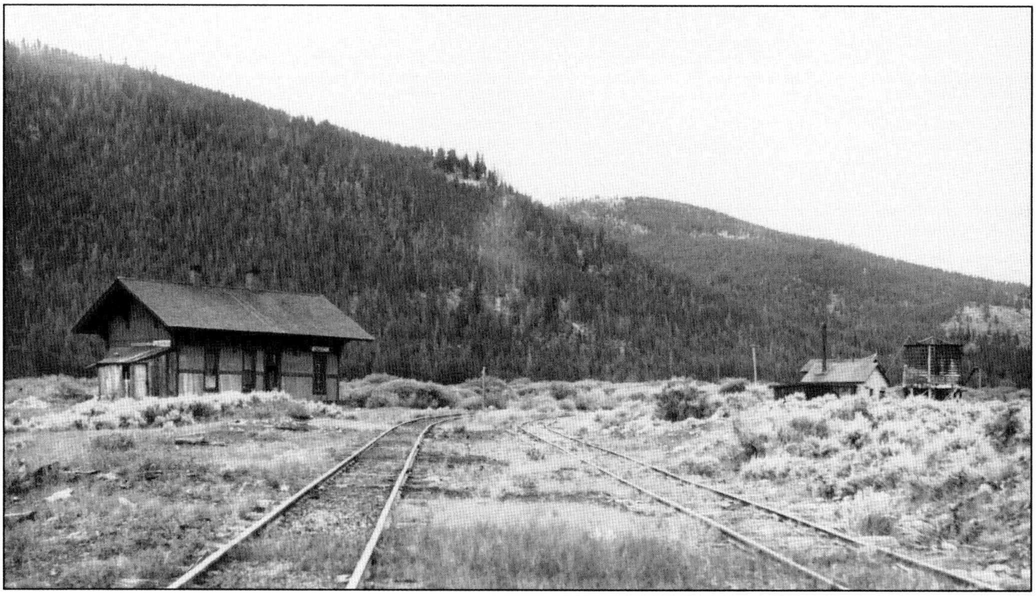

Dickey after Abandonment. The ICC ruled that the Colorado & Southern Railroad could take up the tracks and sell its equipment, effective April 10, 1937. The people and merchants of the county and Denver lost a long and hard-fought battle to retain rail service. The amount of ore produced by the mines did not warrant the expense the company would incur in maintaining service, especially in the winter. (Used with permission from the collection of Bob Schoppe and the Denver, South Park & Pacific Historical Society.)

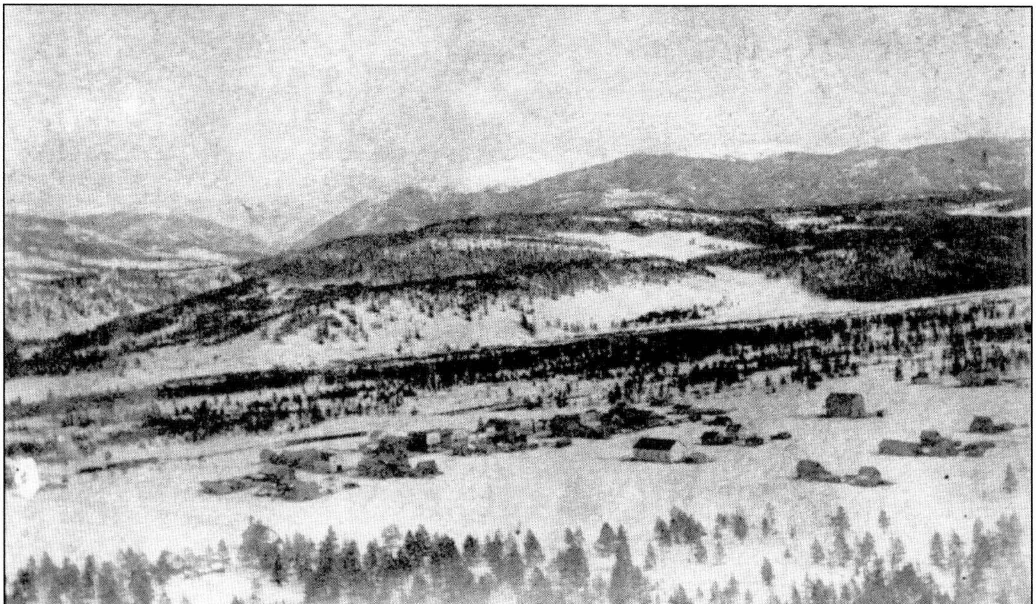

Railroads in Dillon. Dillon moved twice in 1882 so that both railroads and their facilities would be located near the town. The twin trestles crossing the Ten Mile Creek are visible in the center of the image. Most of the buildings in Dillon lined Main Street. The 1883 schoolhouse sat on Hamilton Street, along with the Hamilton Hotel, visible at far right. Swan Mountain rises beyond the town. (Used with permission from the Ed and Nancy Bathke Collection.)

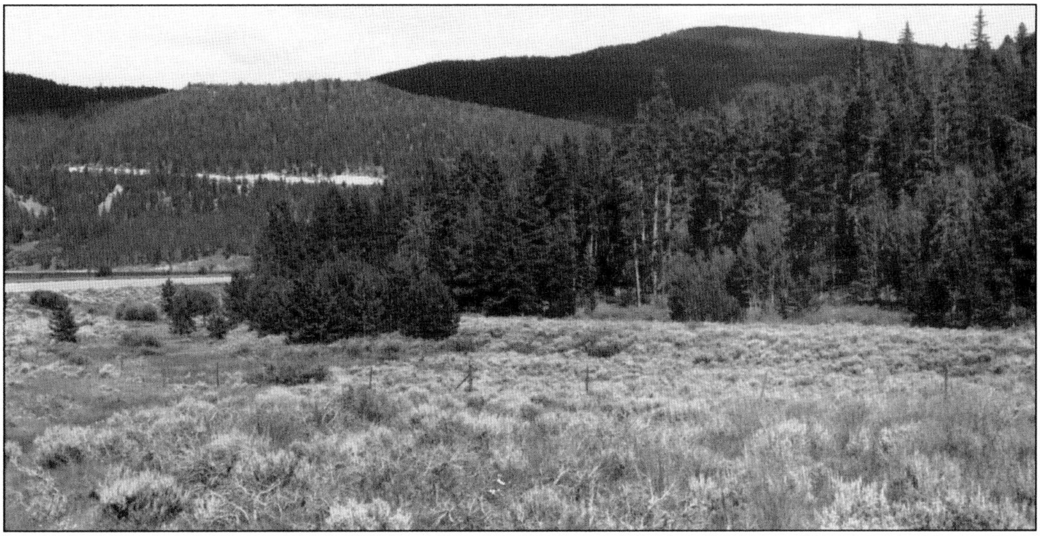

DENVER, SOUTH PARK & PACIFIC RIGHT-OF-WAY. The sagebrush-covered right-of-way is visible to the west of Highway 9 as the road makes a bend toward Frisco. The raised right-of-way joins and then becomes the recreational path. Passing the site of the Hathaway-Lamping charcoal kilns, the path skirts the base of Mount Royal and enters the Ten Mile Canyon.

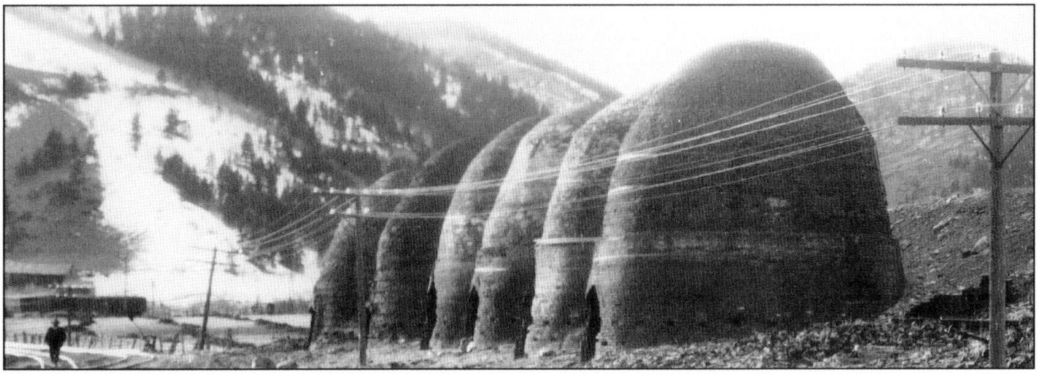

CHARCOAL KILNS AT WEBSTER. At least 50 charcoal kilns operated around Frisco. Each firing consumed 25 to 35 cords of wood. One cord produced about 75 bushels of charcoal. Filling the kiln took four men 12 hours. Charring lasted four to six days. After waiting another 10 days for the charcoal to cool, the men spent a full day emptying the kiln through a small door at the base. (Used with permission from the collection of Bob Schoppe and the Denver, South Park & Pacific Historical Society.)

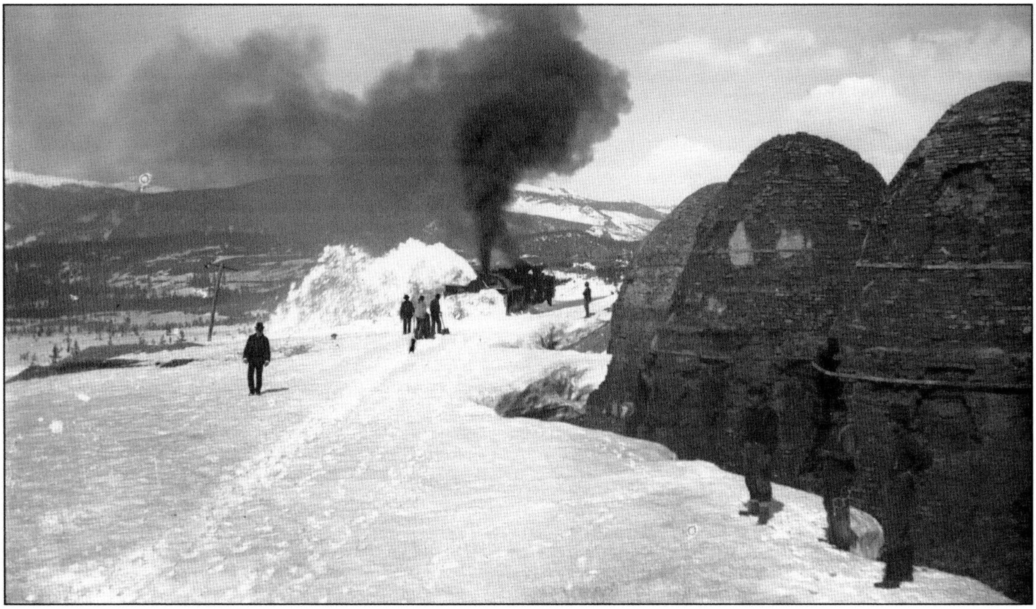

The Abandoned Hathaway-Lamping Charcoal Kilns, c. 1899. The beehive-shaped, 20- to 30-foot-tall kilns provided coke for blacksmiths, ore smelters, and blast furnaces. Inside the kilns, the stacked wood smoldered, slowly changing to pure carbon that gave off a high amount of heat when used as a fuel. The kilns, constructed of local clay and brick, operated under the direction of Frisco residents Joe Lamping and John Hathaway. (This C. H Scott photograph used with permission from the John Manley Collection.)

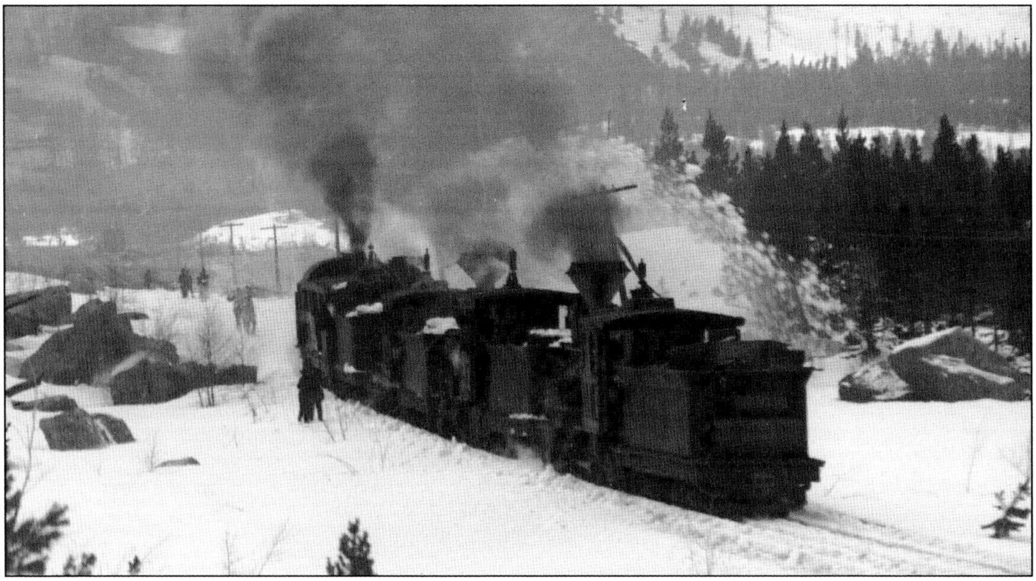

Entering Frisco. Altitude and climate worked against the railroads, especially in winter. Bitter cold, howling wind, blowing snow, raging floods in spring, landslides, and avalanches increased operating costs and endangered workers, riders, and equipment. Keeping the tracks clear of snow, ice, and rocks could be almost as difficult as laying the tracks in the first place. The companies found it extremely challenging to maintain schedules. (This C. H Scott photograph used with permission from the Todd Hackett Collection.)

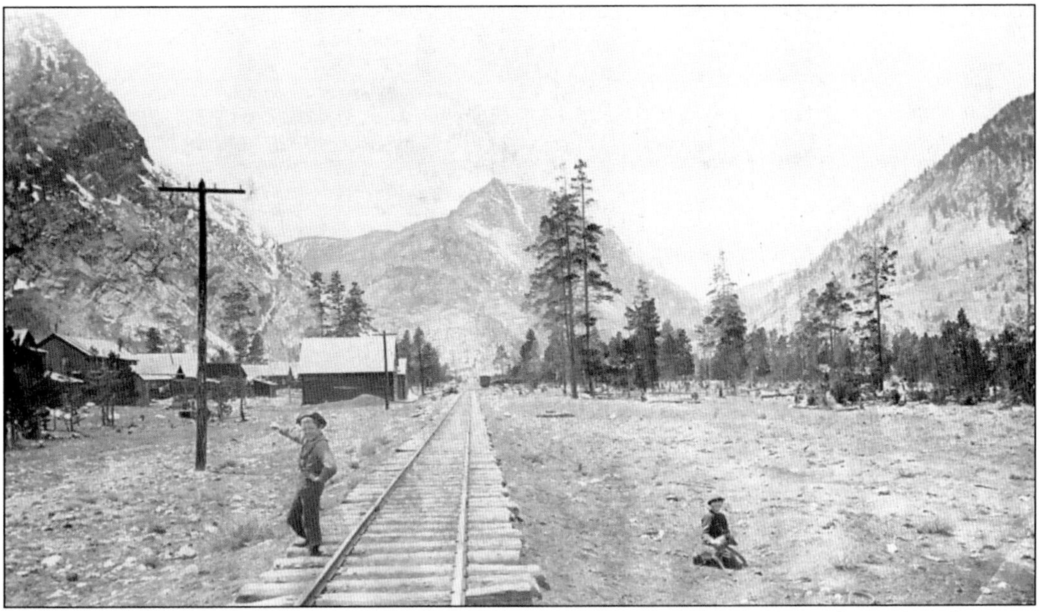

Right-of-Way in Frisco. Hoping to take advantage of its location along the railroad, Frisco town leaders donated land between Main and Galena streets to the Denver & Rio Grande for its right-of-way. The narrow-gauge tracks had three feet between the rails. Standard-gauge railroads laid their tracks four feet, eight and a half inches apart.

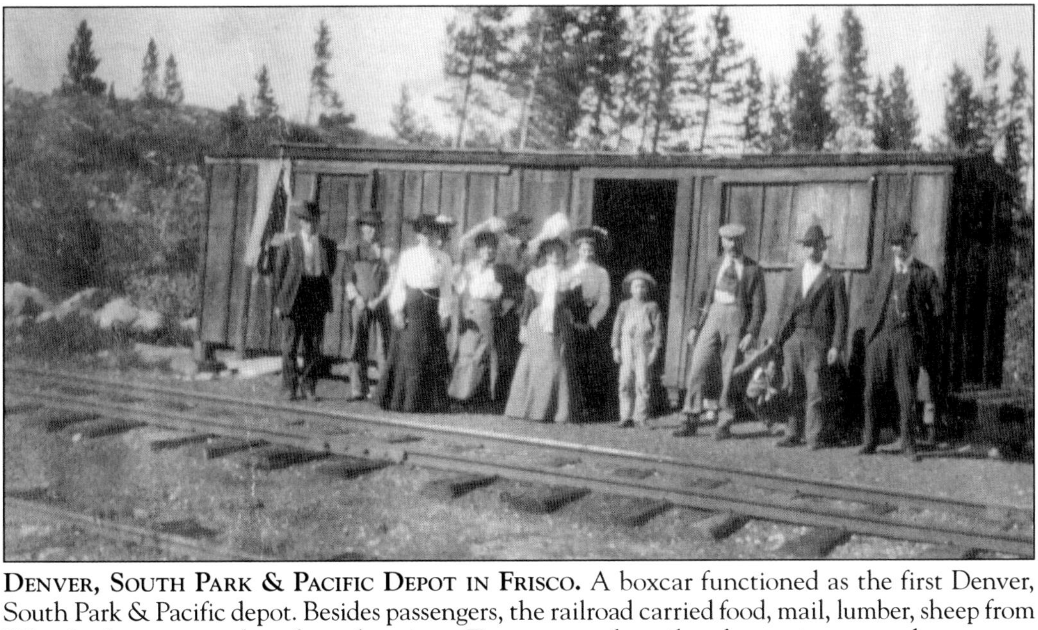

Denver, South Park & Pacific Depot in Frisco. A boxcar functioned as the first Denver, South Park & Pacific depot. Besides passengers, the railroad carried food, mail, lumber, sheep from Wheeler Junction, and ore from the mines. To cut costs, the railroad sometimes seated passengers in a combination car with freight at one end and people at the other. Women, especially, did not appreciate riding in the same car as the freight.

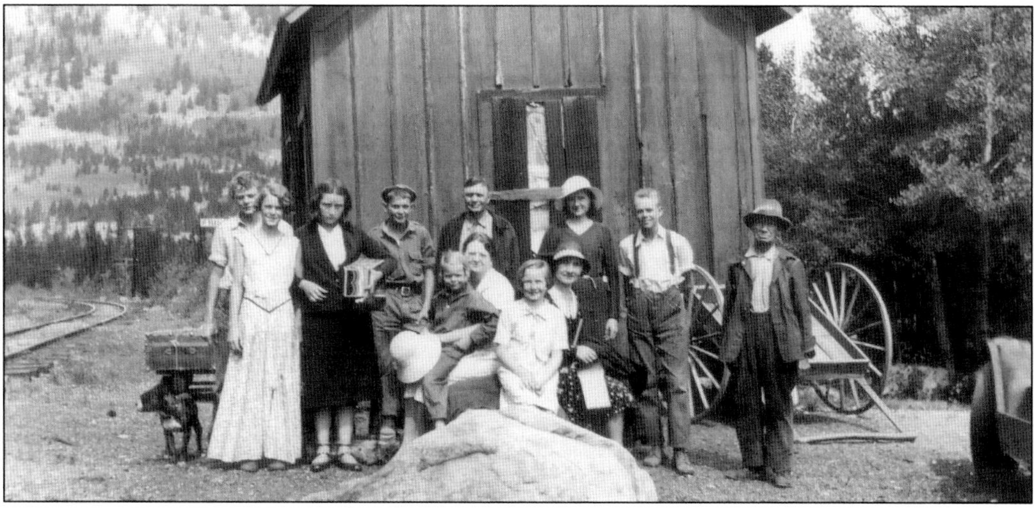

Waiting for the Train. This family group waits for a train at the second Denver, South Park & Pacific depot in Frisco. The railroad laid its tracks at the base of Mount Royal and constructed its depot there. The town hoped to interest the Denver, South Park & Pacific in establishing its headquarters in Frisco and donated many town lots to the company for that purpose.

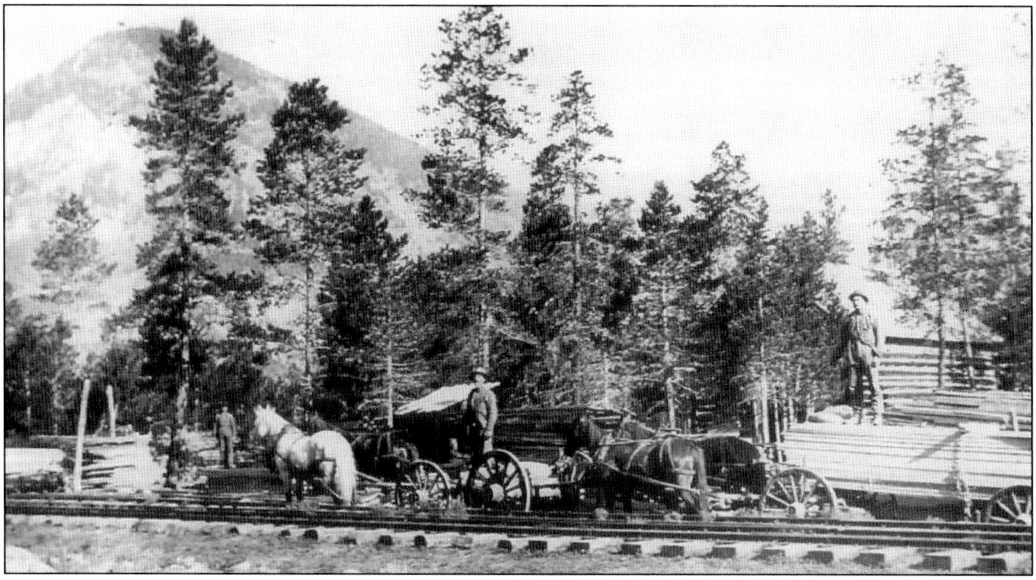

The Demand for Lumber. Numerous sawmills near Frisco and throughout the Ten Mile Canyon provided the tremendous amount of sawn lumber required for mines, railroads, heating, and buildings. Wagons carried the supply to the depot. By the turn of the 20th century, hillsides had been totally stripped of mature trees. Logging continued through summer and winter. Tall stumps indicate the depth of the snow when loggers cut the trees.

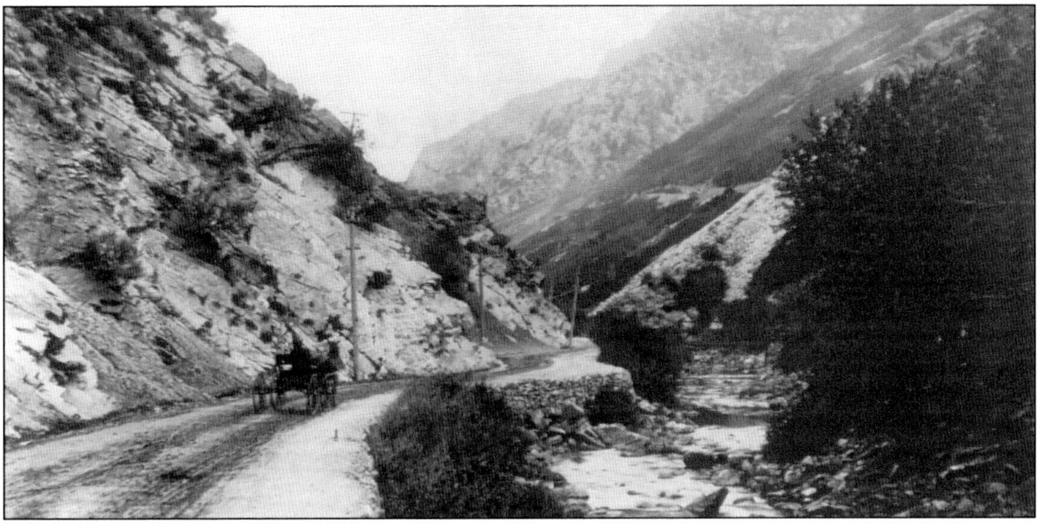

The Narrow Ten Mile Canyon. The canyon held two railroads, one meandering stream, and one wagon road. Because it was there first, the Denver & Rio Grande tried to prevent the Denver, South Park & Pacific from building in the canyon. A judge ruled that the South Park could proceed as long as its facilities came no closer than 50 feet to the center of the Rio Grande right-of-way.

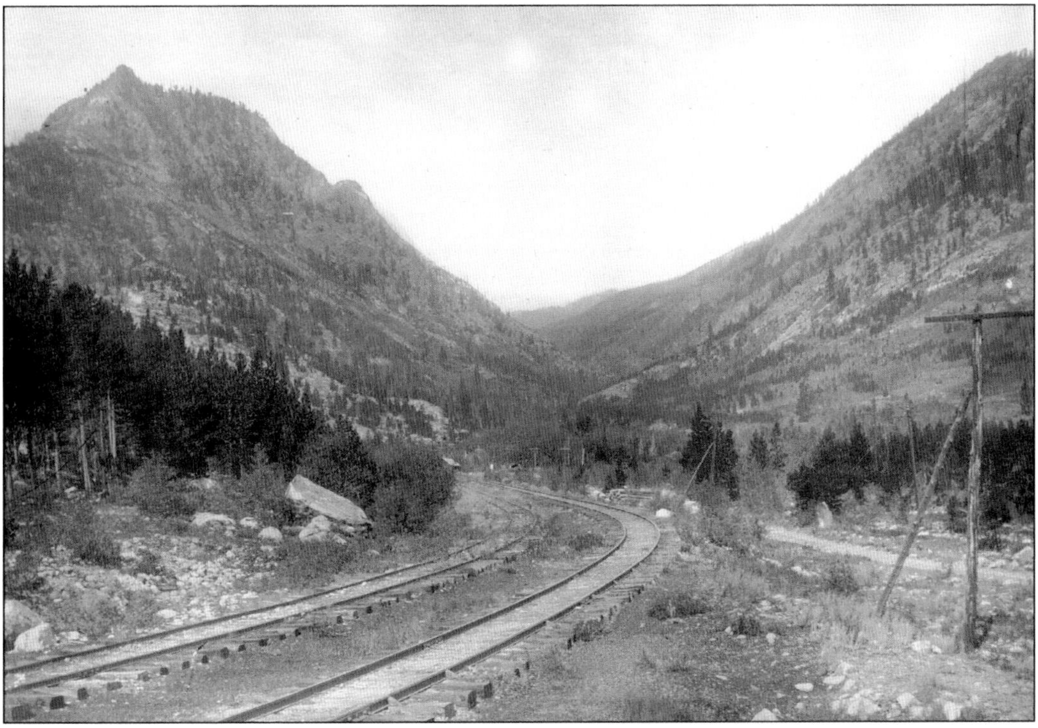

Narrow-Gauge. Railroads chose narrow-gauge because of the advantages. Sharp turns—so necessary in the mountains—required less blasting. Shorter ties saved money, as did the smaller, lighter engines and cars. Men laid the tracks quickly. They spiked the rails directly onto untreated ties of spruce and yellow pine spaced 18 inches apart. Cinders from passing engines became ballast.

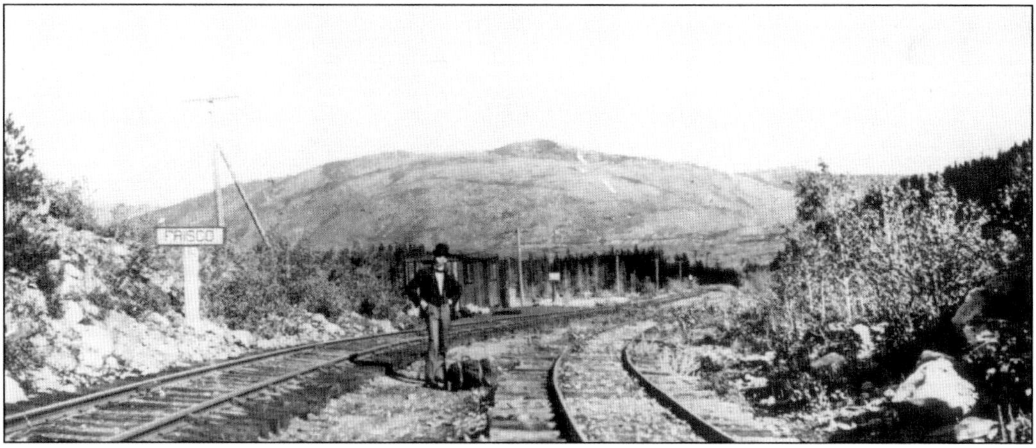

DENVER, SOUTH PARK & PACIFIC TRACK AND SPUR. The Denver, South Park & Pacific's tracks ran along the eastern side of the Ten Mile Canyon. Because none of the railroad's facilities could be closer than 50 feet to the center of the Denver & Rio Grande right-of-way by court order, one of these tracks was a spur serving the mines on the east side of the canyon.

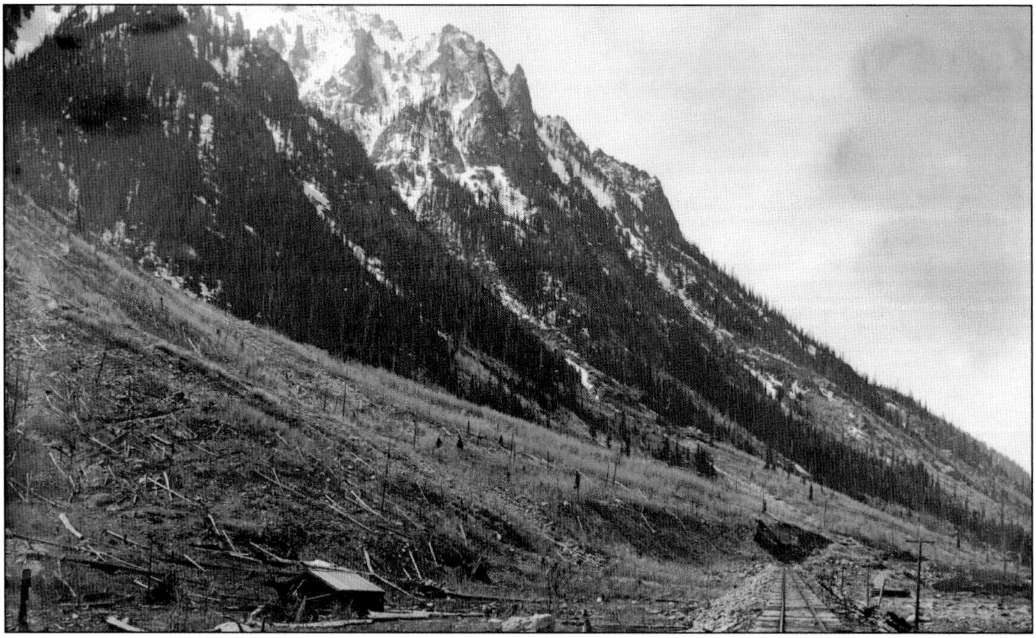

DIFFICULT CONSTRUCTION. Construction in the canyon presented many difficulties. Benches wide enough to hold the tracks had to be blasted into steep mountainsides or through unstable land and rock slides. Gullies were bridged with intricate trestles or filled with tons of rocks and boulders. Because of the rush to complete the line, crews did little grading. Each year, spring melt water and crumbling rocks created further challenges. (Used with permission from the Ed and Nancy Bathke Collection.)

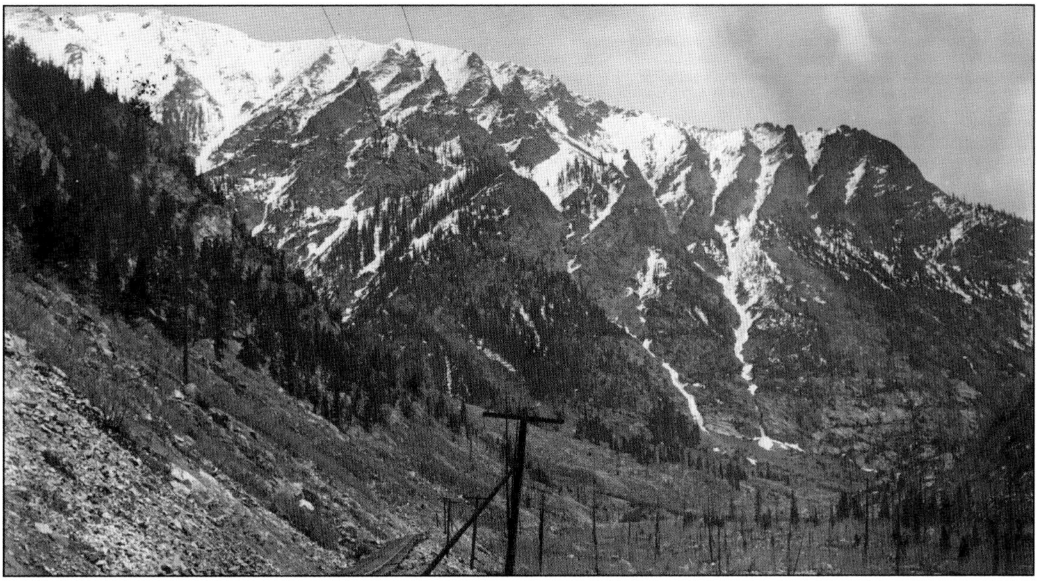

DSP&PRR. Tracks perched precariously on hillsides. The narrowest of benches formed the right-of-way. Unstable hillsides carried track and ties down slope. Rails bent. Trains lurched and swayed. In many places, the top speed for freight trains was 12 miles per hour. This was how the DSP&PRR earned its nickname: Damn Slow Pulling and Pretty Rough Riding. (Used with permission from the Ed and Nancy Bathke Collection.)

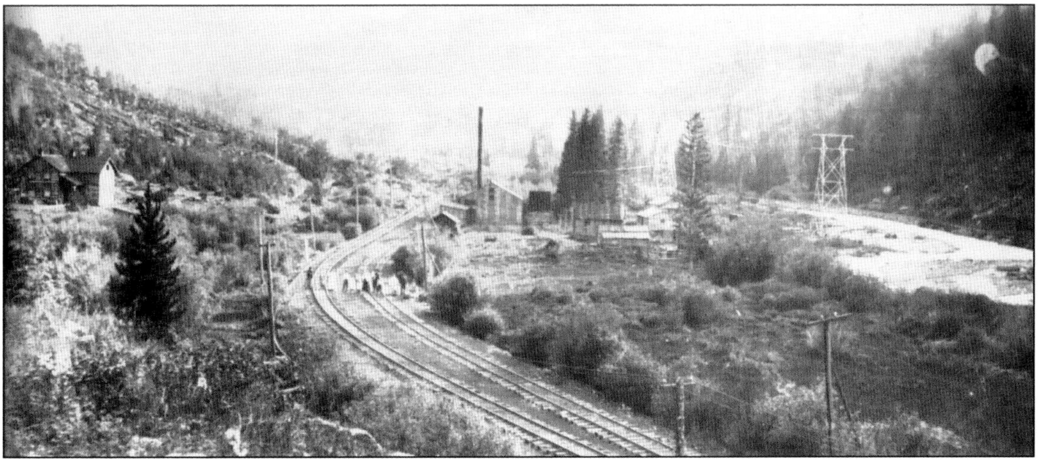

Panorama of Curtin. Sometimes wide and sometimes narrow, the Ten Mile Canyon became a major thoroughfare for goods and people. Here, the Denver, South Park & Pacific main line and spur hugged the eastern side of the canyon. The section house stood on a rise overlooking the tracks. The power plant, with its towering smokestack, provided power for nearby mines. The Ten Mile Creek flowed west of the settlement. (Used with permission from the collection of Bob Schoppe and the Denver, South Park & Pacific Historical Society.)

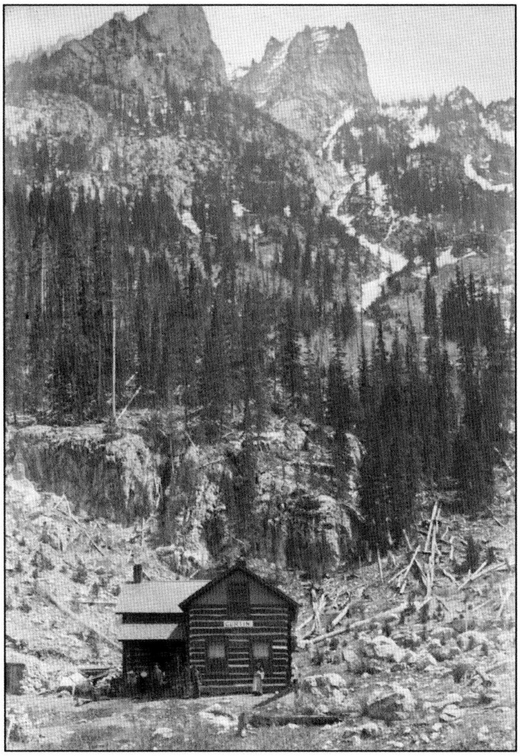

Section House at Curtin. The one-and-a-half-story log section house at Curtin sat on the eastern side of the canyon along the Denver, South Park & Pacific tracks at an elevation of 9,259 feet. A spur, named for nearby Uneva Lake, ran 728 feet beside the main track. The stop was named for Daniel Curtin, who supervised 160 men laying track in the canyon. (Used with permission from the Ed and Nancy Bathke Collection.)

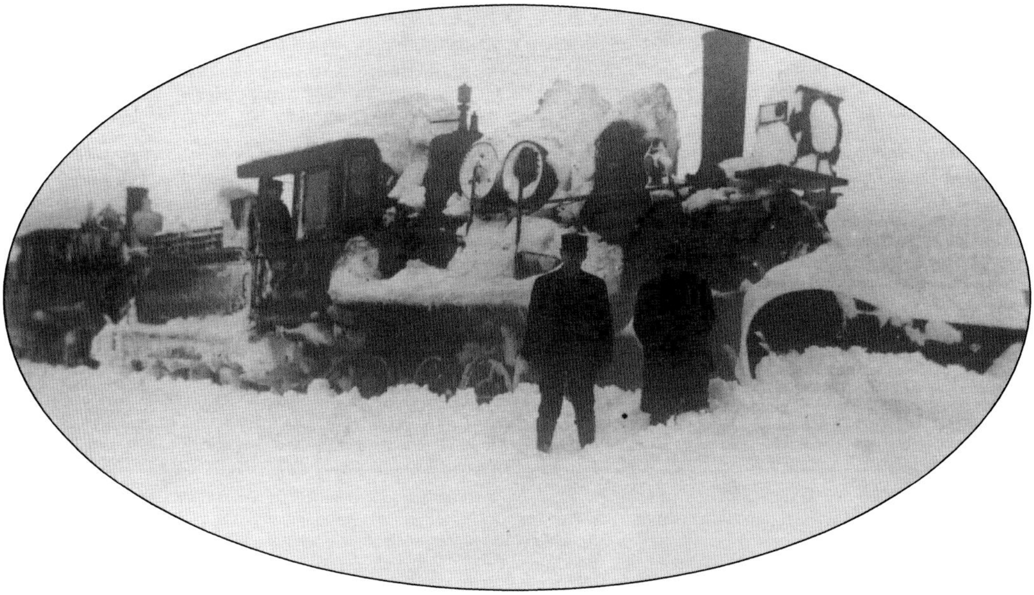

Bucking Plow in Dickey. Winter presented recurring problems, with snow causing the biggest one. In snow not deep enough to require the services of the rotary plow, a bucking plow pushed through the drifts. These wedge plows, some so large they hid the engine behind them, cleared the tracks. Priest flangers developed by the Denver, South Park & Pacific and installed behind the front wheels prevented the build-up of snow and ice on the inside of the tracks that could cause the train to derail. (Used with permission from the Ed and Nancy Bathke Collection.)

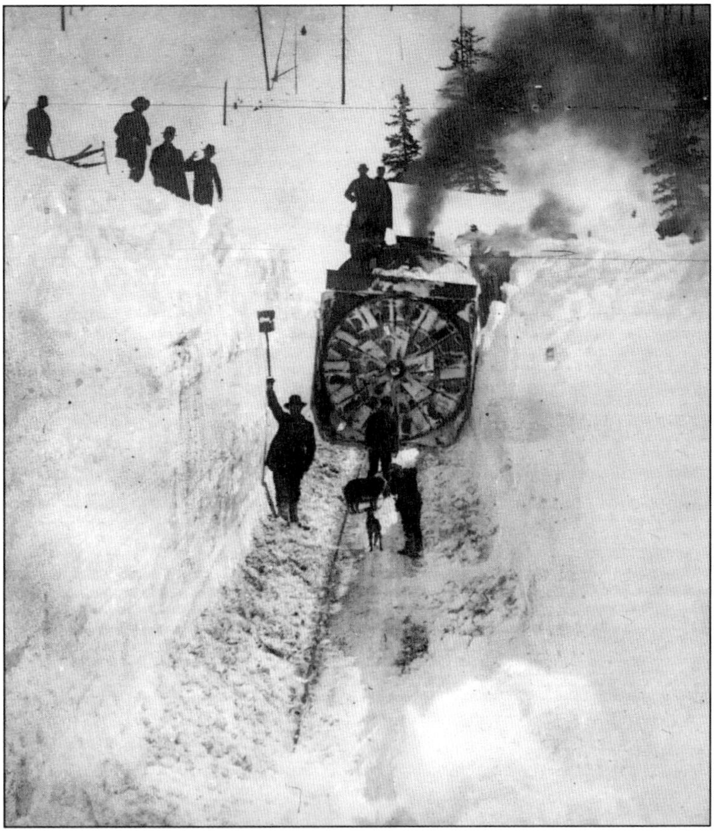

Rotary Snow Plow. Snow became so deep in the Ten Mile Canyon that the railroads needed rotary plows to clear the tracks. Working like a modern snowblower, the rotary plow chewed its way through a drift, throwing the snow up to 30 feet from the track. A coal-fired boiler powered the plow. Because it was not self-propelled, the plow required as many as four to six engines pushing it.

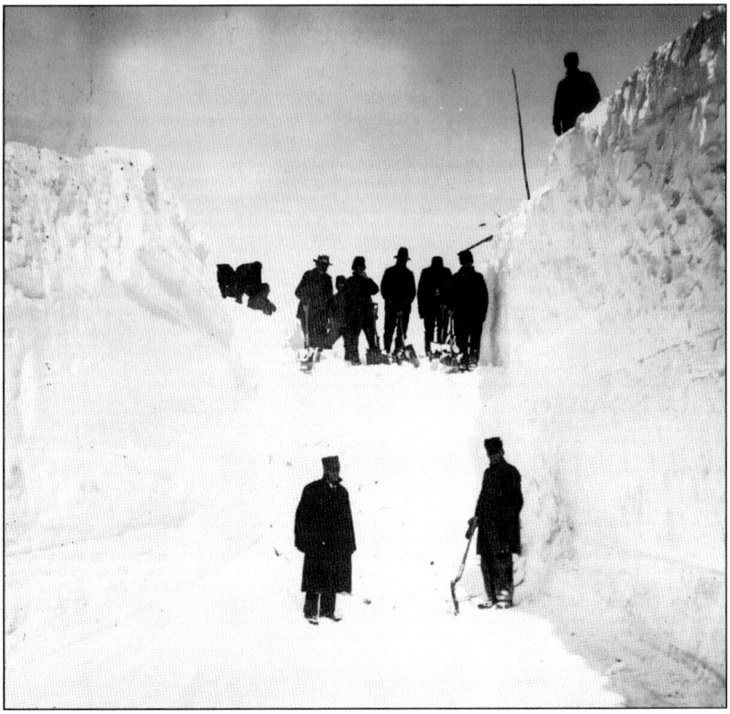

Helping the Rotary. Shovelers worked hard in the Ten Mile Canyon, where the potential for slides and avalanches remained high. One slide in 1886 between Kokomo and Frisco covered 7,000 feet of track. The crippling slides in the canyon had names. One slide that occurred each year near the Uneva spur had the name "Big Tim" or "Big Mike." Note the imprint of the rotary blades behind the two men. (Used with permission from the collection of Bob Schoppe and the Denver, South Park & Pacific Historical Society.)

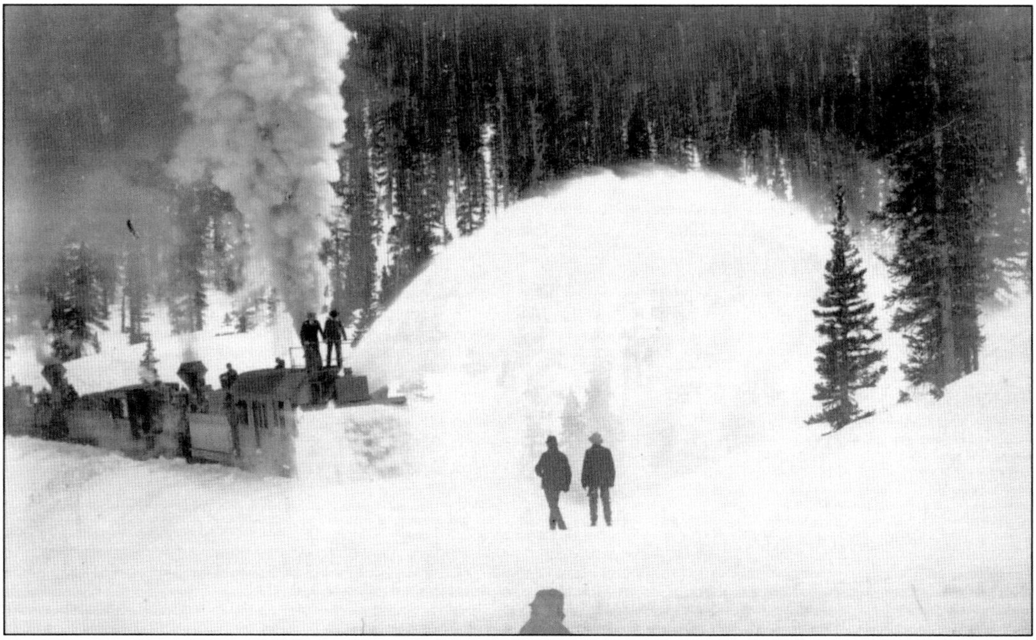

Throwing Snow. A rotary snow plow threw the snow either to the right or left, depending on the angle of the rotating blades. Naturally, downhill was the preferred direction, but if telephone or telegraph poles had been installed on the downhill side of the tracks, snow had to be blown uphill and could slide back down on the tracks. In this undated photograph, the rotary blows the snow uphill. (Used with permission from the Ed and Nancy Bathke Collection.)

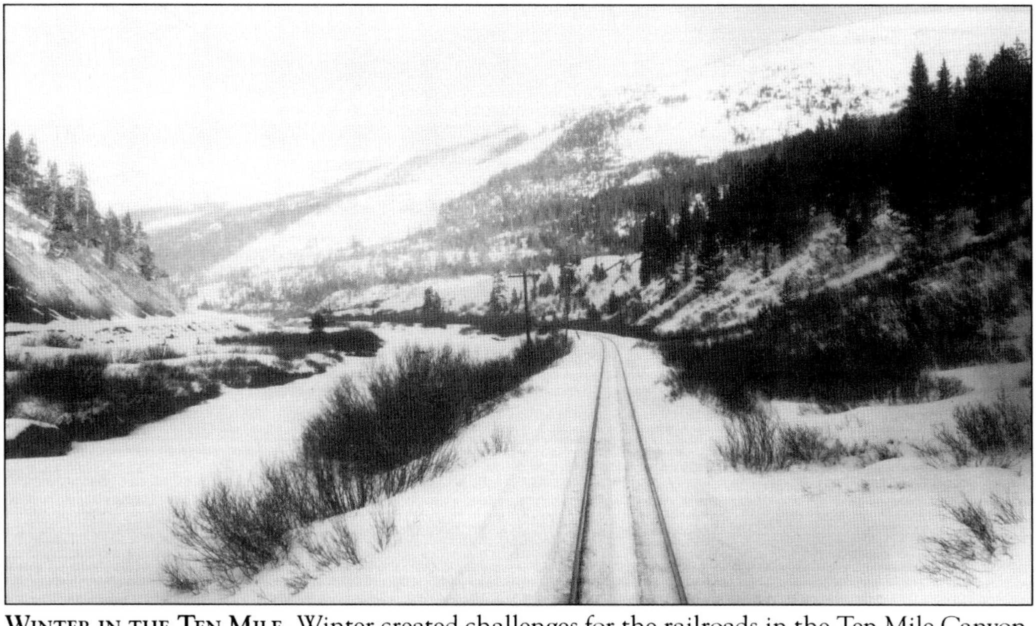

Winter in the Ten Mile. Winter created challenges for the railroads in the Ten Mile Canyon. The year 1899 proved particularly difficult. The last train made it through the canyon on February 1. Clearing began May 13 and continued into September. By October, between one and three trainloads of lumber and mining timbers per day left Wheeler—just in time for snow to begin falling again. (Used with permission of the Colorado Railroad Museum.)

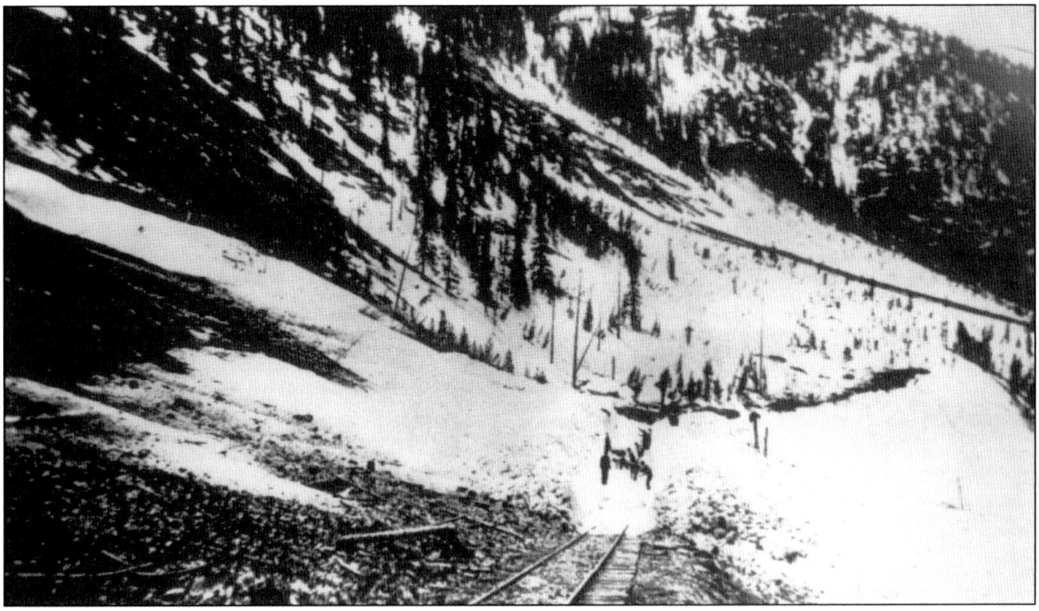

Avalanche in the Ten Mile Canyon. Bitter cold, howling wind, and blowing snow created hazardous travel conditions for trains and passengers. Avalanches, often caused by rumbling engines and shrill whistles, buried the tracks in snow, rocks, and uprooted trees. When clearing an avalanche required dynamite, crews had to replace the tracks damaged by the dynamite before the railroad could resume service.

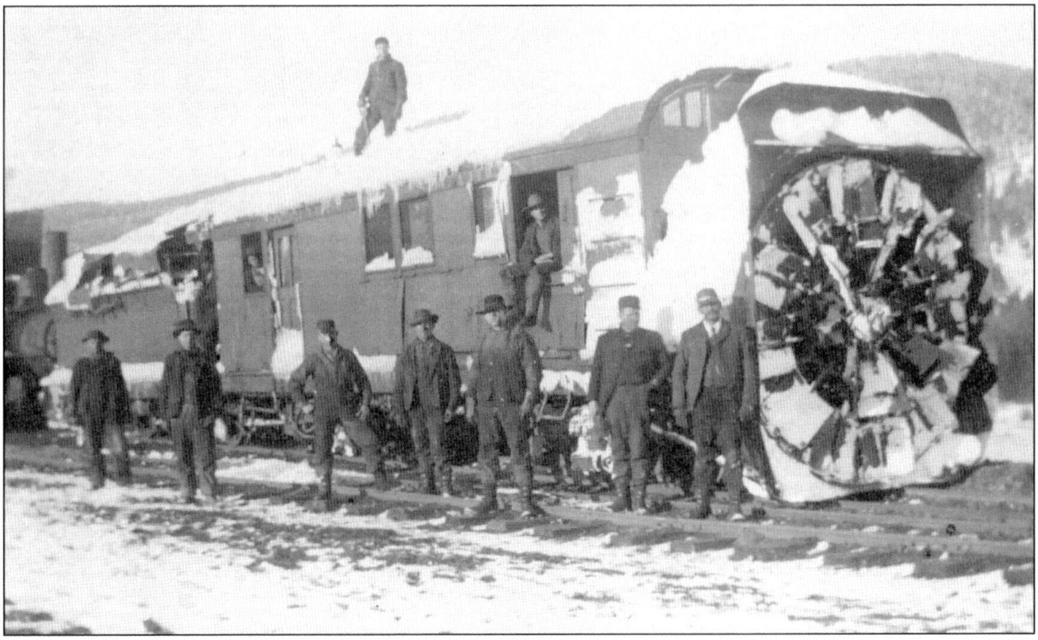

A Harsh Winter. The winter of 1898 demanded the services of the rotary plow. Snow slides containing boulders and trees interrupted service in the Ten Mile Canyon. At one time in early February, three slides blocked the tracks. The first, 300 feet long and eight feet deep, covered the tracks one mile west of Frisco. Another slide, near Curtin, measured 300 feet long and 10 feet deep. (Used with permission from the Ed and Nancy Bathke Collection.)

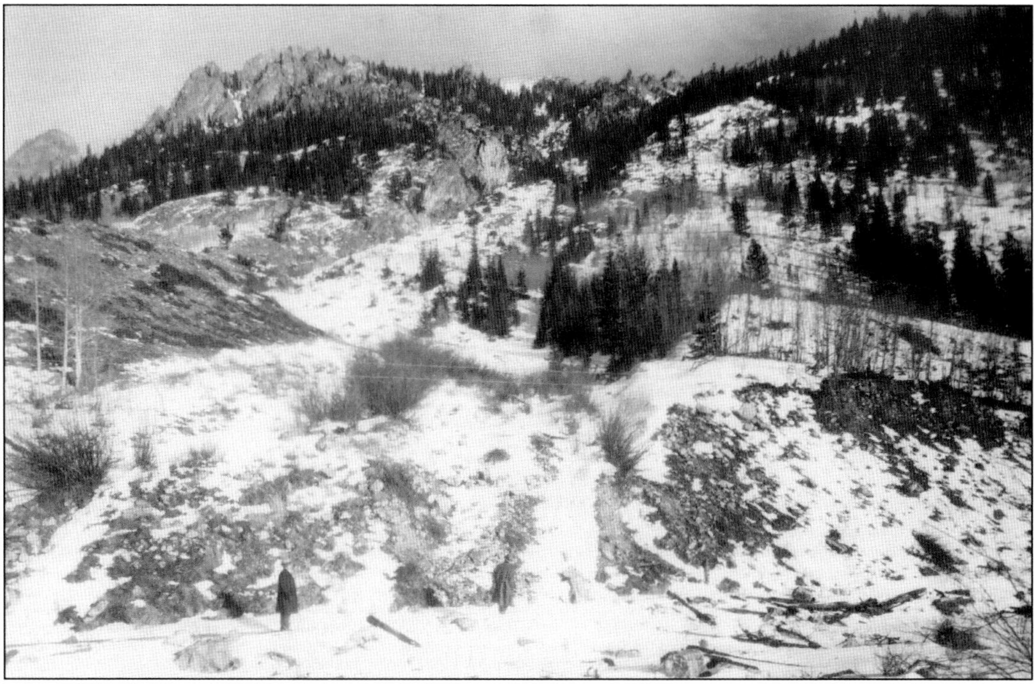

Instant Flying Beef Steaks. The unstable, weathered rocks of the Ten Mile Canyon produced many avalanches over the years. An avalanche does not contain only snow; boulders and tree trunks can also be part of the rapidly moving mass. One tall tale describes how a rotary plow produced instant flying beef steaks as it cut through an avalanche that swept away a herd of cattle. (Used with permission from the collection of Bob Schoppe and the Denver, South Park & Pacific Historical Society.)

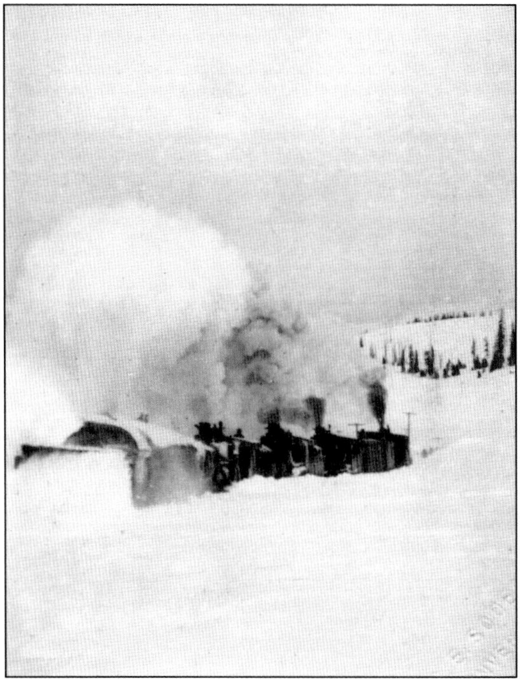

Heavy Snow. Deep snow required four engines to push this rotary snow plow. Sometimes the last engine faced backwards in case the rotary became stuck and the train had to back up through newly fallen snow. Shovelers lived in the boxcar outfitted for eating and sleeping that is seen between the third and fourth engines. The men rode the tracks all winter, going wherever they were needed.

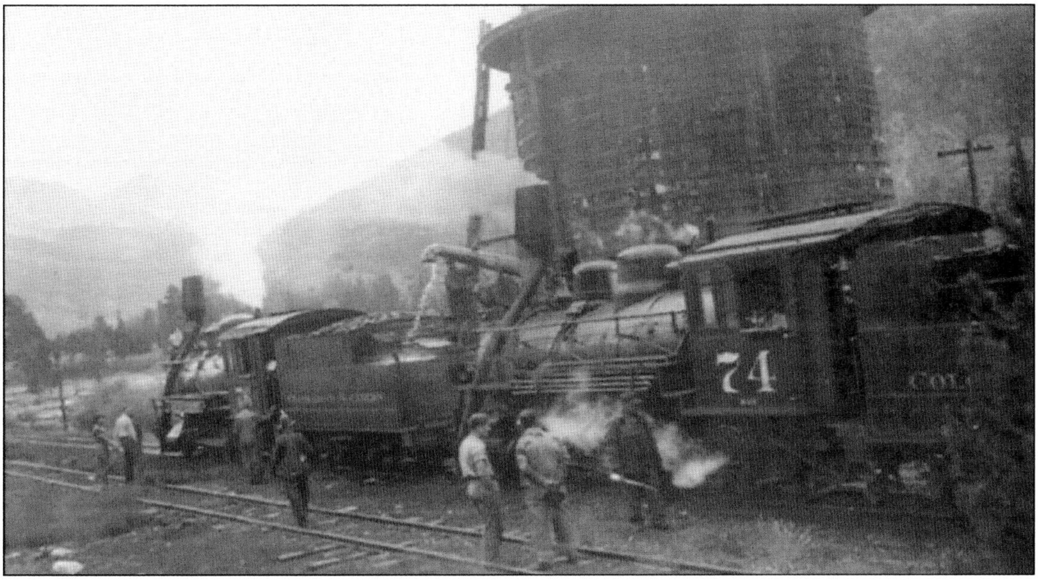

TAKING ON WATER AT SOLITUDE. Engines stopped for water at Solitude (presently the site of Copper Mountain resort), before proceeding. Water tanks caused problems because of leakage. While water in the tanks usually did not freeze, leaks caused some magnificent ice falls beside and sometimes on the tracks. To prevent water in the tender from freezing, the fireman diverted some of the hot water from the engine into the tender. (Used with permission from the collection of Bob Schoppe and the Denver, South Park & Pacific Historical Society.)

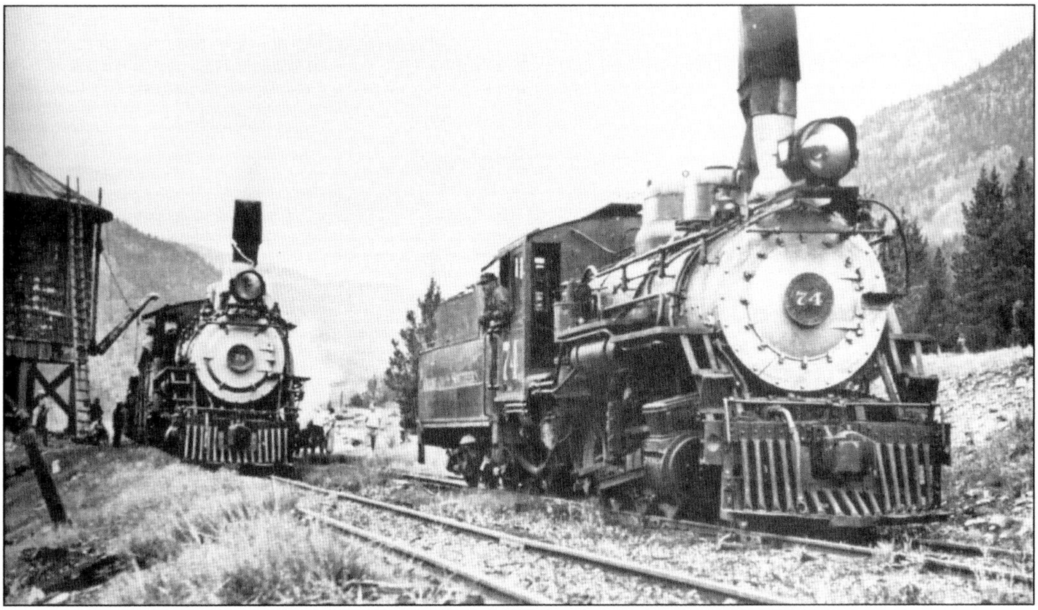

WATER FOR THE ENGINE AT SOLITUDE. Steam engines consumed large amounts of water. An improper amount of water in the boiler could result in an explosion. Crews refilled the tender at tanks along the tracks. The fireman took great care in opening the valve on the water tank to start the water flowing. At any moment, the spout could swing quickly upward, spilling water over the tender and fireman. (Used with permission from the collection of Bob Schoppe and the Denver, South Park & Pacific Historical Society.)

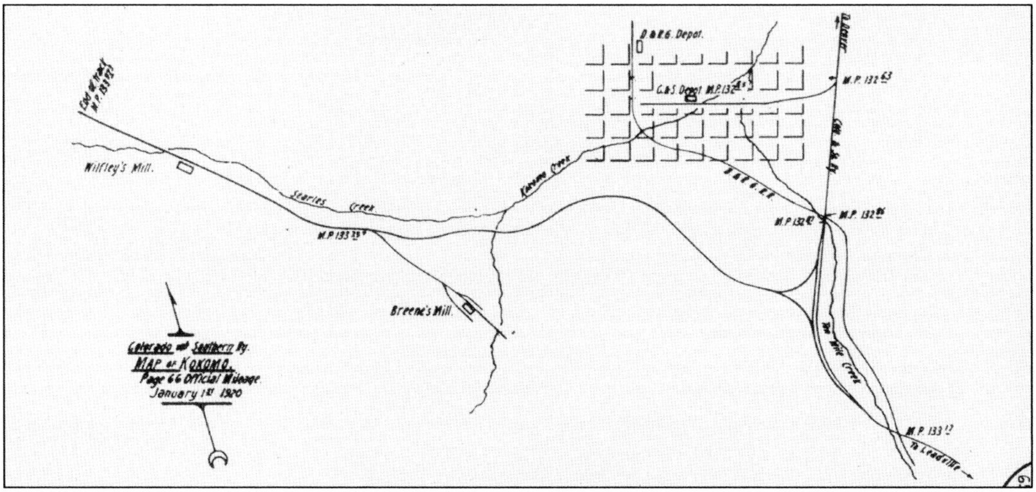

COLORADO & SOUTHERN MAP OF KOKOMO. The Colorado & Southern Railroad built several spurs in Kokomo. One, built in 1895, led to Wilfley's Mill; another, built in 1908, led to Breene's Mill. Workers constructed a wye for turning engines as part of the Wilfley spur. The Colorado & Southern depot sat beside the downtown spur. The spurs to Wilfley's and Breene's Mills have not been covered by the Climax molybdenum mine's tailings ponds. (Used with permission from the collection of Bob Schoppe and the Denver, South Park & Pacific Historical Society.)

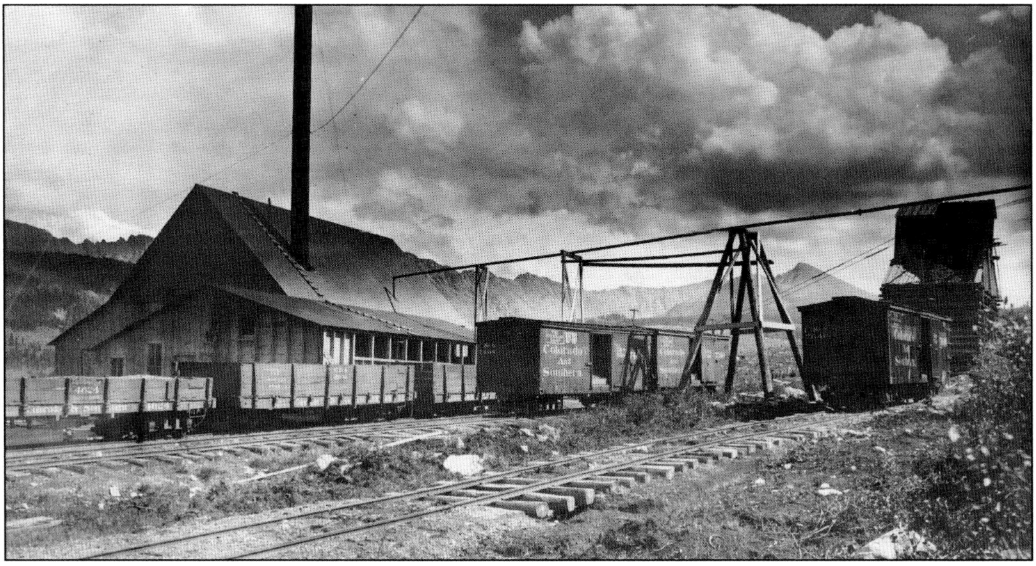

THE TRANSPORTATION ADVANTAGE. Mills located on railroad spurs enjoyed an advantage when shipping ore to smelters in Leadville and Denver. The lower costs made mining operations more profitable. The area pictured here, identified as Breene's Mill on a 1918 railroad map, was located on a spur of the Colorado & Southern Railroad. Note the ladders on the roof to aid in extinguishing any fires caused by the milling operations. (Photo courtesy Denver Public Library, Western History Collection, X-61439.)

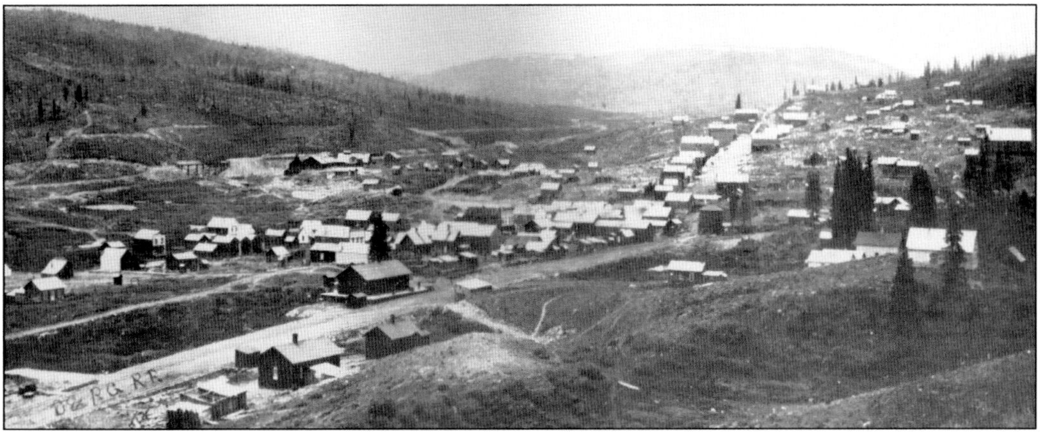

KOKOMO, LOOKING SOUTHWEST, C. 1885. The Denver & Rio Grande depot, built on the main line running through town, appears just left of center and east of the tracks. The two Denver, South Park & Pacific trestles crossing over the Denver & Rio Grande tracks appear in the distance. The White Quail complex stood between the two trestles. (Used with permission from the collection of Bob Schoppe and the Denver, South Park & Pacific Historical Society.)

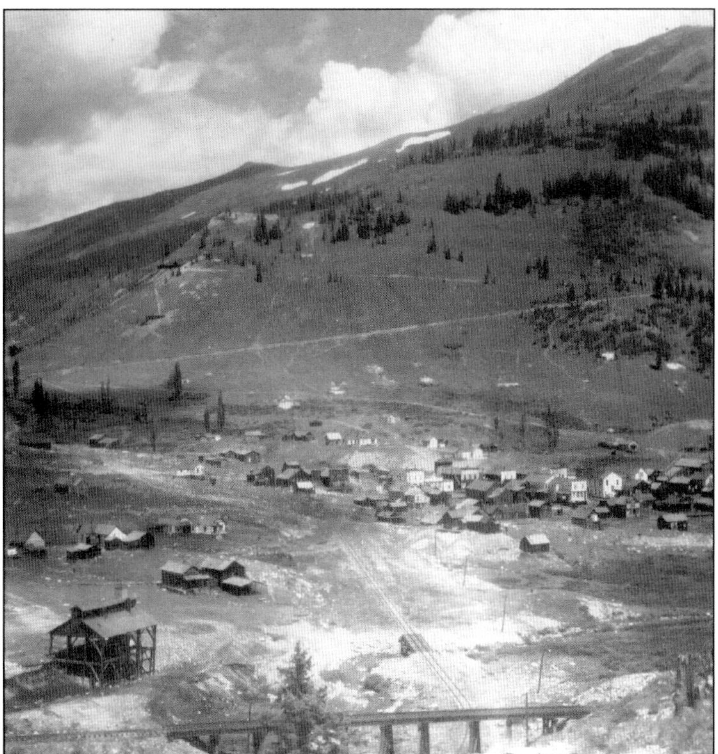

LOOKING NORTHWEST OVER KOKOMO. The Denver & Rio Grande hindered the construction of the Denver, South Park & Pacific facilities in many ways. In September 1883, at the instigation of the Denver & Rio Grande, several owners of unproductive placers filed injunctions to prevent the railroad from building on their land. To continue construction, the Denver, South Park & Pacific bought one of the worthless claims for $11,000. (Used with permission from the Ed and Nancy Bathke Collection.)

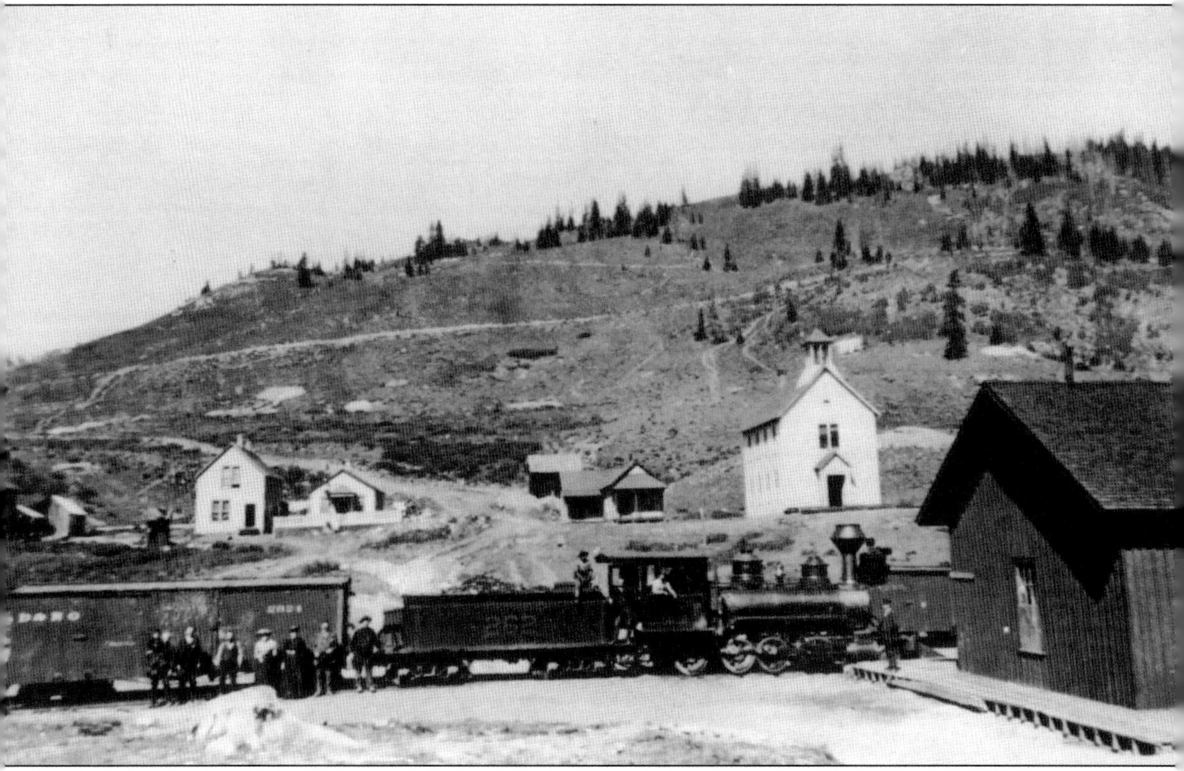

DENVER & RIO GRANDE TRAIN BESIDE KOKOMO DEPOT. Miners and others generally welcomed both railroads in the Ten Mile Canyon. They felt that competition would keep prices lower. The newspaper editor in Breckenridge remarked that the competition would increase trade, cut travel time to Denver, open markets for ores at reasonable rates, stimulate prosperity, and hasten development. The legal battles between the two companies created little sympathy among residents.

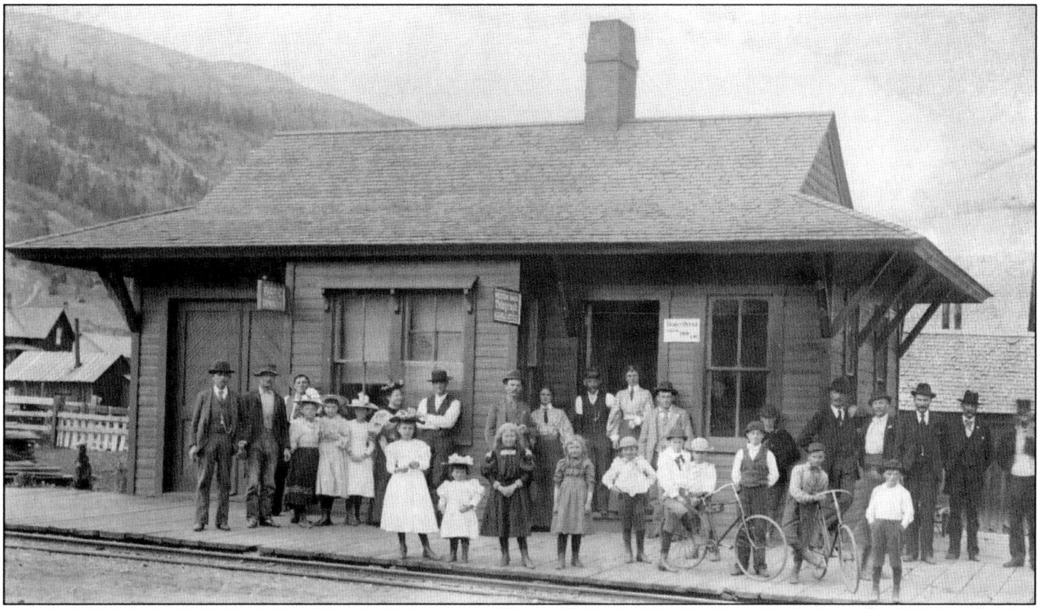

The Denver, Leadville & Gunnison Depot in Kokomo. Dressed in their finest clothing, these residents of Kokomo posed on the loading platform of the former Denver, South Park & Pacific (later the Colorado & Southern) depot on a summer day. The stationmaster stands in the doorway. The men at right wear lapel jewelry identifying them as members of a fraternal organization such as the Odd Fellows or Masons. (Used with permission from the Dave Cattanni Collection.)

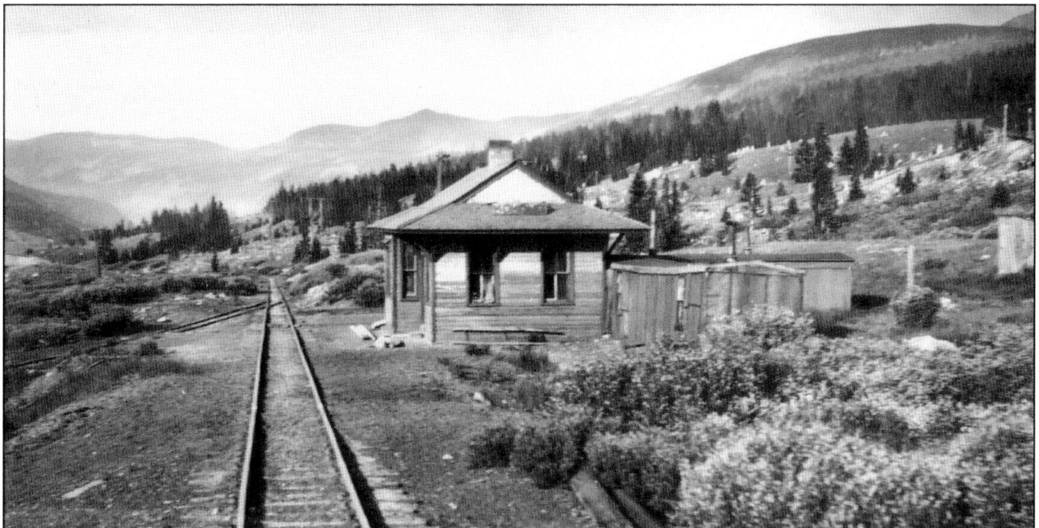

The Denver, South Park & Pacific Depot, Looking Northeast. In this photograph, the depot, which was moved several times, sits on the main track leading to Wheeler. The downtown spur joins the main line just beyond the depot. On the hill, tall tree stumps indicate that lumbering occurred when snow covered the ground. The trees went to sawmills that cut lumber for buildings such as the depot and the buildings behind it. (Used with permission from the collection of Bob Schoppe and the Denver, South Park & Pacific Historical Society.)

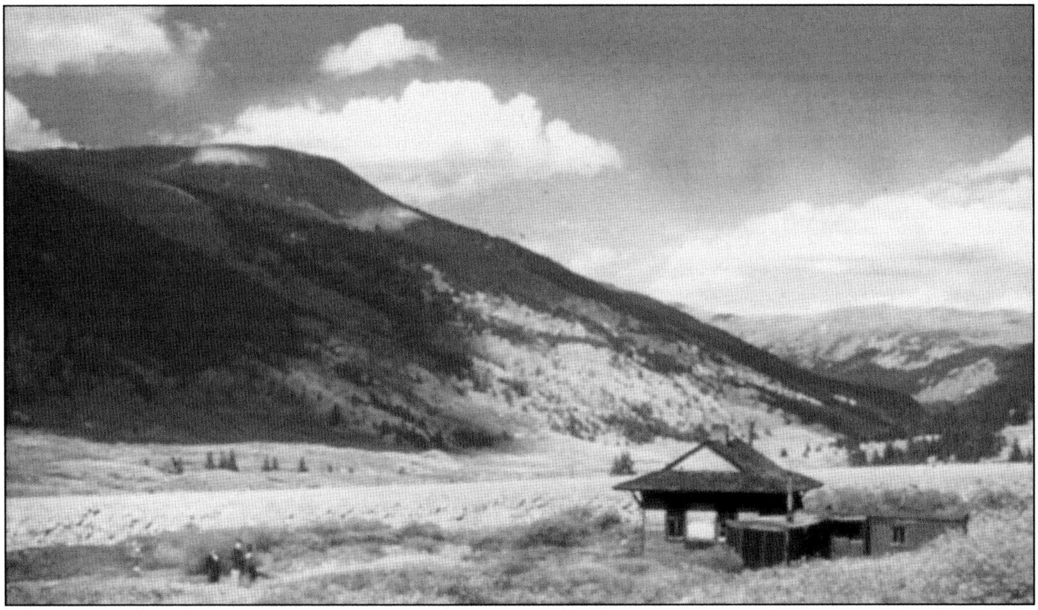

THE COLORADO & SOUTHERN DEPOT IN JUNE 1946. Identified by its distinctive roofline, the depot and a few of the old boxcar outbuildings still stand. A road no longer open to traffic runs across the former railroad right-of-way. Today, the depot is gone but this part of the Kokomo town site has not yet been covered by the tailings from the Climax molybdenum mine. (Used with permission from the collection of Bob Schoppe and the Denver, South Park & Pacific Historical Society.)

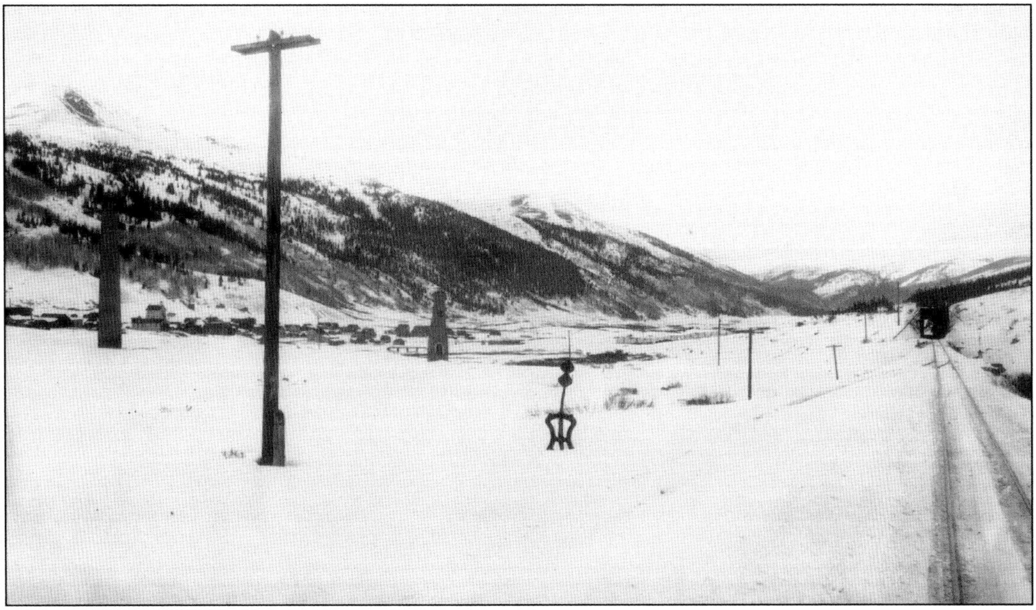

KOKOMO IN 1929. With Kokomo in the distance, the two smokestacks indicate the location of the White Quail mill. Right of the smokestack in the center of the photograph is the trestle that was part of the spur running through town. The harp switch stand indicates the location of the wye on the Wilfley spur. To the right, the snowshed that covered the tracks south of the depot still stands. (Used with permission of Colorado Railroad Museum.)

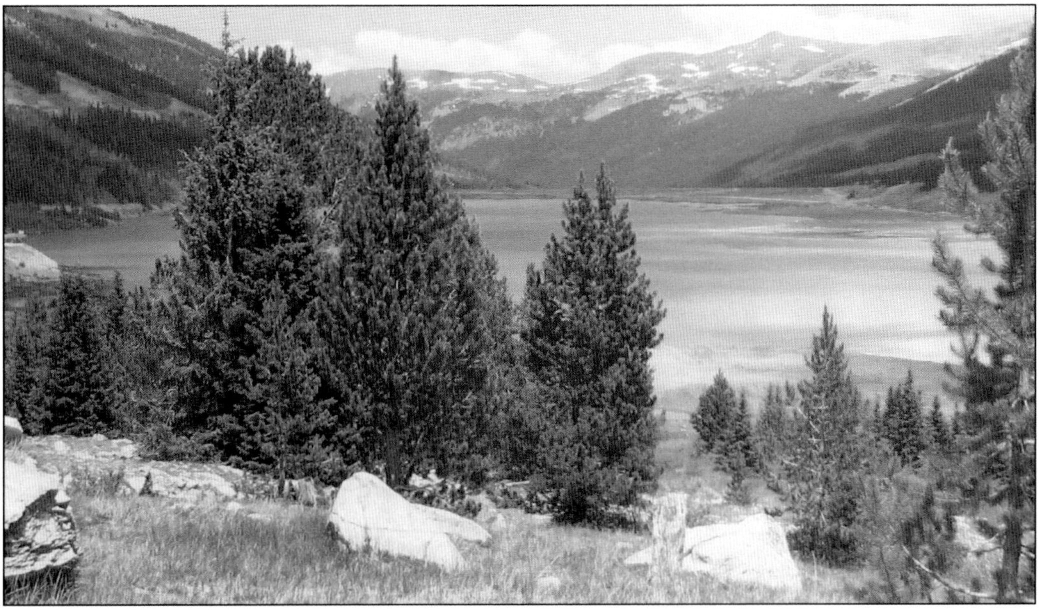

Kokomo Town Site in 2009. The owners of the Climax molybdenum mine purchased the entire upper Ten Mile valley for their tailings ponds in 1959. The company bought private land, mining claims, and public property such as streets and school grounds. To obtain additional acreage, the company engaged in land swaps with the US Forest Service. Tailings and water in the ponds almost completely cover the town site. (Used with permission from the collection of Bob Schoppe and the Denver, South Park & Pacific Historical Society.)

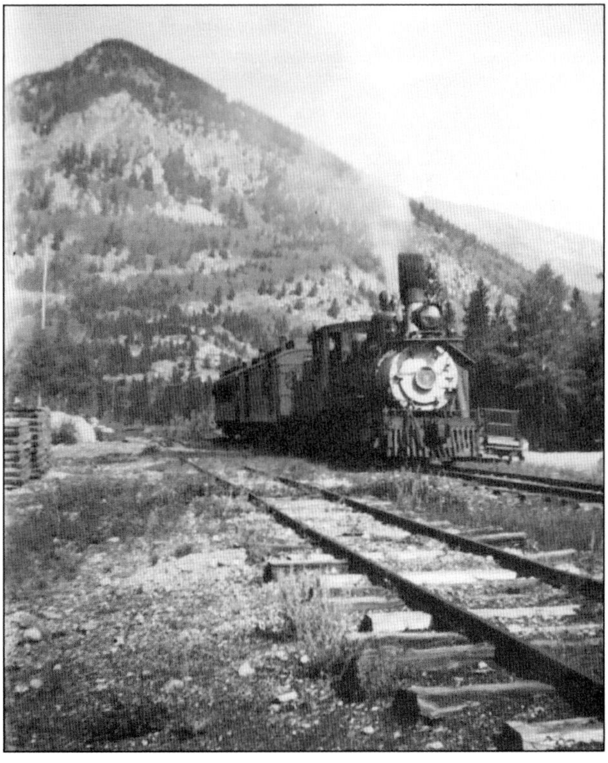

Bankruptcy. Financial problems dictated corporate changes. Reorganized to avoid bankruptcy, the Denver, South Park & Pacific Railway Company became the Denver, Leadville & Gunnison Railway Company in 1889. Faced with continuing fiscal instability, the newly formed company was purchased by the Colorado & Southern in 1898 and then the Chicago, Burlington and Quincy in 1908. These new owners had little interest in maintaining the narrow-gauge line. (Used with permission from the collection of Bob Schoppe and the Denver, South Park & Pacific Historical Society.)

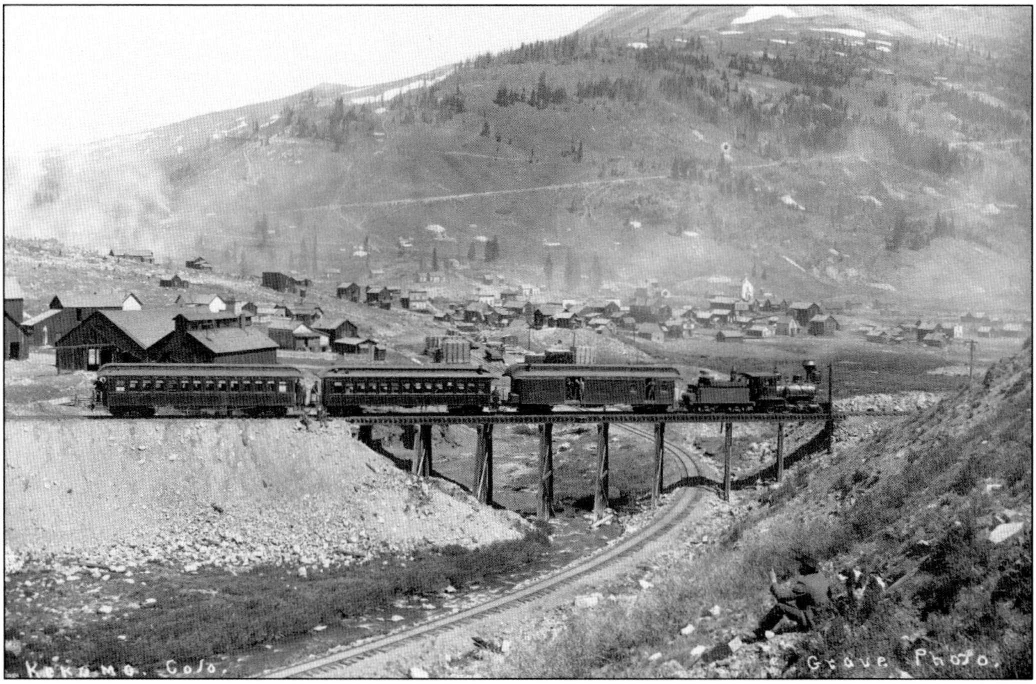

A Denver, Leadville & Gunnison Train at Kokomo in 1899. Where the width of the canyon became too narrow to maintain a distance of 50 feet from the center of the Denver & Rio Grande right-of-way, a judge ruled that the Denver, South Park & Pacific could build two crossings over the Rio Grande tracks on trestles. To slow construction, the Rio Grande stationed locomotives at the construction sites. (Used with permission from the collection of Bob Schoppe and the Denver, South Park & Pacific Historical Society.)

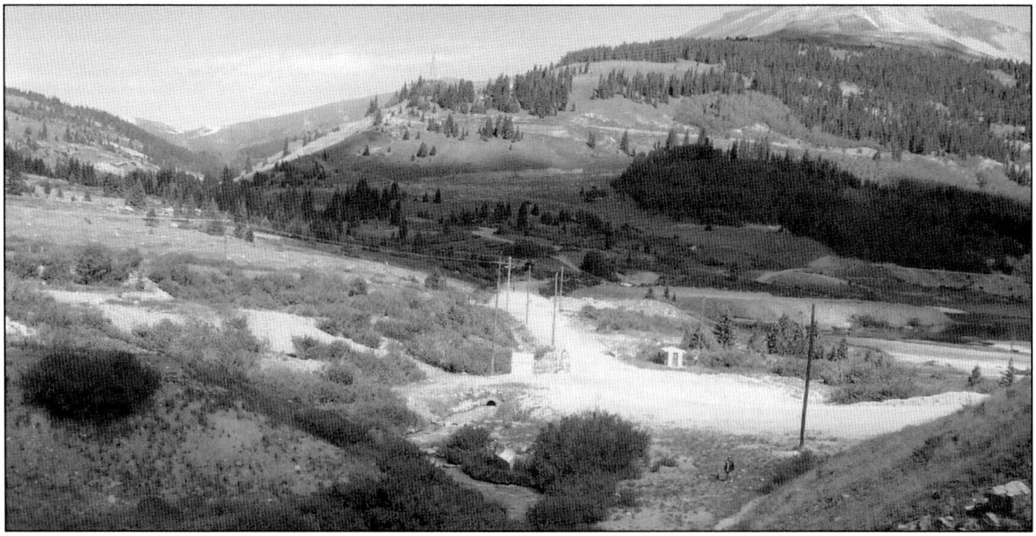

Location of Trestle Remains in 2010. Nothing remains of the trestle except for a few timbers. This part of the town of Kokomo has not yet been covered with tailings from the Climax molybdenum mine. A greatly reduced Ten Mile Creek flows beneath the road. Vegetation has slowly reclaimed the slopes once stripped bare by timbermen. (Used with permission from the collection of Bob Schoppe and the Denver, South Park & Pacific Historical Society.)

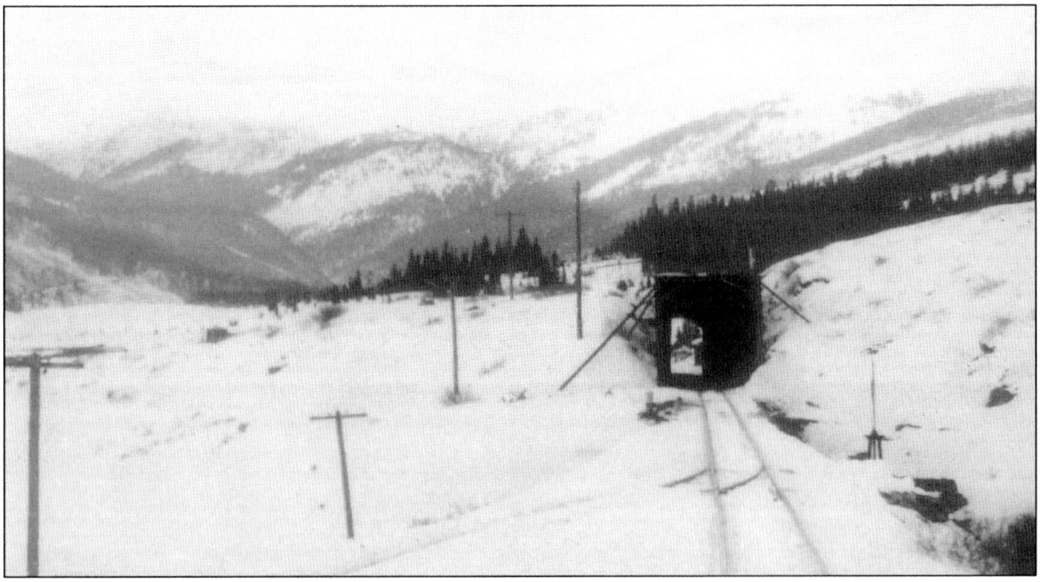

The Snowshed in 1929. The 544-foot-long snowshed covered the tracks just to the north of where the downtown spur joined the main track and south of the depot, which is visible through the snowshed. The railroads built wooden snowsheds where avalanches threatened danger to people and equipment. Unfortunately, cinders from the engines often set the snowsheds on fire, requiring replacement and causing added expense for the railroads. (Used with permission of the Colorado Railroad Museum.)

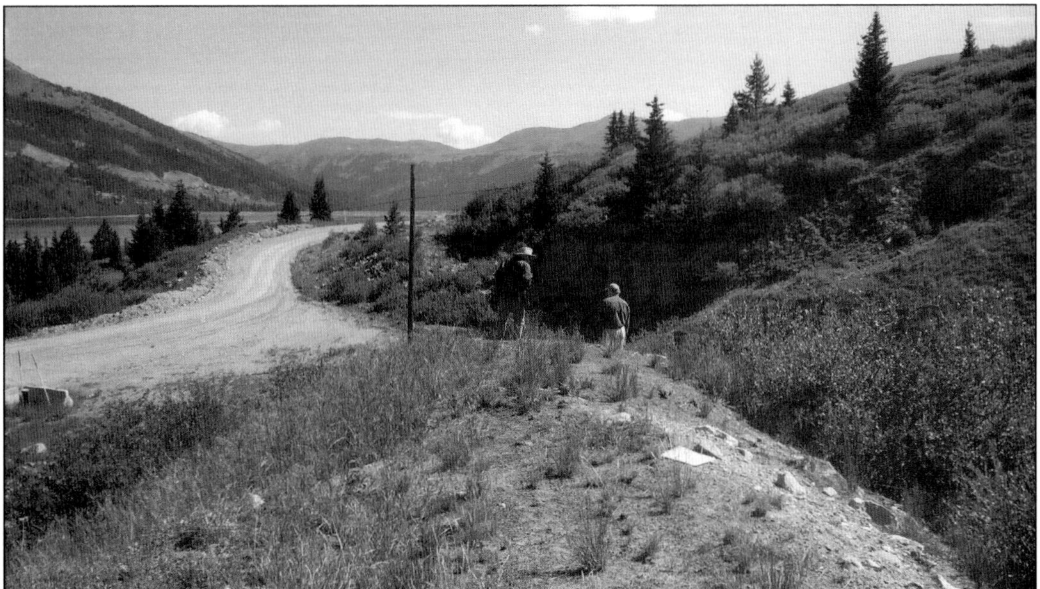

The Trestle in 2010. Two men stand where the Denver, South Park & Pacific trestle crossed the Denver & Rio Grande tracks near Kokomo. The right-of-way is seen in the foreground. The snowshed stood beyond the trestle. The depot, which had been moved several times, stood to the north of the snowshed. This part of Kokomo has not yet been covered by the Climax molybdenum mine's tailings ponds. (Used with permission from the collection of Bob Schoppe and the Denver, South Park & Pacific Historical Society.)

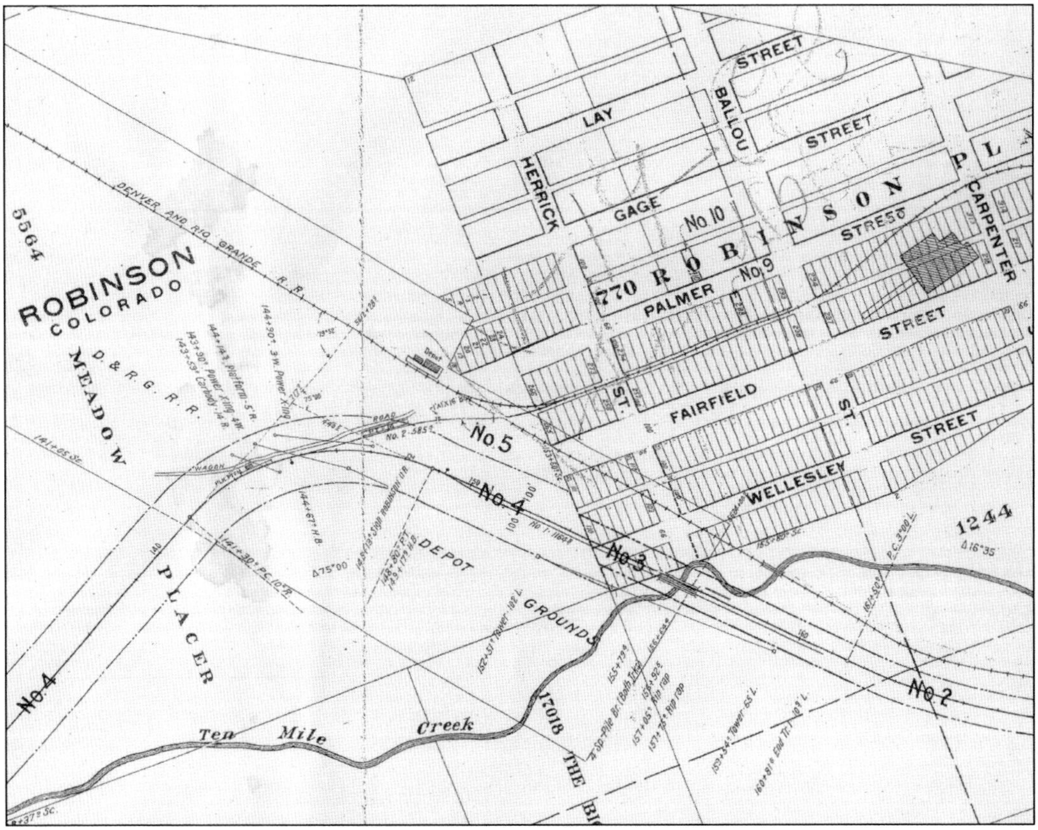

THE DENVER & RIO GRANDE TRACKS IN ROBINSON. The tracks skirted the southeastern section of town, with a spur leading northwest through alleys and along streets. The two buildings at the depot site sat beside the main track, just southwest of where the spur joined the main line. Railroad workers had to struggle in heavy snow while laying the track over Fremont Pass from Leadville in 1881. (Used with permission from the collection of Bob Schoppe and the Denver, South Park & Pacific Historical Society.)

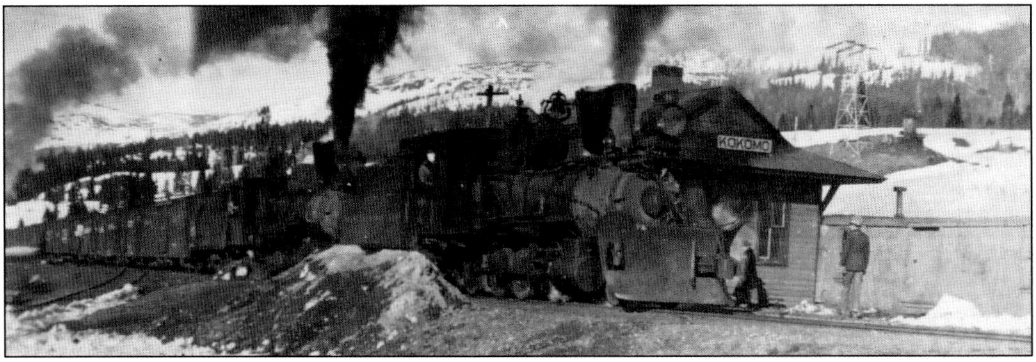

BURNING AND HAULING COAL. Smoke and cinders announced the arrival of the train. Coal, a large part of the tonnage carried by the railroads, came from the King mines at Como and Baldwin mines in Gunnison. Owned by Union Pacific, the mines provided coal for Colorado & Southern engines. The railroads preferred Baldwin coal despite its higher cost. It burned at a higher temperature, producing less ash and fewer clinkers. (Used with permission from the collection of Bob Schoppe and the Denver, South Park & Pacific Historical Society.)

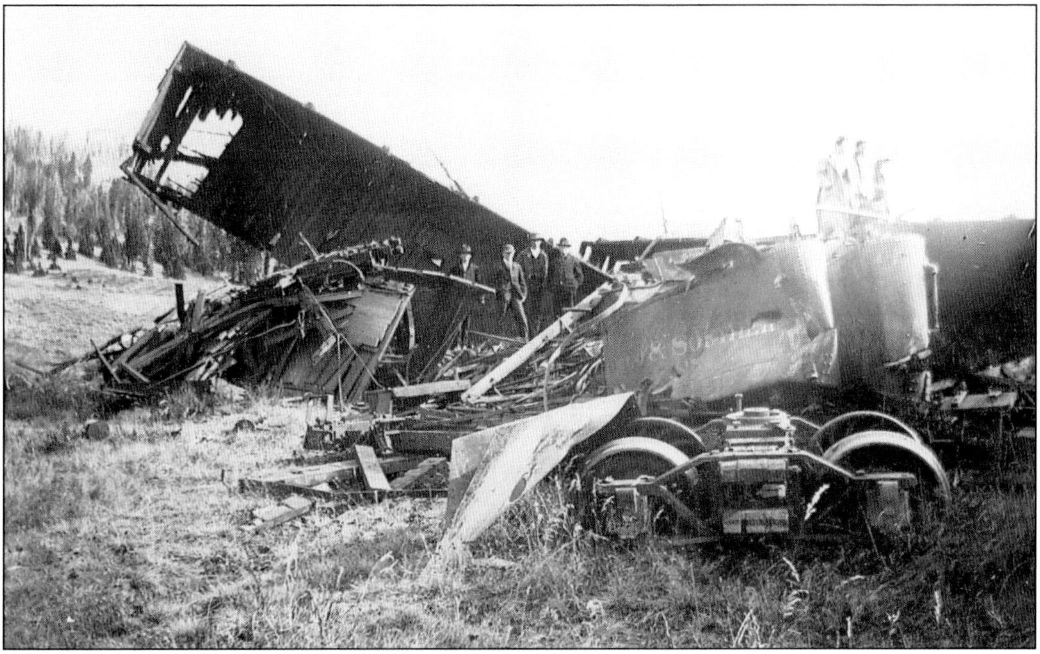

Oops! Buddy Schwartz, the engineer of Colorado & Southern engine 55, survived this October 1907 wreck on Fremont Pass between Climax and Kokomo. One month later, two fully loaded freight cars with their brakes not set rolled downhill from Kokomo to Frisco, derailing and spilling clothing along the right-of-way. (Used with permission from the Clair Dungan-Tom Klinger Collection.)

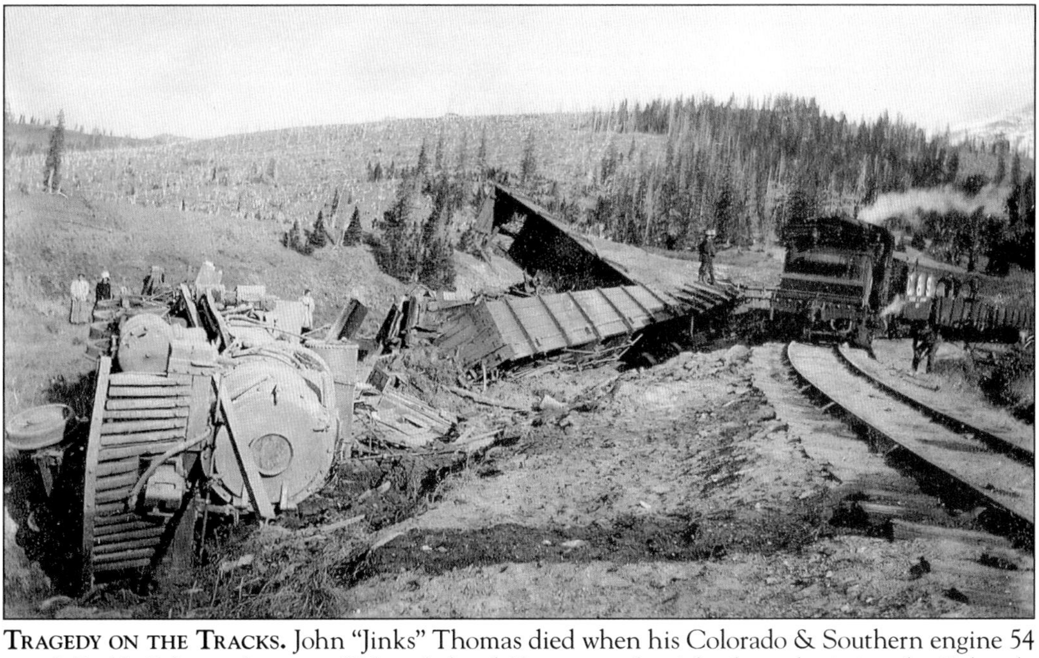

Tragedy on the Tracks. John "Jinks" Thomas died when his Colorado & Southern engine 54 struck Buddy Schwartz's engine 55 from behind. Despite workers' deaths and injuries, the Colorado & Southern boasted in 1905 that after 26 years of operation, it was the only American railroad with any length of service that had not killed a passenger. (Used with permission from the Clair Dungan-Tom Klinger Collection.)

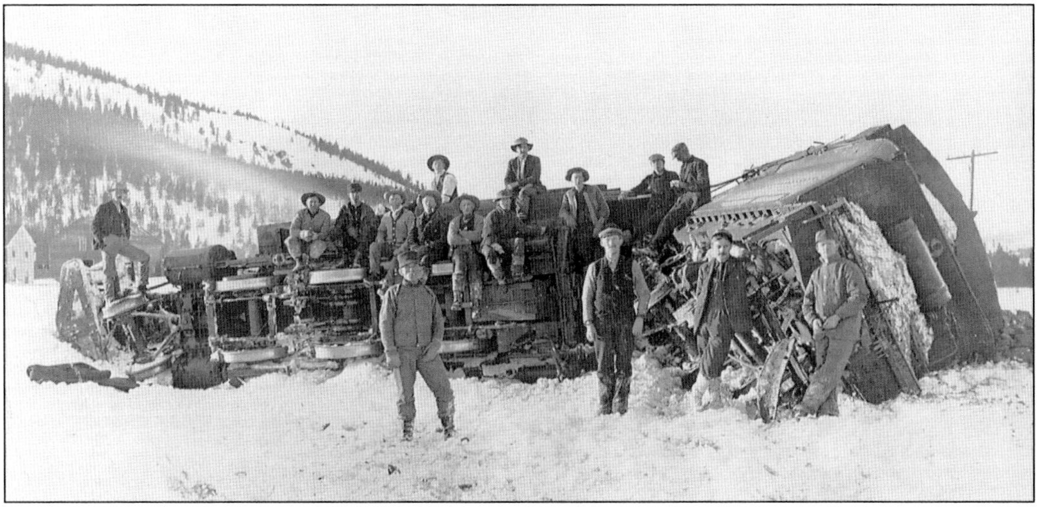

EXCITEMENT IN 1910. With Dillon and Lake Hill in the background, these workers posed for the photographer before tackling the difficult task of putting the engine and tender back on the track. Winter conditions made their jobs even more dangerous. Some accidents were not preventable. In 1905, after a 500-pound boulder smashed into a passenger car at Wheeler, five men worked to remove it. (Used with permission from the R.H. Kindig-Tom Klinger Collection.)

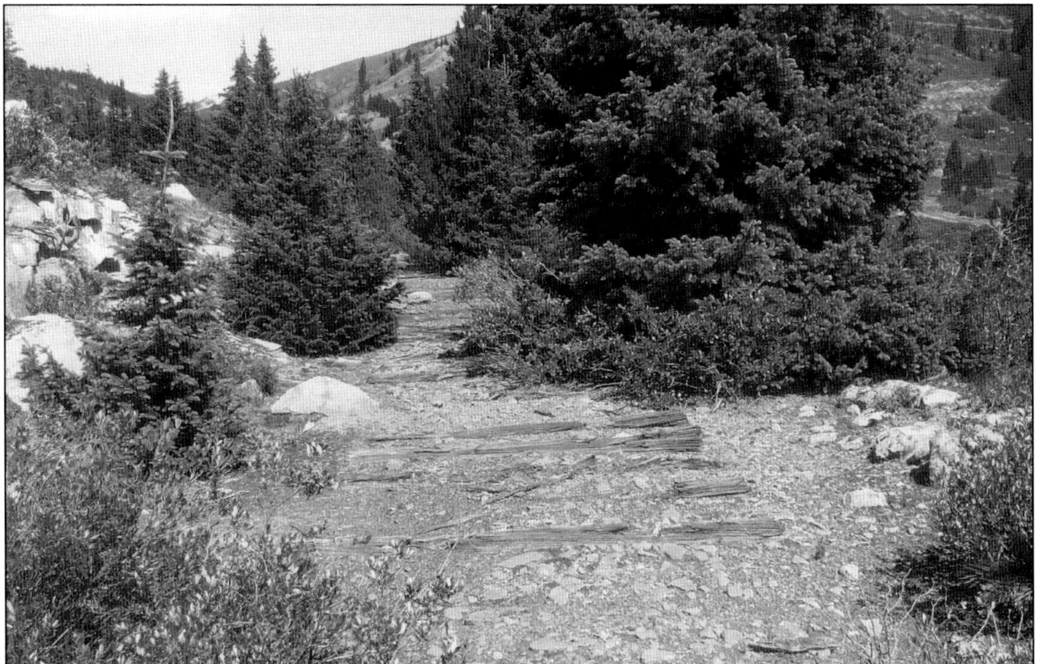

REMINDERS OF A LONG-GONE ERA. In 2010, decaying railroad ties are all that remain on the Denver, South Park & Pacific right-of-way near Kokomo. Although the narrow-gauge engines no longer pull passengers and freight from station to station, the local summer and winter recreational economy still depends on an efficient transportation network to carry goods and people into, through, and out of Summit County. (Used with permission from the Bill Fountain Collection.)

Six

Agriculture
A High-Altitude Enterprise

Ranching began near Frisco and in the Ten Mile Canyon when herdsmen drove their cattle and sheep over the Continental Divide in summer to graze on the lush grasses that had provided food for the American bison for centuries. Residents welcomed the farmers and ranchers because locally grown products cost less than those carried great distances by wagons.

One of the earliest ranches might have been the Union ranch, located at the junction of the Ten Mile Creek and Blue River. The owners sold meat and dairy products. On another ranch, one half-mile east of Frisco, Lawson and Cadwalader grazed a dairy herd on 300 acres of land. The southern Ten Mile had its share of ranches, too. Dairy herds that produced milk for Kokomo and Robinson fed on irrigated hay fields.

The Homestead Act of 1862 allowed a US citizen to claim 160 acres of the public domain for the cost of a small filing fee. The Deming, Rutherford, Giberson, Thomas, and Wheeler families, among others, took advantage of this and homesteaded ranches in the Frisco area.

Ranches consisted of fields for crops and winter grazing, as well as corrals, barns, houses, and a variety of small buildings. Families grew crops that matured in the short, frost-free season, such as carrots, turnips, cauliflower, radishes, "mountain" head lettuce, peas, cabbage, potatoes, and onions.

Individual ranches tended to be large because of the acreage required to raise hay, timothy, clover, and alfalfa for winter feed. Haying began in August and might continue until October if snow or heavy rain delayed the harvest. The fall roundup followed haying. Ranchers branded calves while culling yearlings, calves, and older cattle for shipment to Denver. Ranchers conducted another roundup in the spring, mainly to brand the newborn calves.

Ranches around Frisco produced more than just cattle. Sheep grazed on the alpine meadows near Wheeler Junction during summer months. Both railroads carried carloads of sheep to distant markets.

Today, the ranch lands are gone, with cattle, sheep, barns, and corrals replaced by a reservoir, an interstate highway, a Walmart, a Safeway, a ski resort, and a transportation center, as well as condominiums and businesses.

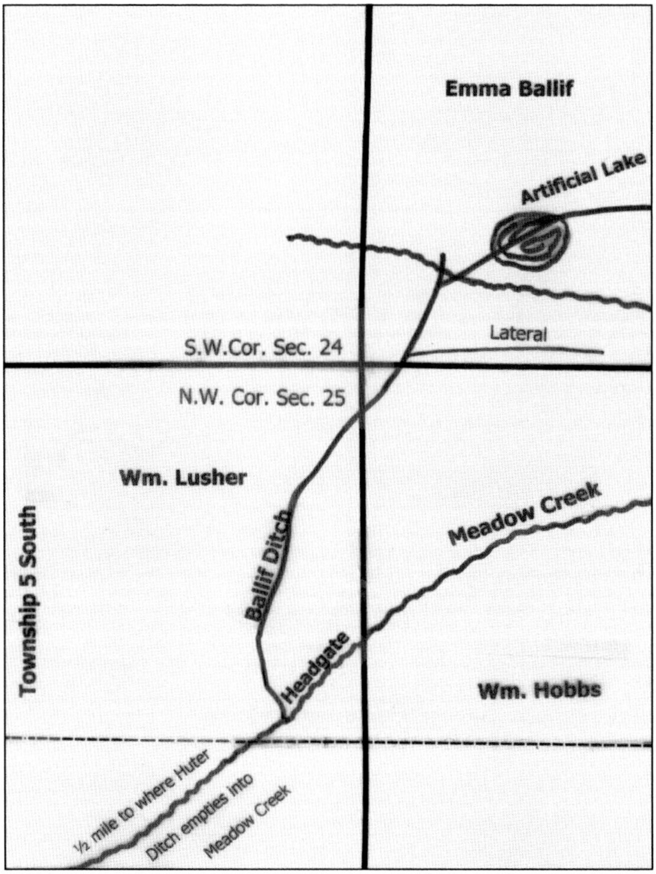

Undated Map showing Portions of the Ballif, Hobbs, and Lusher Ranches. Giberson Bay, an embayment on the western shore of Lake Dillon, now covers the portions of the ranches shown in the map. The Ballif ditch crossed the Lusher ranch before reaching Meadow Creek. A headgate regulated the flow of water entering the ditch. (Map drawn by author.)

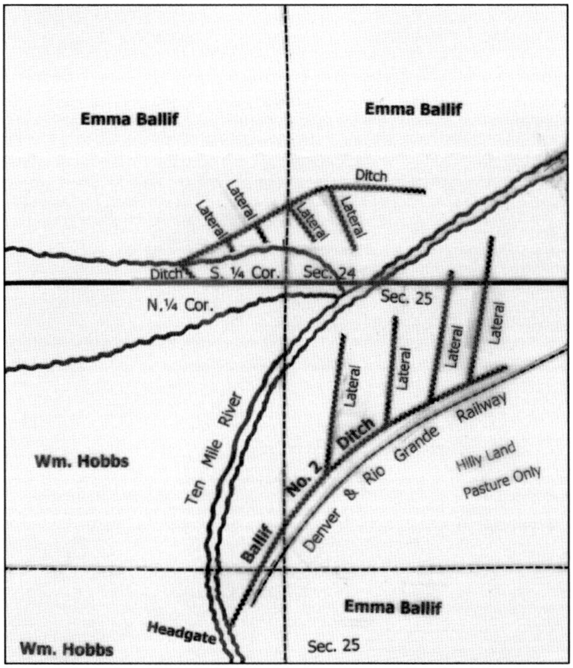

Undated Map Showing Portions of Ballif and Hobbs Ranches. Frisco and Giberson Bays, two embayments on the western edge of Lake Dillon, cover the portions of the Ballif and Hobbs ranches shown on the map. A complex of ditches with lateral extensions irrigated and drained the gently sloping meadows. Notice the section labeled hilly land useful only for pasture. (Map drawn by author.)

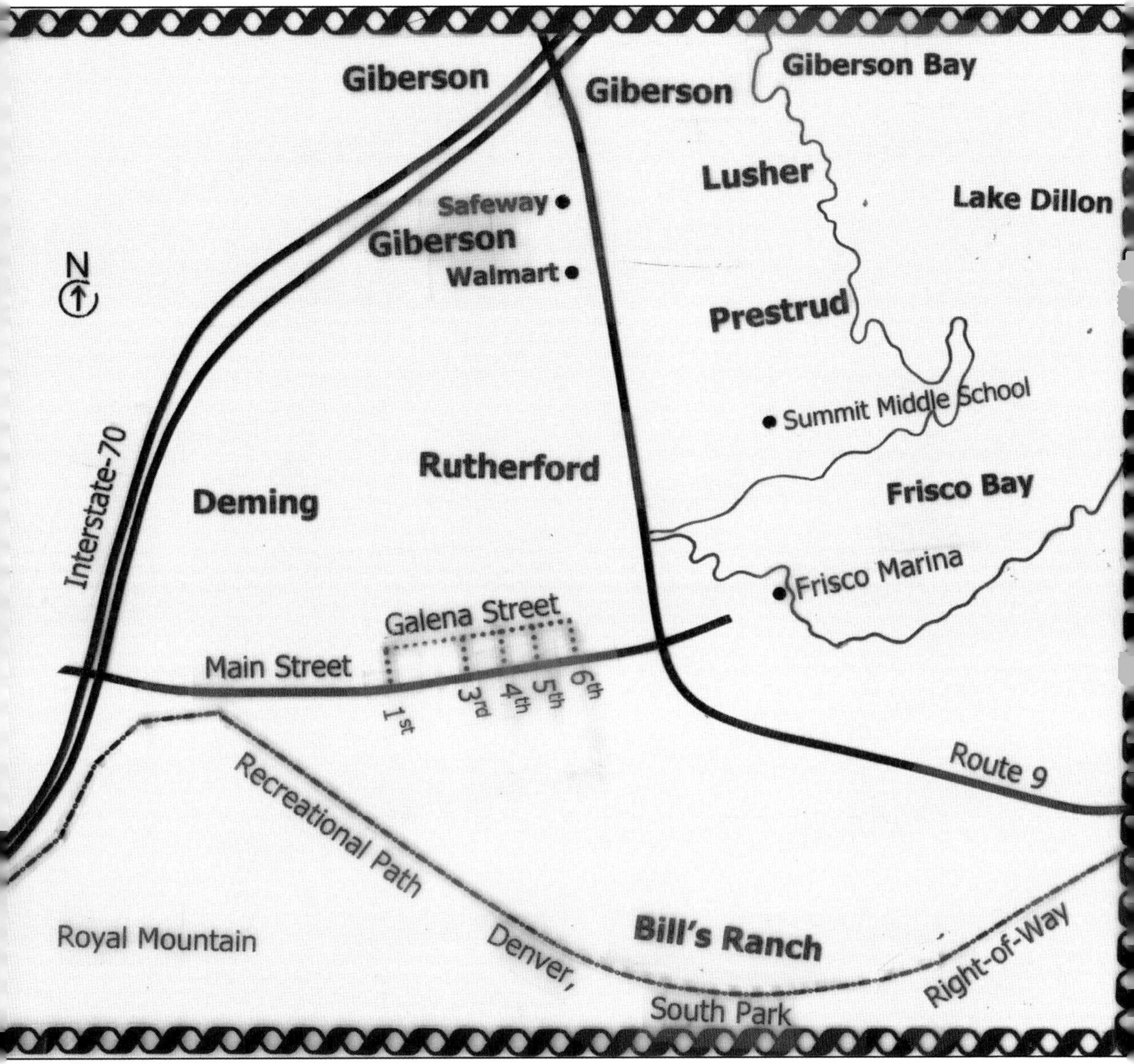

Map Showing Frisco Area Ranches Superimposed on Present-Day Road Map. Houses, condominiums, businesses, a marina, a transportation center, and recreational facilities occupy land that once provided feed for cattle and homesteads for families. The recreational path follows the Denver, South Park & Pacific right-of-way. Lake Dillon covers portions of the Giberson, Lusher, and Prestrud ranches. (Map drawn by author.)

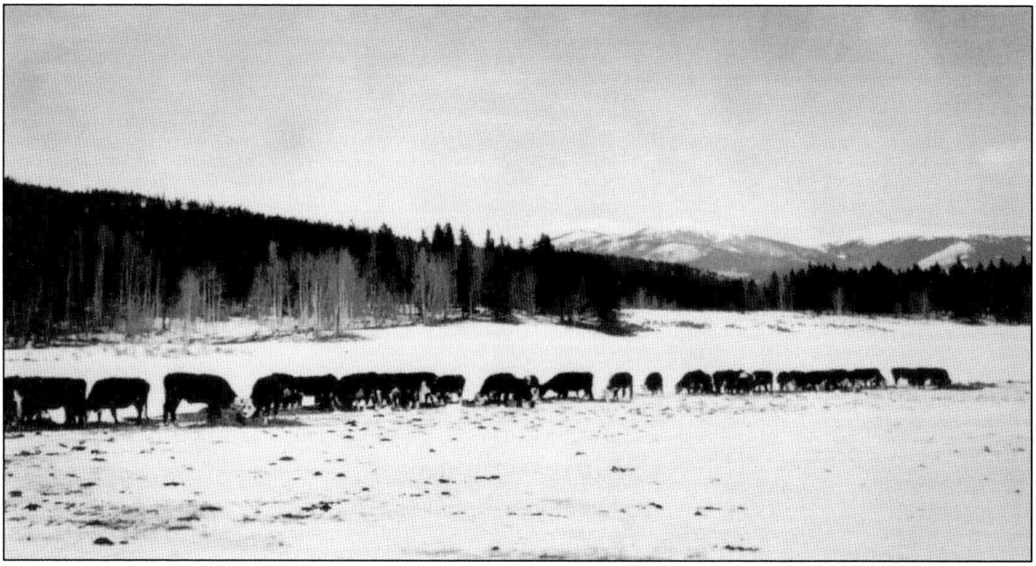

Lusher Meadow. During the winter, cattle ate feed grown during the summer months and stored in barns and fields during haying time. Cattle shipped to Denver represented a sizeable portion of a ranch's income each year. The cattle—mostly Herefords and, later, Angus—fed on the stubble left after harvesting until the snow became too deep. Then ranchers used hay sleighs to haul feed to the hungry animals.

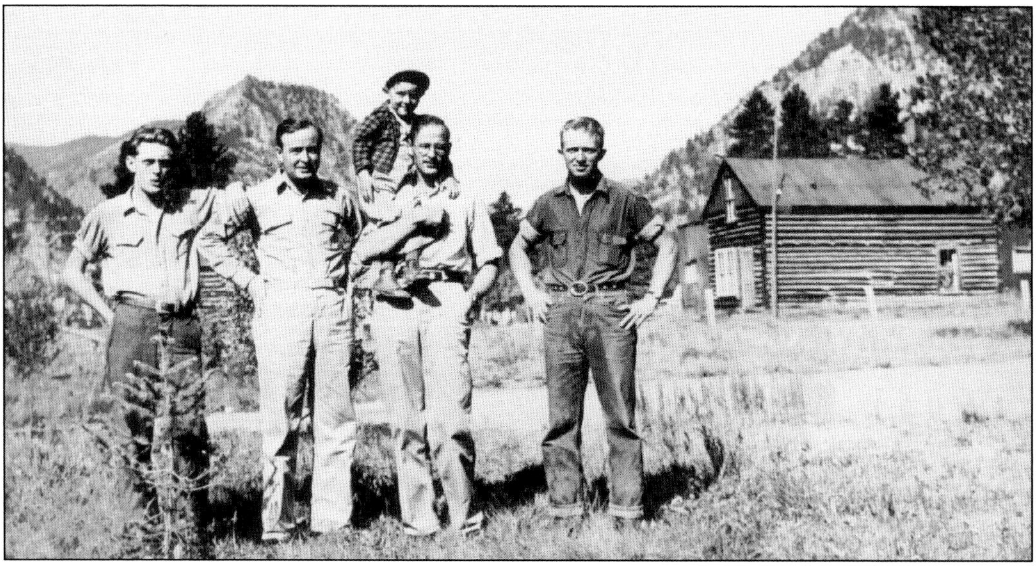

The Deming Ranch. The Deming family took advantage of the Homestead Act of 1862 and claimed 160 acres in 1890. To supplement income from the ranch, the men in the family worked in mines, ran trapping lines, and found employment at local sawmills. The women in the family worked from dawn to dusk maintaining the home, cooking, washing, cleaning, sewing, and tending the family garden.

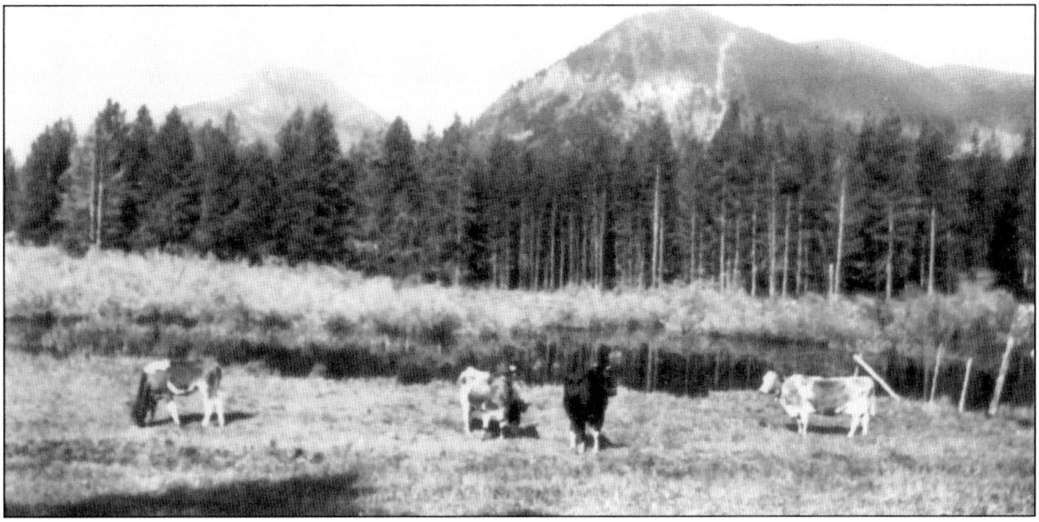

Milk Cows on the Rutherford Ranch. The biggest problem facing ranching families such as the Rutherfords was not the weather, which they had learned to anticipate, but the prices they received for animals and crops. They were at the mercy of situations beyond their control. Low prices for cattle and sheep and high prices for rail transportation caused constant worries.

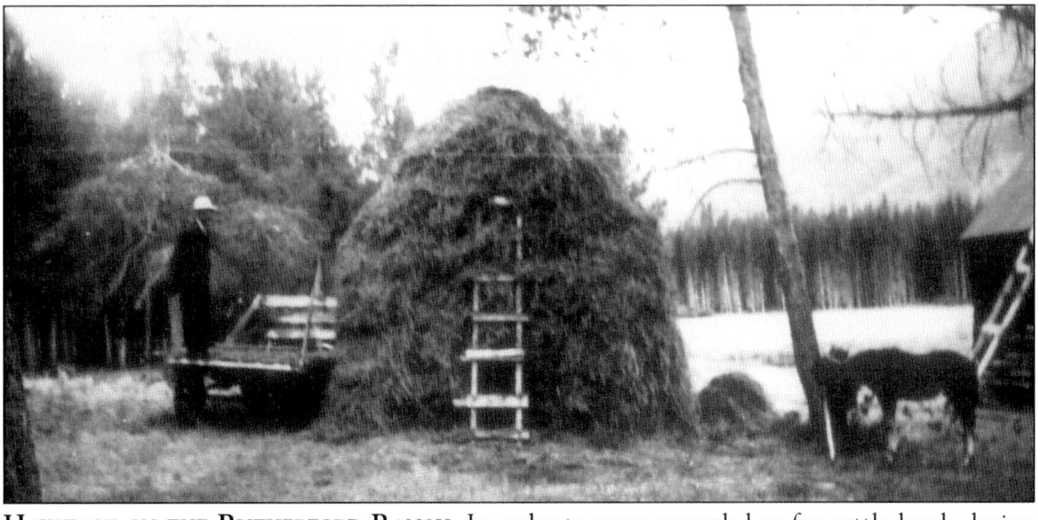

Haystack on the Rutherford Ranch. In order to grow enough hay for cattle herds during dry summer months, many ranchers dug water ditches to irrigate and drain pastures, fields, and meadows. Because flood irrigation was the method of choice, standing water had to be removed from the fields as well; just as in mining, too much water caused as many problems as too little.

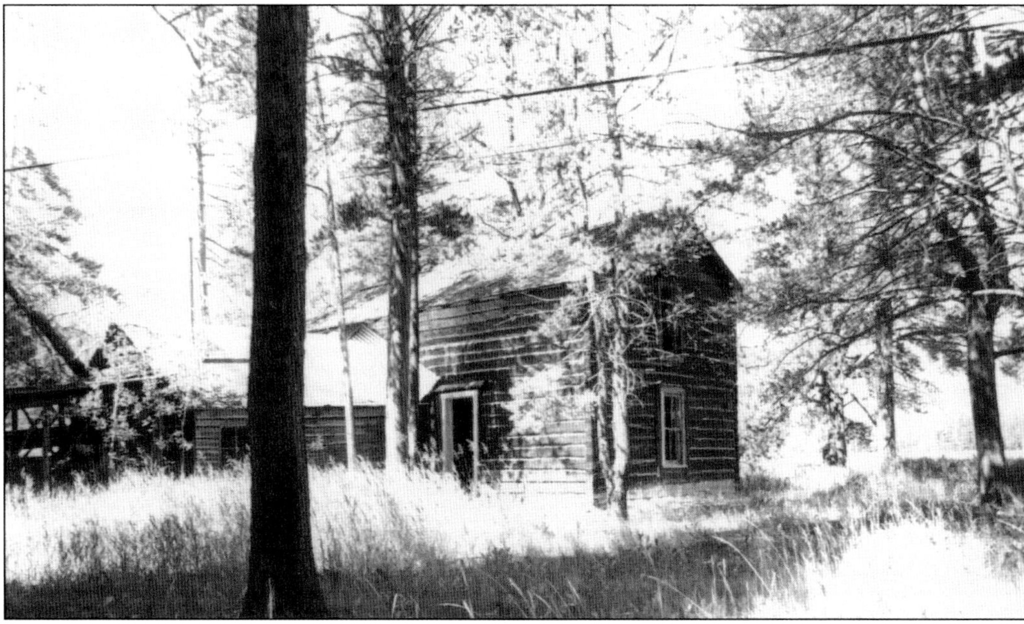

Bill's Ranch House. Jane Thomas and her two sons, William (Bill) and Walter, purchased 145.7 acres of ranch land, located south of town, from the federal government. Needing a market for his dairy products, in 1930 Bill wrote to 100 carefully selected people in Denver offering them free property if they would build cabins within a year. Bill's venture proved successful, eventually becoming Frisco's first subdivision and first second-home development.

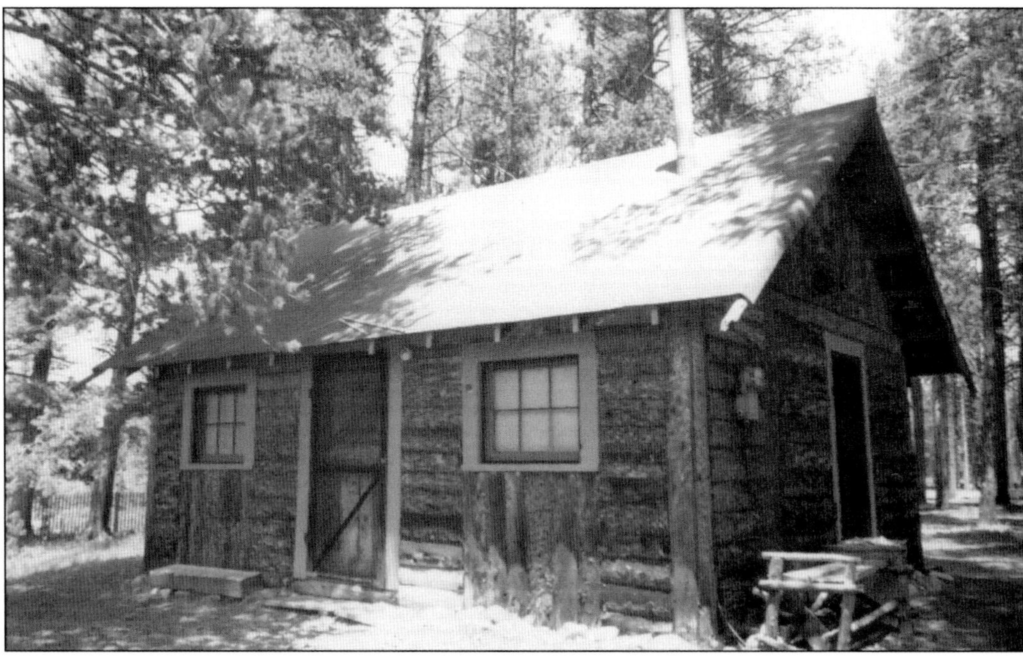

Niemoth Cabin at Bill's Ranch. Of the 100 people who received letters—addressed to "Mr. Man"—from Bill Thomas, only two replied to the offer. One of the respondents, a minister named Mr. Dexheimer, told his congregation. Several church members came and chose their lots. One family was the Niemoths, who built this cabin on their free land.

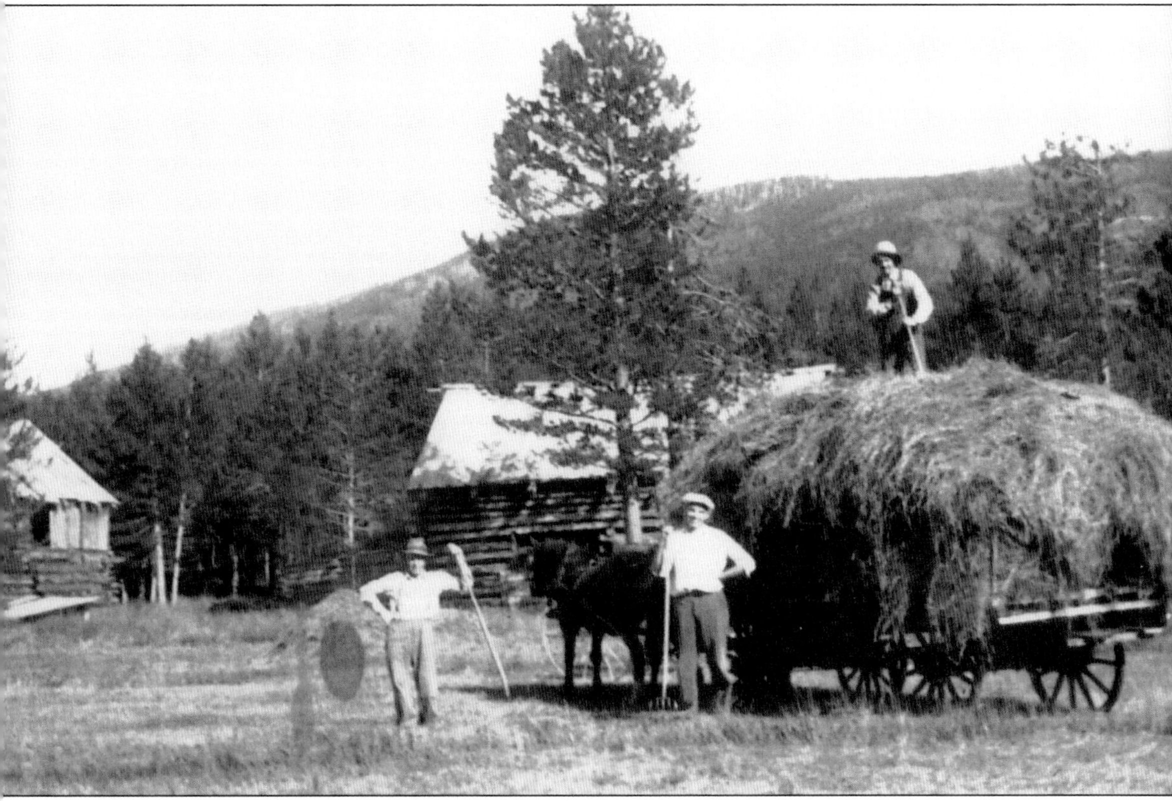

Hay Wagon on Bill's Ranch. Summit County ranches grew a large crop of hay for local use. In 1917, the ranches produced 8,500 tons of hay, valued at $102,000; two years later, the crop totaled 10,357 tons with a value of $130,000. Not all of the hay stayed in the county; ranchers shipped any surplus by rail to markets as far away as Kentucky.

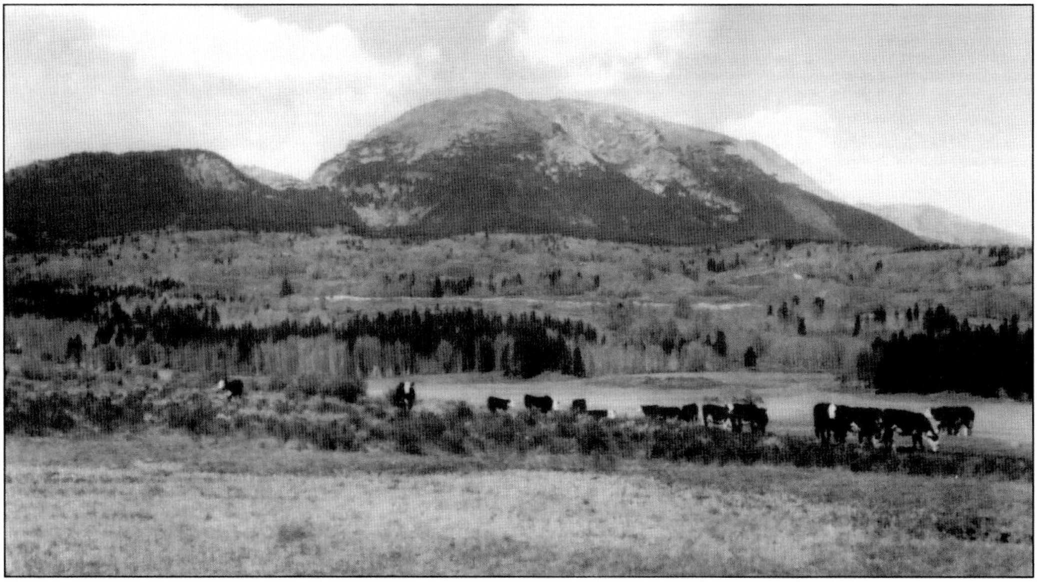

Howard and Lura Belle Giberson's Ranch. Cattle grazed the grasses in the meadows on the Giberson ranch, which extended from the slopes of Buffalo Mountain to land now under the water of Lake Dillon. Although there were exceptions, few cattle came into the county to maintain or increase herd size. Usually, calves born each spring replaced those cattle sent to market.

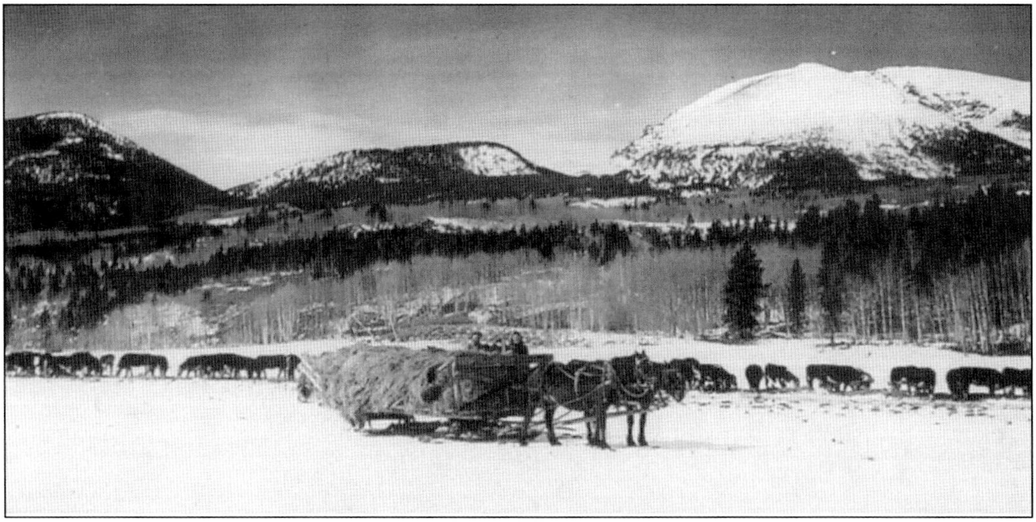

Feeding Cattle on the Giberson Ranch. When snow became too deep for cattle to graze on field stubble, ranchers like the Gibersons brought in hay on wagons from the supply stacked in fields or stored in barns. The Gibersons held a cattle sale each year. Buyers hauled their purchases to Denver on the train and, later, by truck. (Photograph loaned by Peggy Alexander on behalf of Sue Giberson-Chamberlain and Howard and Lura Belle Giberson.)

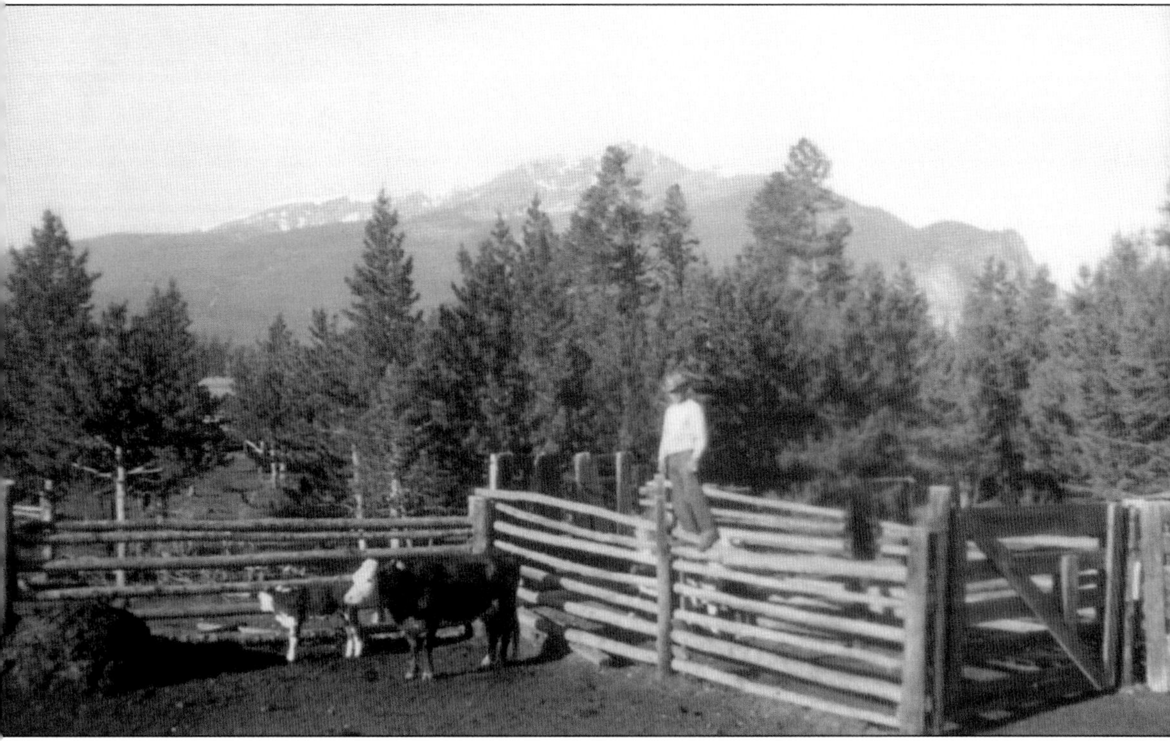

Corrals on the Giberson Ranch. Eventually, only meat cattle grazed in the meadows of the Giberson ranch. The 720-acre ranch included the former Lusher ranch with house and barn that stood near the present-day Holiday Inn. The Safeway, Walmart, and Best Western now occupy land that had been part of the Giberson ranch. Remnants of the meadows where the cattle grazed remain to the west of Giberson Bay. (Photograph loaned by Peggy Alexander on behalf of Sue Giberson-Chamberlain and Howard and Lura Belle Giberson.)

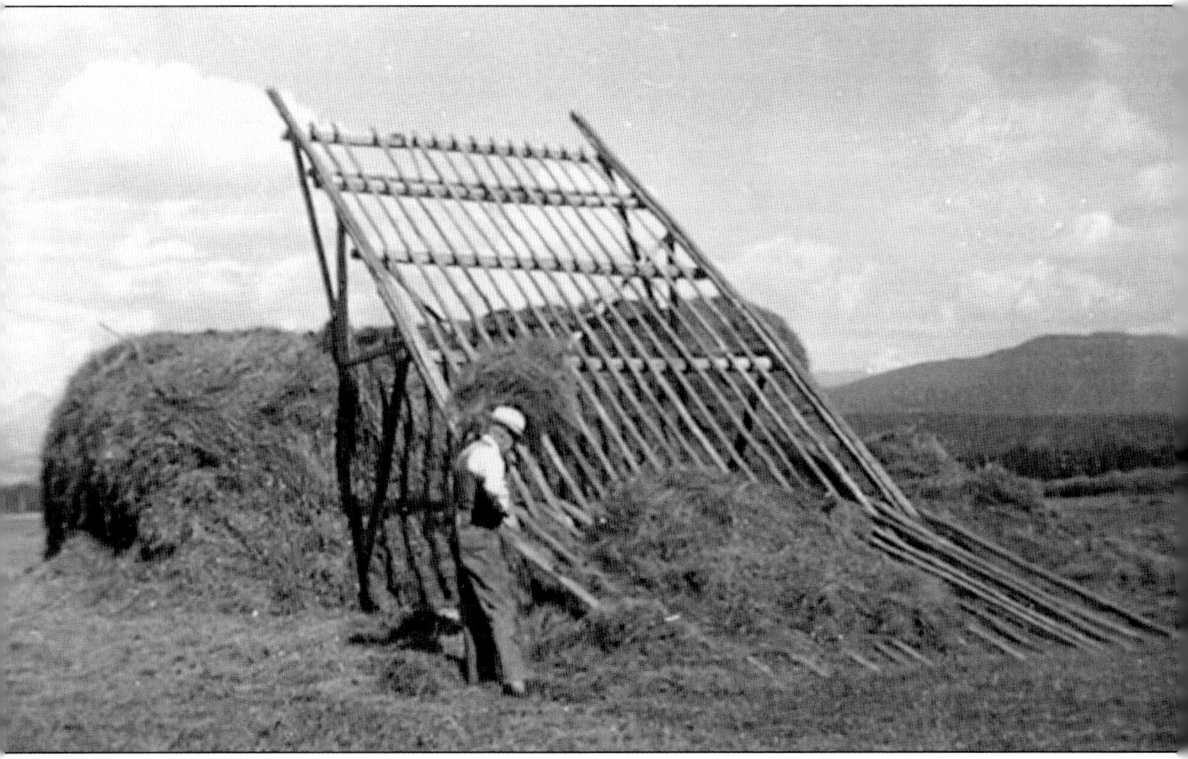

Hay Stacker on the Giberson Ranch. Wooden plungers, pushed by horse or tractor, piled the hay for storage in fields. Fencing kept the cattle away until the hay was needed. Ranchers also used the plunger to push cut hay up the incline and into a barn through an opening in the roof for winter storage. (Photograph loaned by Peggy Alexander on behalf of Sue Giberson-Chamberlain and Howard and Lura Belle Giberson.)

DAIRY PRODUCTS ON THE GIBERSON RANCH. Like others, the Gibersons sold dairy products to local residents and shipped cream to Denver by train. In addition, they raised pigs, chickens, and a few rapidly maturing vegetables. The women churned cream into butter and used some of the cream to make cheese. A ready, eager market existed in nearby Frisco. (Photograph loaned by Peggy Alexander on behalf of Sue Giberson-Chamberlain and Howard and Lura Belle Giberson.)

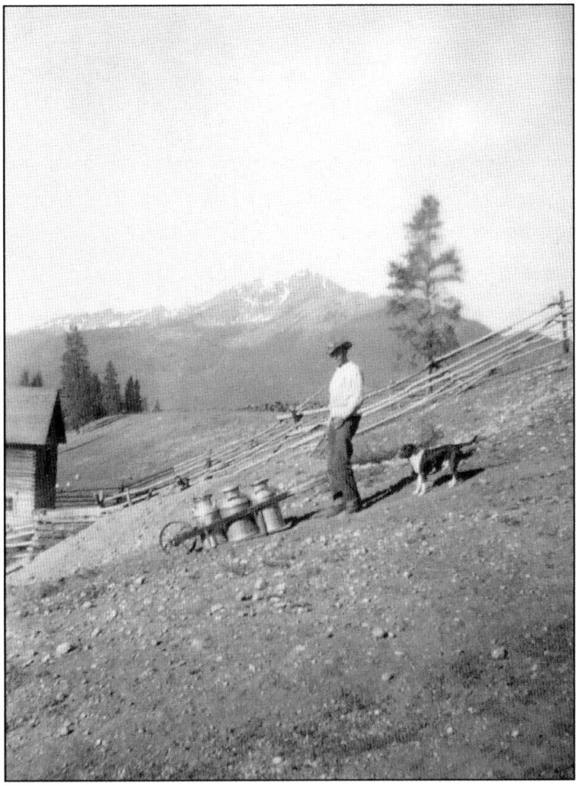

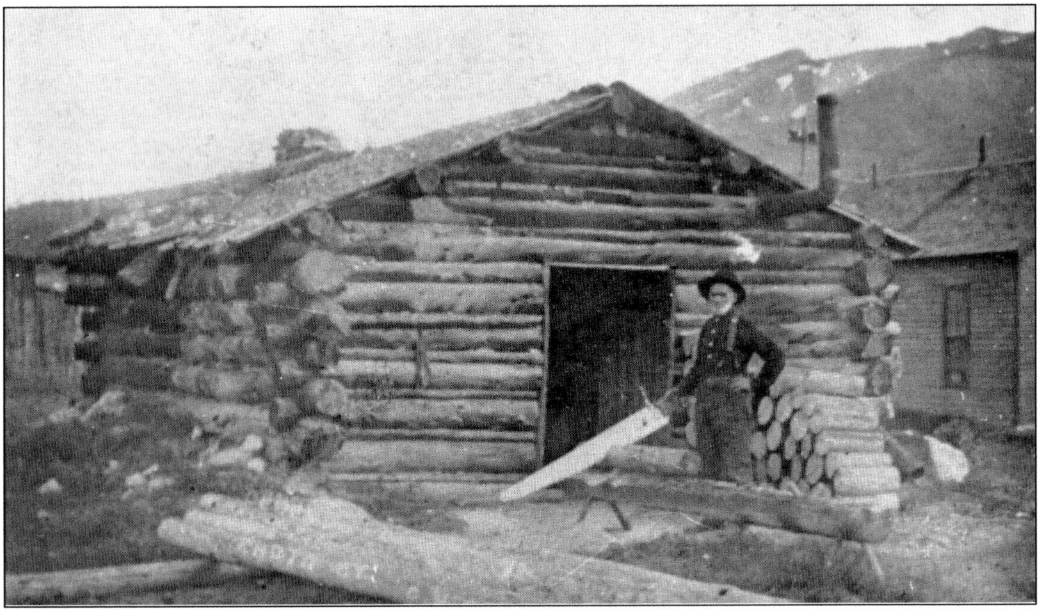

TIMBER HARVEST. Loggers cut vast amounts of lumber to supply mining, residential, and transportation needs. Men used one- and two-person saws to cut timber even during winter months, when snow covered the ground to great depths. Sawn logs were needed for constructing cabins, houses, bridges, stores, and buildings at mines. Railroads laid an average of 3,000 ties per mile, consuming huge quantities of sawn logs. (Courtesy History Colorado.)

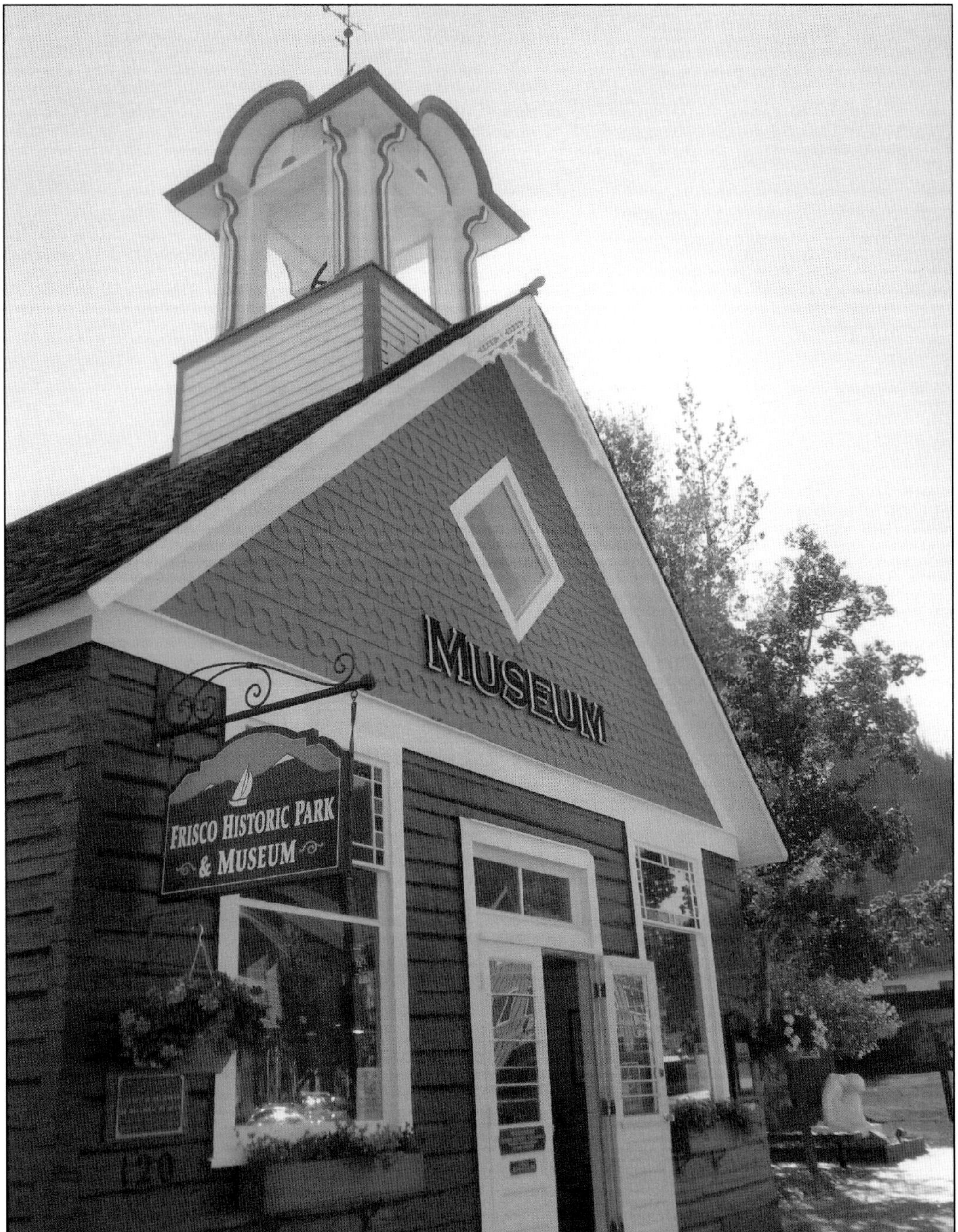

About the Frisco Historic Park & Museum. The Frisco Historic Park & Museum, operated by the Town of Frisco, helps visitors learn about Frisco's historical and cultural heritage. The schoolhouse, still on its original site and now listed on the National Register of Historic Places, opened its doors to the public as a museum in 1983. During the ensuing years, the town added 11 other restored historic structures, each displaying artifacts from Frisco's past. (Courtesy Simone Belz.)

BIBLIOGRAPHY

Clawson, Janet Marie. *Echoes of the Past: Copper Mountain, Colorado.* Denver, CO: Waddell Litho, 1986.

Dempsey, Stanley, and James E. Fell Jr. *Mining the Summit, Colorado's Ten Mile District, 1860-1960.* Norman, OK: University of Oklahoma Press, 1986.

Gilliland, Mary Ellen. *Lula, a Portrait in Pictures and Prose of a Keystone, Colorado Family.* Dillon, CO: Summit Historical Society, 1990.

Poor, M.C. *Denver, South Park and Pacific, Memorial Edition.* Denver, CO: World Press, 1976.

Mather, Sandra F. *Summit County.* Charleston, SC: Arcadia Publishing, 2008.

Pritchard (Mather), Sandra F. *Men, Mining, and Machines, Hardrock Mining in Summit County, Colorado.* Breckenridge, CO: Summit Historical Society, 1996.

———. *Roadside Summit, Part II, The Human Landscape.* Breckenridge, CO: Summit Historical Society 1992.

Speas, Sam, as told to Margaret Coel. *Goin' Railroading: A Century on the Colorado High Iron.* Boulder, CO: Pruett Publishing Company, 1985.

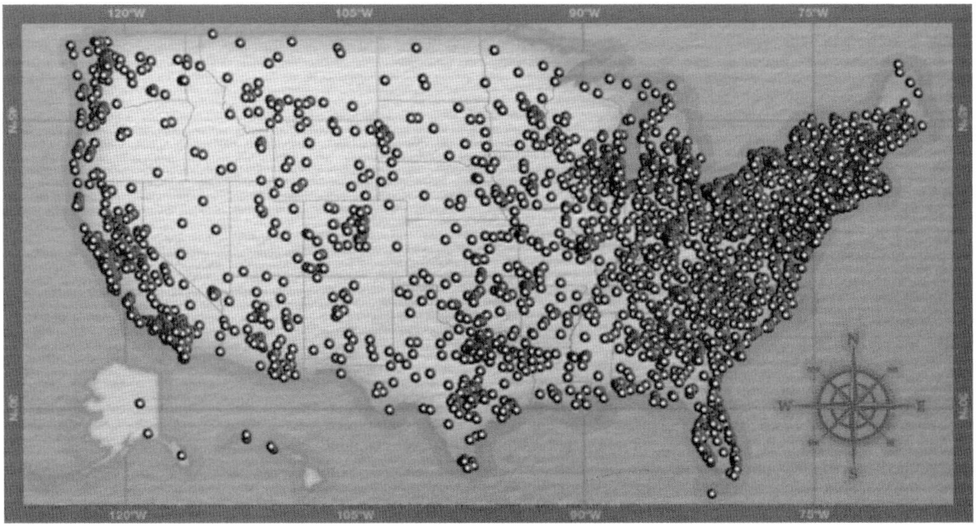